STANDING AT THE THRESHOLD

STANDING AT THE THRESHOLD

Working through Liminality in the Composition and Rhetoric TAship

EDITED BY
WILLIAM J. MACAULEY JR.
LESLIE R. ANGLESEY
BRADY EDWARDS
KATHRYN M. LAMBRECHT
PHILLIP LOVAS

UTAH STATE UNIVERSITY PRESS
Logan

© 2021 by University Press of Colorado

Published by Utah State University Press
An imprint of University Press of Colorado
245 Century Circle, Suite 202
Louisville, Colorado 80027

The University Press of Colorado is a proud member of the Association of University Presses.

The University Press of Colorado is a cooperative publishing enterprise supported, in part, by Adams State University, Colorado State University, Fort Lewis College, Metropolitan State University of Denver, Regis University, University of Colorado, University of Northern Colorado, University of Wyoming, Utah State University, and Western Colorado University.

∞ This paper meets the requirements of the ANSI/NISO Z39.48–1992 (Permanence of Paper)

ISBN: 978-1-64642-088-9 (paperback)
ISBN: 978-1-64642-089-6 (ebook)
https://doi.org/10.7330/9781646420896

Library of Congress Cataloging-in-Publication Data

Names: Macauley, William J., editor. | Anglesey, Leslie R., editor. | Edwards, Brady (Professor of English), editor. | Lambrecht, Kathryn M., 1988–, editor. | Lovas, Phillip, editor.
Title: Standing at the threshold : working through liminality in the composition and rhetoric TAship / edited by William J. Macauley Jr., Leslie R. Anglesey, Brady Edwards, Kathryn M. Lambrecht, and Phillip Lovas.
Other titles: Working through liminality in the composition and rhetoric TAship
Identifiers: LCCN 2021001168 (print) | LCCN 2021001169 (ebook) | ISBN 9781646420889 (paperback) | ISBN 9781646420896 (ebook)
Subjects: LCSH: Graduate teaching assistants. | English language—Rhetoric—Study and teaching (Higher) | Academic writing—Study and teaching.
Classification: LCC LB2335.4 .S83 2021 (print) | LCC LB2335.4 (ebook) | DDC 378.1/25—dc23
LC record available at https://lccn.loc.gov/2021001168
LC ebook record available at https://lccn.loc.gov/2021001169

The University Press of Colorado gratefully acknowledges the support of the University of Nevada, Reno, toward the publication of this book.

To the Department of English and the graduate school at the University of Nevada, Reno, who are dedicated to developing future generations of faculty members and academic researchers. And to our families, friends, and colleagues who encouraged us throughout the development of this collection. Bill wants to specifically dedicate this project to the TAs he has worked with, who both sparked this collection and provided him with direct experience of the complexities and challenges they face in their roles and responsibilities as TAs teaching writing.

CONTENTS

FOREWORD

Andrea Williams and Tanya Rodrigue

Several seminal articles in rhetoric and composition scholarship, such as Lucille Parkinson McCarthy's "A Stranger in Strange Lands: A College Student Writing Across the Curriculum" (1987) and David Bartholomae's "Inventing the University," (1986) discuss the difficulties students face in entering and dwelling in foreign academic territories. Learning how to write, speak, engage in a discourse community, learn, be, and what Bartholomae refers to as "try on" disciplinary identities, habits, and practices across courses and disciplines is difficult. Graduate teaching assistants (GTA) are not any different than undergraduate students in this respect: they are exploring new territory—both in the discipline as they move from novice to experts and in the classroom as they shift from student to teacher. Many also dwell in new territory as administrators and peer mentors.

The liminal position of TA work requires considerable improvisation, as TAs are expected to perform unfamiliar roles, often with little preparation, in new territories. Improvisation, which we define as the opportunistic act of identifying and using the available means to make a performance work, can be intimidating for experienced teachers and is even more so for novice teachers. TAs may feel anxious or have questions such as "What pedagogical methods should I use? How should I act as a teacher? How can I best create ethos as a disciplinary expert and teacher? How do I negotiate my identity and needs as a person and as a teacher in the classroom? Are my students learning anything from me?" Yet as Andrea knows from working closely with TAs for more than two decades, TAs are sometimes reticent to share their anxiety and struggles, draw on available resources, and/or work to advocate for space to discuss writing pedagogy. Certainly TA education may help mitigate such feelings TAs may have as new graduate students, new teachers, and new administrators, but as this collection explores, the very nature of TAs' liminal role calls for improvisation. This theme of improvisation runs throughout this collection as its authors use the challenges they face as pedagogical actors to develop new and creative ways of imagining and inhabiting the TA roles they play. Perhaps most important, this collection, written by TAs for TAs, initiates productive conversations concerning common questions about teaching assistantships, thereby assuaging concerns and reassuring TAs they can in fact be effective practitioners even in the liminal space they occupy. Further, this collection supports the importance of TA education and having a scholarly space to discuss TAs' questions, concerns, and anxiety.

Using a range of theories and methods, the authors explore the affordances and constraints of liminality to empower TAs and help them build effective pedagogies, whether by drawing on the rhetorical tradition of imitation to rethink what it means to innovate (Caccia); analyzing gestures to position TAs as embodied teachers (Campbell and Fiscus-Cannaday); exploring how TAs with disabilities can advocate for themselves (Donegan); or reframing failure as a productive lens for pedagogical development (Schoettler and Saur). This collection not only illuminates the dilemmas posed by TA liminality, offering potential ways to work both with and against this liminality, but also makes a compelling argument for the importance of developing and sustaining TA-education programs that create *teacher communities* (Schoettler and Saur) wherein TAs are able to tell their stories and share their vulnerabilities and needs as new teachers; develop mentorship (Donegan) and modeling (Caccia); use "preflection" (Mauer, Matzker, and Dively) and reflection (Schoettler and Saur); and foster self-efficacy (Schoettler and Saur), self-compassion, and interdependence (Lambrecht, though she doesn't use these terms). These important themes and issues are all deserving of the exploration provided here.

In demonstrating a strong commitment to teaching, many of the authors in this collection argue that liminality is a productive space in which to learn and grow as teachers. To this end, they present concrete pedagogical strategies TA readers may adopt or adapt in the classroom. For example, in "From Imposter to 'Double Agent': Leveraging Liminality as Expertise," Kathryn M. Lambrecht advocates that TAs recognize they are in fact developing teachers and scholars and encourages them to be as kind and generous to themselves as they are to their developing students. This move may help create solidarity between TAs and students, thus enhancing learning. Similarly, Megan Schoettler and Elizabeth Saur, in "Beyond 'Good Teacher' / 'Bad Teacher': Generative Self-Efficacy and the Composition and Rhetoric TAship," advocate TA-led professional development. They encourage TAs to deconstruct the unproductive good/bad binary in describing themselves. Schoettler and

Saur argue that TAs develop a strong sense of self-efficacy by reframing negative experiences as productive learning experiences can help themselves become more reflective practitioners.

The assembly of these personal stories, studies, and explorations by and for rhetoric and composition TAs is in itself an important act of solidarity, whereby the individual and the local are transformed into a collective testimony about identities and experiences that have largely been excluded from disciplinary discussions and scholarship. Creating such a scholarly record affirms TAs and makes a case to the institutions where TAs are located that many of the problems they face are the result of the fraught roles they occupy rather than of individual shortcomings. These authors offer creative and timely ways to help TAs navigate some of the quandaries and challenges they encounter as they move through and temporarily dwell in liminal positions during graduate school. Simultaneously, these authors provide valuable pedagogical lessons and insights that will have a lasting and positive impact on TAs and their teaching beyond graduate school.

REFERENCES

Bartholomae, David J. 1986. "Inventing the University." *Journal of Basic Writing* 5 (1): 4–23.
McCarthy, Lucille Parkinson. 1987. "A Stranger in Strange Lands: A College Student Writing across the Curriculum." *Research in the Teaching of English* 21 (3): 233–65.

ACKNOWLEDGMENTS

The creation of *Standing at the Threshold* has been a significant undertaking, which we as the editors would not have been able to create without the help of many of our friends and colleagues. This project began from simple beginnings in one of Dr. Macauley's graduate courses at the University of Nevada, Reno, as an assignment for his graduate students to challenge themselves with something bigger than the class. Both during and after the course, Dr. Macauley encouraged us to share both our ideas and our work with the larger graduate teaching community. Because of his encouragement, this collection has become a labor of love for each of the editors.

We are indebted to Utah State University Press for taking a chance on this collection and being willing to endure our endless questions. To Rachael Levay, whose patience, guidance, and perseverance have been both essential and unbelievably constant. And to the reviewers who spent time with our collection at various stages of the process and gave us valuable feedback so we could complete the work you see here.

We would also like to thank everyone who has been a part of this project, from each of our contributors who took the time and the care to share their research and stories with us (and now you) to those graduate students who were in the ENG 729 course where this collection began and contributed to the creation of the collection at its earliest stages. And finally, we thank the hundreds and hundreds of graduate students and faculty who inspire us on a daily basis to continue doing what we love. We continue to learn from each and every one of you, and we hope this collection shows just a little of that inspiration you have passed to us.

STANDING AT THE THRESHOLD

INTRODUCTION
Rhetoric and Composition TA Observed, Observing, Observer

William J. Macauley Jr.

I was teaching a course called Problems in Contemporary Rhetoric and Composition in the spring of 2015. The course focused largely on intersections of composition, neuroscience, social psychology, and young-adult psychology. The idea was to coordinate our intentions in teaching writing with research and scholarship in other fields toward understanding our students more deeply, thus creating opportunities to reconsider our pedagogies and practices toward increasingly informed teaching of writing. This course design originated from my work in student-writer agency and self-efficacy, as well as understanding disconnects among composition, agency, self-efficacy, cognitive development, and the psychosocial conditions our typical students might experience. I admit that the turn toward how our profession/field was understood and portrayed was a surprise, but the linkages seemed to make a lot of sense. For many, teaching writing at the college level is introduced through TAships and the orientations/trainings that accompany them. The graduate students with whom I was working that semester pointed out that their preparation for teaching writing had not enabled their feeling agentive, self-efficacious, or adequately prepared for that important work, especially if the research from other fields indicated such teaching could potentially have long-lasting and even psychological or physiological impacts on their FYC students. They felt ill prepared and underqualified, and discussions of agency and self-efficacy only seemed to amplify their senses of unreadiness.

As our conversations continued, and we read more of the scholarship on TA preparation,[1] we found what could be fairly characterized as a binary view of the field: one either set the writing programs as the priority OR one focused on the care, nurturing, and professional preparation of neophytes. To focus solely on the program or on the neophytes is possible, I suppose, but I have never met a WPA who does either, and all the WPAs I know describe the tough choices and often very difficult compromises they must frequently make to protect both. However, this

DOI: 10.7330/9781646420896.c000

unsatisfying dualism seems to persist, but few of those discussions happen "where the rubber meets the road." Neither have we found many instances of TAs speaking for themselves in the literature. The scholarship seems to be published at some distance from the TAs; TAs are spoken for and about without their often speaking for or about themselves. That is the place where this collection began: we agreed that TAs' own voices should be much more present in these conversations, that TAs have knowledges that would benefit a number of audiences in this area. So, a primary interest for this collection was then set: TAs, both current and former, speaking directly to readers and speaking for themselves about their programs, preparations, and connections to the field.[2]

Four key concepts became essential to these voicings. First among those key concepts is *who speaks*. It has been our experience that TAs are discussed or sometimes quoted, but by and large they have had very little direct input into the scholarship *as scholars and/or researchers* about their experiences. This is an obvious problem we set out to address, not to the exclusion of other perspectives or voices but as an essential and strategic complement to them.

Liminality is a second key concept. For us, it refers to TAs working between roles and responsibilities rather than the process of crossing a threshold or accessing what is on the other side of a threshold. There is also a sense for us that these movements of rhetoric and composition TAs crossing thresholds, these transitions, are not unidirectional but recursive and repetitive. Liminality, for us, also means that being between or in transition is being neither exclusively students nor fully teachers, and potentially recognizable as neither. Although scholars have discussed liminality in relation to learning and threshold concepts, their discussions tend to be focused on the process that is to come or that has already happened rather than on what liminality means/does as an experience in and of itself (Cody and Lawlor 2011; Irving and Young 2004; Land et al. 2005). For us, in this collection, liminality alone is a limited lens because it can accept ends justifying means without critically engaging exactly what those means are for the TAs who experience them. In short, the liminality of the rhetoric and composition TAship is not a one-time jumping of the gap to credentialing but the accumulated reality of jumping back and forth repeatedly between the two, often for a number of years.

Thresholds, as we discuss them generally in rhetoric and composition, are based on Jan Meyer, Ray Land, and Caroline Baillie's work (2010) in threshold concepts that asserts the impossibility of moving forward without threshold concepts and their profound impacts after acquisition.

Linda Adler-Kassner and Elizabeth Wardle (2015) have articulated threshold concepts for the teaching of writing through their collection *Naming What We Know*, which includes either five or thirty-four threshold concepts, depending on how one counts. In our case, here in this collection, thresholds are certainly informed by these works, but we think about them more as what is accumulated by TAs in a number of contexts and roles in the runup to crossing over from student to faculty, even as TAs bounce back and forth between teacher roles and student roles. So, while the ideal of a threshold concept may be a one-time passage of profound impact, in this collection we are thinking of thresholds as something a bit different. We are thinking about professional and institutional presence as TAs move back and forth between student and teacher, recipient and provider, institutional "client" (if you will) and practitioner. In this case, we understand thresholds as repeated experiences rather than singular locations, as ongoing transformations rather than distinct exigencies. We are also thinking about how rhetoric and composition TAs' experiences as TAs inform/distort perceptions of what might be on the other side of that threshold, about how those TAs' experiences mis/align with what is to come as professionals in rhetoric and composition.[3] We also question what the outcomes of such consonances and dissonances might be for neophytes making their ways into rhetoric and composition. Rather than assuming or trusting that threshold concepts might provide or ensure stable intellectual or pedagogical contexts for rhetoric and composition TAs once they have moved out of their TAships, it is worth considering the experiences of TAs *during their TAships* as indicators to them of conditions and challenges to come.

Misinformation, those dissonances mentioned above, is a fourth key concept in building this collection. There have always been ample opportunities for misunderstanding composition, and particularly troubling have been those misconceptions that discount/undermine our work as writing teachers. Certainly, there are many examples of how our work is misunderstood by central administration, faculty in disciplines outside English, and even by colleagues within our English departments but in different areas of English studies. However, of primary concern for this collection are distortions emanating from writing program inductions, from what TAs are learning about the profession from their TAship experiences. We can (and inadvertently too often do) contribute negatively to neophyte development in our own profession through choices such as treating all FYC-teaching TAs the same regardless of experience, interests, and/or engagement with teaching writing. Another way we often confound our own interests is by continuing the "information-dump" orientation right before the semester begins or going along with "get-someone,-anyone,-in-front-of-that-FYC-class" staffing practices that too often confound the work of WPAs when they don't have full control over the courses for which they may nonetheless be held responsible. Both are necessarily reflections of the contexts within which our writing programs exist, to be sure. A more cynical reader might say these are accurate portrayals of a career in teaching writing. However, TAships and graduate programs in rhetoric and composition are necessarily but not inordinately optimistic; they tend not to just be about what seems likely given current conditions but about what *should be* given that to which we, the field(s) and the devoted professionals within it, have devoted ourselves to making manifest.

Not complex is recognizing the absence of TA voices from these discussions. We, in this collection, do not mean to suggest TAs have been misrepresented or deliberately excluded. Certainly, in the research and scholarship of Heidi Estrem and E. Shelly Reid (2012), Rebecca Nowacek (2011), Jessica Restaino (2012), Tanya Rodrigue and Andrea Williams (2016), Mary Soliday (2011), and others TAs are very present and well represented. However well TAs have been represented though, they have not often been the researchers, scholars, or voices speaking with authority on TA issues. No longer should TAs seem like repeating specters, somewhat visible but only partially and only through special lenses, repeating activities over and over, year after year, cohort after cohort, never interacting directly with those who may sense their presence without being able to fully see them. Those of us looking for the TAs (in the literature) remain unable to fully engage with them, and they (TAs, through the literature) remain unable to fully engage with us. Thus, one of the purposes of this book, beyond helping incoming and future rhetoric and composition TAs prepare for their TAships, is to turn on the full-range UV lights, so to speak, so WPAs and writing program educators who "sense" TAs' presence are able to really see them.

Liminalities, thresholds, and misinformation together are quite complex. Together, they begin to articulate the uniqueness and depth of the rhetoric and composition TAship. While rhetoric and composition TAships are liminal in the sense of being between, they are complicated by their also being thresholds TAs cross more than once, from which TAs don't acquire just one concept via a single crossing and that also foreshadow what work in rhetoric and composition actually is or could be. While there is little question TAs can fairly be characterized as both student and teacher, they can also be understood as in motion from one to the other, never solely one nor the other. We understand rhetoric and composition TAships as exceeding any of these concepts individually and engaging all of them simultaneously—and engaging multiple iterations of each of them, as well. Rhetoric and composition TAs are living in both an overt and a more subtle liminality in the sense that they are moving back and forth between student and teacher, but they are also potentially moving back and forth between the realities of the program in which they are studying and the one within which they are teaching, the local program and the field more generally, the aspect of rhetoric and composition they teach in and the aspect in which they hope to work after TAing, the present conditions of the field as expressed locally and the future conditions of the field as expressed wherever they are employed after grad school.

So, are these dualities or continua? In some ways they are both and neither because they are thresholds; the TAship is knowledge essential to moving forward for these graduate students, and they can't move forward without it (for a number of reasons).[4] And, TAs' understandings of their work and their fields afterward will be forever changed by their TAships. However, the threshold is not singular; it is multiple and repeated because the contexts change, because the learning and exposure to the field and profession change, because the roles and responsibilities and opportunities change. This doesn't make any of the thresholds not thresholds but instead multiplies them along conceptual lines of inquiry, growth, and development. In other words, the threshold concept of what a faculty member is and does, for example, will not come in one experience or iteration; it will not be gained completely in one threshold crossing. It is so complex and situated it must be iterative and cumulative. It remains a threshold concept because it must be understood to move forward, and it changes the learner forever once it is understood, but this learning does not happen all at once. Some might argue that this discounts this example as a true threshold concept, but I argue that it better argues for the complexity inherent in what might truly be considered a threshold concept. The rhetoric and composition TAship is replete with numerous complex and recursive thresholds that must be crossed repeatedly because, even if the TAship structure is stable, the field and the world outside the TAship are not.

And, of course, in all of this, there is an ever-present risk when a substantial contingent is not included in the conversation. What are TAs experiencing? What perspectives and experiences are TAs finding most impactful? There, of course, are no singular answers, and students who are looking for one thing and don't find it may feel misled. Faculty who teach toward one perspective and find students disinterested may become equally disappointed. That's why who speaks is such an important part of both this area of scholarship and this collection, so the varieties of perspectives are available. Triangulation is not simply a research method but a practice of careful thoughtfulness that allows consideration of multiple perspectives, larger understanding, and overlapping confirmations. Thus far, TAs have not been able to speak for themselves in terms of their own preparations; this collection hopes to begin to change that and, by doing so, increase the understanding of what the rhetoric and composition TAship is and does.

We need to hear rhetoric and composition TAs because they are the only ones who can show us what these experiences are in this moment, and in the next, and the next. They need us to be aware in order to ensure that what they are experiencing actually does prepare them for their work during their graduate studies and after. We need to hear their voices in order to know what information is resonating for them, and they need us to respond so their liminality is not quicksand and the thresholds they approach are not forced, uninformed choices. These are the concerns, questions, implications past and current rhetoric and composition TAs should be able to share directly with future TAs, WPAs, and writing program educators, and we think their voices have been muted too long.

In the interest of including these voices, this collection is built around three conceptions of participating in the rhetoric and composition TAship. The first is accessing the TAship in rhetoric and composition, learning how to make one's way into it. It makes sense to start here, and our authors offer meaningful insights on not only how to "get into" a TAship in rhetoric and composition but how to do so in rich and rewarding ways. A second move is living a rhetoric and composition TAship. In this section, the focus becomes the interaction between the individual and the roles and responsibilities they must take on. As the individual evolves and unfolds, so does the TAship. The third move is transcending the rhetoric and composition TAship. There will come a point for every TA when, rather than serving the TAship, the TAship serves them. This final section focuses its attention there, exploring and discussing options for becoming via the TAship. Overall, especially for the new or about-to-be-new rhetoric and composition TA reader, this collection attempts to reveal an arc of experience our authors and editors have shared and value.

The collection opens with a foreword from Andrea Williams and Tanya Rodrigue emphasizing the inherent call for improvisation in the rhetoric and composition TAship that is closely paired with TA reticence to admit not knowing exactly what to do at all times. Williams and

Rodrigue set out one of the most salient and least visible liminalities/ thresholds for TAs. From there, the collection moves readers through rhetoric and composition TAships. Lew Caccia argues that imitation has a rich history of utility and productive application within rhetoric and composition apprenticeship and that it should not be forgotten as a strategy now. Lillian Campbell and Jaclyn Fiscus-Cannaday, in chapter 2, encourage a sensitivity to embodied teaching practice, a critical awareness providing insights and evidence to support more diversified approaches and thinking about how the teaching is actually done. In both these chapters, awareness and critical engagement with teaching, as both observed and experienced, are essential strategies for accessing the rhetoric and composition TAship.

The next set of chapters (chapters 3–5) focuses more attention on inhabiting the rhetoric and composition TAship. Jennifer K. Johnson makes a salient argument that understanding the differences among TAs, by both institutional representatives and the TAs themselves, creates both opportunity and an understanding of the need for opportunities in those TAships. Kylee Thacker Maurer, Faith Matzger, and Ronda Leathers Dively dig deeply into liminality itself and how it relates to graduate student WPAs. Student WPAs' competing roles and responsibilities "trouble" the more familiar TAships in rhetoric and composition, for the TAs especially. Finally, in this section, Rachel Donegan discusses ableness and its impact on TA identity, student impressions of TAs with disabilities, and how the profound culture of ability and accomplishment complicates and, in some ways, works counter to the inclusion of TAs who are differently abled. In all three chapters, TA identity raises questions about the seeming homogenization of many writing program education designs; these authors argue that identity should not only inform TAships but be directed at making them less one size fits all.

In the final pair of chapters (chapters 6 and 7), the authors are focused on what might be characterized as transcending the limitations of TA roles and training. Kathryn Lambrecht, in chapter 6, argues that balance can be accomplished among the multiple and varying roles experienced by TAs in rhetoric and composition. She not only argues for balance but shows readers how balance might be accomplished, which calls for an identity outside the TAship that guides the work within it. Megan Schoettler and Elizabeth Saur argue that key to a sense of well-being in a rhetoric and composition TAship is what they call "generative self-efficacy," which presents a cogent argument for breaking out of good teacher/bad teacher dichotomies and supports TAs' not only being themselves but building themselves as agentive professionals and teachers. The collection closes with an afterword by Jessica Restaino, a recognized and dedicated researcher in this area, who argues that the collection, as part of a larger currency in research and scholarship in this area, offers readers an opportunity to appreciate and explore the liminalities inherent in TAships and beyond. Together, these pieces explicate an arc of experiences TAships can include that runs the gamut from improvisation and accessing the rhetoric and composition TAship to inhabiting it and finally transcending it or recognizing its uniqueness among so many other liminalities. Together, they reveal the richness these TAships can convene through the voices of those who have lived these lives and those who are devoting their research to those experiences.

This depiction of an evolving rhetoric and composition TAship is designed first for new TAs, who need some kind of support from the field as they embark on their new roles and responsibilities. The collection provides these readers with opportunities to understand firsthand what being a TA in rhetoric and composition can be/mean. This collection can also be used by WPAs and/or writing program educators who experience any dissatisfaction with their programs or the outcomes for their TAs. These insights and voices can provide them with perspectives they may not be able to have on their own. Finally, anyone approaching anew, redesigning, or inheriting writing program education can use this book to complement and enhance their understandings of how and when TAs in rhetoric and composition can most benefit from their interventions and attentions.

In the end, this is a labor of love, for our field and our students, for our programs and our courses, but for none of these more than rhetoric and composition TAs themselves. They are essential to the continued success and operation of writing programs in colleges and universities across the country and beyond. Their contributions have not been appreciated sufficiently yet, and this collection is a step toward their having the opportunity to speak their truths. We could not be more excited about the potential of this area of scholarship, more flattered to have these contributors trust us with their work, or more grateful to be learning from these gifted researchers, scholars, and writers.

NOTES

1.   I want to acknowledge here that I am /we are focusing on those rhetoric and composition TAs who plan to continue in rhet/comp in their later careers, which is one of the challenges of TA development for writing program education. Elsewhere in this introduction and in the collection itself, this will certainly not be the case.

2. The argument here is not a complex one. If we want to understand in firsthand ways what TAs in Rhetoric and Composition are experiencing, it is smart to hear their voices as much as possible, to treat them as informed participants rather than research subjects, especially considering that we are training them to do this kind of scholarly work anyway.

3. We wonder whether Rhetoric and Composition faculty can be encouraged to accept less than ideal working conditions because their TAships, many times conflicted, difficult, and led by professionals in their own field, may suggest that what they can experience as TAs is the norm, to be expected, just part of the reality of a career in Rhetoric and Composition.

4. Standard approaches can assume too much about TAs, about who they are, what they bring to the table, and what they do not. The diversification of the Rhetoric and Composition TAship in terms of discipline, identity, prior experience, financial/familial concerns, social/cultural difference, and/or academic background make assumptions about what TAs collectively have in place—thus making that threshold more complex for both the TAs and those who guide their progress. It can also make this work that much richer and more nuanced.

REFERENCES

Adler-Kassner, Linda, and Elizabeth Wardle, eds. 2015. *Naming What We Know: Threshold Concepts of Writing Studies*. Logan: Utah State University Press.

Cody, Kevina, and Katrina Lawlor. 2011. "On the Borderline: Exploring Liminal Consumption and the Negotiation of Threshold Selves." *Marketing Theory* 11 (2): 207–28.

Estrem, Heidi, and E. Shelly Reid. 2012. "What New Writing Teachers Talk about When They Talk about Teaching." *Pedagogy: Critical Approaches to Teaching Literature, Language, Composition, and Culture* 12 (3): 449–80.

Irving, Allan, and Tomas Young. 2004. " 'Perpetual Liminality': Re-Readings of Subjectivity and Diversity in Clinical Social Work Classrooms." *Smith College Studies in Social Work* 74 (2): 13–227.

Land, Ray, Glynnis Cousin, Jan H. F. Meyer, and Peter Davies. 2005. "Threshold Concepts and Troublesome Knowledge (3)*: Implications for Course Design and Evaluation." In *Improving Student Learning: Diversity and Inclusivity*, edited by Chris Rust, 53–64. Oxford: Oxford Centre for Staff and Learning Development.

Meyer, Jan H. F., Ray Land, and Caroline Baillie, eds. 2010. *Threshold Concepts and Transformational Learning*. Rotterdam: Sense.

Nowacek, Rebecca S. 2011. *Agents of Integration: Understanding Transfer as a Rhetorical Act*. Carbondale: Southern Illinois University Press.

Restaino, Jessica. 2012. *First Semester: Graduate Students, Teaching Writing, and the Challenge of Middle Ground*. Carbondale: Southern Illinois University Press.

Rodrigue, Tanya, and Andrea Williams, eds. 2016. "Teaching Assistants and Writing Across the Curriculum." Special Issue, *Across the Disciplines: Interdisciplinary Perspectives on Language, Learning, and Academic Writing* 13 (3):1–5.

Soliday, Mary. 2011. *Everyday Genres: Writing Assignments across the Disciplines*. Carbondale: Southern Illinois University Press.

1

IMITATION, INNOVATION, AND THE TRAINING OF TAS

Lew Caccia

In my experience, I have noticed many TAs bring to the composition courses they teach a definite sense of how to succeed as a writer.[1] For these TAs, the strategies for effective writing are specific to the environment. It seems TAs transfer their prior expectations as students and stress approaches toward product and process for which they have been affirmed. I have observed some TAs recall their preference toward immediate benefit, or "payback," for an in-class exercise or assignment spread over at least two class meetings.[2] Other TAs sometimes note their discomfort with assignments or activities perceived as having too many restricting requirements. Less evident is the rhetorical practice that can help enact pedagogical theory and facilitate dominant academic writing practices: *imitatio.*

Conversations about imitation are rare in pedagogy today. Perhaps this lack is expected given the dialectic that has existed between imitation and innovation in classical rhetoric and contemporary composition studies. Kathleen Vandenberg observes the studies as "concerned more with the relationship between composition students (as imitators) and teachers (as models) insofar as those relationships have potentially been sites of power, authority, resistance, and 'violence' (albeit not physical)" (2011, 112). Drawing from the perspective of social science philosopher Rene Girard, who believed that human development and rivalry are based on "mimetic desire," Vandenberg affirms the eighteenth century as an approximate chronological divide. Heretofore, the basis for theoretical and applied logic was primarily theological, thus favoring imitation as an educational and professional practice. During the eighteenth century, the ascendancy of science and technology gave rise to logic that favored innovation. Since then, imitation and innovation have existed in tension linked with the binary dissociations of product and process, form and content, originality and correctness. Teachers have hesitated

DOI: 10.7330/9781646420896.c001

to use imitation because, for many, it connotes strict verbatim transfer and inhibits personal expression.

Responding to Vandenberg's call to "illuminate debates over imitation pedagogy in composition studies" (2011, 112) in ways that inform teaching approaches and their relationship with classical rhetoric, this article envisions locating imitation at the forefront of writing-pedagogy education and explores the bases for doing so. Specifically, by drawing on classical rhetoric and contemporary representations of mimetic models, I explore how those engaged in TA training could productively use imitation to complement TAs' prior academic success and their already substantive professional experience in nonacademic settings or prior teaching experience in secondary or alternative postsecondary environments. While a mastery of content—and the ability to ascribe the method by which the content is generated or executed—is essential to reproduce the style, tone, and rhetorical purpose demonstrated in pedagogical practice, informed imitation also integrates multiple models properly selected for emulation. As this essay explains in more detail, attention to pedagogy as imitative practice foregrounds mimesis as a new alteration by which a level of resemblance exists between the original essence and the derivation from which a novel understanding can emerge (figure 1.1). The degree of resemblance can vary among derivations, and the process of emulative selection can be a source of difficulty for imitators. Cicero speaks of such difficulty in *De Oratore*, acknowledging imitation as an affordance that preserves precision. Navigating the constraints posed by both imitative and inventive practice, Cicero recommends "using the best words—and yet quite familiar ones—but also coining by analogy certain words such as would be new to our people, provided only they were appropriate" (1967, 1.34.155).

In this generative performance, Cicero enjoys the availability of choice while entertaining the responsibility of freedom. As Cicero found among the best words both the quite familiar ones and those that are appropriately coined, Quintilian too recognized the limited scope, even the contextual impossibility, of extended verbatim transfer. Regarding one case, Quintilian explains, "We simply cannot help contriving many of [the best possible words], and of various kinds, because Latin idiom is often different from Greek" (2001, X.v.3). The case put forth by Quintilian requires an adequate resemblance between the original and the translation. While the imitator enjoys the choice of new words and figures of speech, the imitator still bears the responsibility to retain the original meaning. When effectively executed, the resulting imitation coexists with the original essence, neither superior nor inferior but

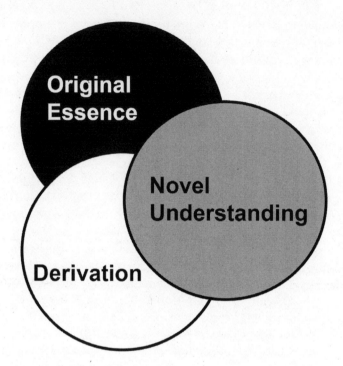

Figure 1.1. Mimesis as new alteration

complementary in a way that advances new knowledge or awareness appropriate to the context of original goals and outcomes.

Understanding imitation as an essential pedagogical method also plays a valuable role for its link with technological and evolutionary progress. Philosophical conceptions of reality are defined by the embedded quality of rhetoric within the larger discursive and material contexts of human activity: "If our art is embryonic when compared with that of the future, then the art of the past must be even more undeveloped" (Sullivan 1989, 16). Thus, by connecting the technological mindset with faith in evolutionary progress, new insights emerge only if original forms and past practice are brought to continual, collective awareness. Communicative art, then, exists as a point of analysis and contemplation: "It tries to break up and challenge experience, make us put it back together in different ways" (Lanham 1976, 114). A careful reading of these passages intensifies our awareness that we cannot produce new insights without returning to the past, so we shouldn't just ignore the past. This is not to say anyone is arguing that we should ignore the past, but this point is important because a general understanding of evolution (both as change and as stability) is premised on the operations of imitation. Hence, this is one of the many ways imitation should be acknowledged to TAs as essential to our thinking.

The imitative practice, or lack thereof, demonstrated by TAs is a concern in the scholarship of writing-pedagogy education. E. Shelley Reid (2011) notes liminality between the TAs' writing-pedagogy education and their actual teaching practice. This liminality, which is discussed later in this essay, inhibits formalized mentoring goals and clarity on principled teaching, accounts of teaching challenges, and approaches toward those challenges. Despite the liminality, first-year TAs do typically express an implicit sense of *imitatio* in their expressed desire to enact the knowledge of their faculty mentors and practicum coordinators. For example, some of my TAs have noted in their journals for practicum the method by which their mentor distributes materials to students in the first-year composition class. They note positioning: where the mentor sits, stands, moves to another part of the room. Positioning is also accounted for in the figurative sense, how topical units are sequenced, how lessons are transitioned into one another. From a content perspective, journals note the manner by which lessons are partitioned. For example, one mentee described a class-long lesson on personification that began with definitions and descriptions of objective and subjective writing. TAs also contemplate in terms of differential imitation when questioning whether to cater teaching styles to particular students. They consider imitation in terms of limitation, whether they, for instance, agree with putting as many restrictions into an essay assignment. Mentees just as much consider imitation in terms of delineation, such as whether specific instructional practices can transfer from composition 101 to developmental English or perhaps to composition 102. TAs even consider the intangible or seemingly intangible issues of emotionally intelligent pedagogical practice, issues that include the question of how they too can build a type of relaxed, yet firm, relationship with students. In their own words, first-year TAs clearly desire to learn and build upon their existing expertise.

Because many new TAs draw more closely on their own experiences as students (or those of peers) than they do scholarship or direct mentoring—and because they are thirsty for models—working from that perspective by encouraging thoughtful imitation can be a way to help new teachers develop.

This encouragement should provide methods by which they could learn to engage and critique—in the service of understanding and enacting—instructional paradigms that contribute to dominant academic writing practices. Without a proper theoretical and applied logic,

TAs are situated at a hindrance. Similar to the way they were asked to mimic the essential qualities of academic discourse in first-year composition, we should likewise instruct them to model generative tools and disciplinary vocabulary in first-year teaching. This more thorough rhetorical grounding would provide a means by which TAs take true ownership of pedagogical principles rather than simply perform educational approaches consistent with the programmatic goals, outcomes, and rubrics that inform assessment. As this essay establishes, an appreciation for emulative selection enables speakers and audiences to perceive more acutely the variable quality of repetitive sequence and its role in unconscious workings of evolutionary progress. If discovery is the process by which we advance knowledge, then affording TAs the resources to comprehend the innovative facets of classroom practice through imitative study of their and others' teaching must not be an implicit agenda but an essential, reinforced component of writing-pedagogy education.

DEFINING EMULATIVE SELECTION

As suggested above, one way to construct this grounding within the TA curriculum is through a study of emulative selection, a neglected facet of the larger scope of imitation. I contend that by initiating rhetorical practice into the practicum classroom and thereby accentuating imitation rather than performance, we can move TAs' attention away from extended verbatim transfer and toward the more inventive yet equally complicated aspects. Figure 1.2 offers a mini wordle to help represent some of the imitable discourse processes that can be traced back to antiquity.

Emulative selection could be defined as striving to excel, especially through imitation, by careful choice or representation. A central category among imitable discourse processes, emulative selection has been described in various ways. As Dale Sullivan explains in "Attitudes toward Imitation: Classical Culture and the Modern Temper," several types of imitable discourse processes can be traced to *De Oratore* and *Institutio Oratoria*, including "very close imitative exercises like memorizing, translating, and paraphrasing, to rather loose forms of imitation: modeling and reading" (1989, 13). Imitation is generally and vaguely opposed to innovation and/or expression. This opposition, however, was not the case for the rhetorical tradition. In *De Oratore*, Cicero expands on the point of modeling as he offers an early pedagogical perspective, suggesting "that we show the student whom to copy, and to copy in such a way as to strive with all possible care to attain the most excellent qualities

Reading Paraphrasing Modeling
Memorizing Imitation Translating
Emulative Selection

Figure 1.2. Several types of imitable discourse processes

of the model" (1967, 2.22.90). Differentiating from the most excellent qualities of the model, Cicero offers an early version of imitation as generative work as opposed to repetitive labor, suggesting that "whereby in copying he may reproduce the pattern of his choice and not portray him as time and again I have known many copyists do, who in copying hunt after such characteristics as are easily copied or even abnormal and possibly faulty" (2.22.90). In this account, Cicero claims one can both imitate and critique any given model. Or more prescriptively, Cicero argues that imitation *should* be selective or it risks imitating faulty qualities. Exploring imitation as generative work thus brings an intentionality to imitation we don't—at least in its simplest definition—give it.

Quintilian's fundamental treatment of imitative practice in *Institutio Oratoria* can be applied across communicative forms and purposes. His efforts to incorporate rhetoric into a comprehensive curriculum offer insights that reinforce and extend Cicero's pedagogical awareness. Following Cicero's suggestion to show students whom to copy, Quintilian affirms it is from "authors worthy of our study that we must draw our stock of words, the variety of our figures and our methods of composition, while we must form our minds on the model of every excellence" (2001, 10.2.1). Quintilian complicates imitative practice on several levels, advising students to assume a critical perspective in their approach. One complication put forth by Quintilian is the inseparability of the intrinsic power of language from the effect of the speaker delivering the language. Quintilian goes as far as to assert that "the greatest qualities of the orator are beyond all imitation" (10.2.12). For the purpose of advising caution in the selection of emulative models, Quintilian attributes "talent, invention, force, facility, and all the qualities which are independent of art" as contributing toward the rhetorical force of discourse.

In addition to encouraging students to take a critical stance in selecting whom and what words to imitate (2001, 10.2.14), Quintilian also calls for integrating multiple models, drawing from not only one author or text or style but doing so in a way that coordinates with the students' own talents and purposes. Quintilian thus presents us with an opportunity to develop theories of TAship in rhetoric and composition toward understanding the fullness of liminalities in those positions. TAs do not always enjoy the same social circumstances and power relations as their faculty. Foley-Schramm et al. offer as a case in point the "complex relationships and power dynamics embedded" (2018, 93) in their contributions toward a university-wide writing rubric. Later in this volume, Rachel Donegan offers another case of complex social circumstances and power relations in her description of a graduate student who had difficulty availing herself of the benefits of her official student accommodations. It is sometimes from their own specialized fields of expertise that TAs can attain legitimated authority from their audiences. Maintaining that even the most celebrated authorities have deficiencies subject to corrective evaluation by appointed critics and peers alike, Quintilian expresses his "wish that imitators were more likely to improve on the good things than to exaggerate the blemishes of the authors whom they seek to copy" (2001, 10.2.15). In his comprehensive treatment of rhetorical education, Quintilian thus establishes that not only can students imitate with alteration, they *must* imitate with alteration. By considering how imitation might be an act done deliberately and carefully, we can help new teachers attempt to use rhetoric as a lens to reconsider teaching practices.

As a form of critical engagement, emulative selection may not easily register among types of imitable discourse processes for an assortment of reasons. As mentioned above, given its association with behaviorism and atomistic formalism, treatments have dismissed imitation as automated, even dehumanizing at the expense of creativity and individuality in communicative practice. Classical rhetoric establishes, however, that imitative practice extends well past a student's adherence to rules and forms. Adherence to rules and forms contributes to a student's imitative practice, but it is just one facet of imitation. While we may quibble as to what certain rules and forms suggest about a student's imitative practice, we do recognize rules and forms are important facets of imitation. This is not to say we agree what emulative selection specifies but rather that it affords a picture that helps us identify and account for a student's imitative practice. If we continue to think of imitation only in terms of adherence to rules and forms, we are precluding the range of options the study of imitation has to offer students and their faculty.

To demonstrate what this focus on mimesis looks like, and what it offers TAs, I return to the studies conducted by E. Shelley Reid, Heidi Estrem, Marcia Belcheir (2012) and others who suggest liminality between the TAs' writing-pedagogy education and their actual teaching practice. The scholars arrived at these most carefully grounded conclusions by focusing on what the TAs might say in the presence of their graduate faculty and how their core beliefs and rationales might alternatively manifest in the absence of their faculty. Partly because the subfield of writing-pedagogy education has not yet achieved a formal standing,[3] the quantity of studies measuring liminality between TAs' writing-pedagogy education and their actual teaching practice are limited.[4] The rigorous studies, however, do take multiple measures over an extended period of time and help illustrate the potential for orienting TAs toward imitative practice.

OBSERVING UNCONSCIOUS REPRODUCTION IN DISCOURSE

In attending to emulative selection in relation to the studies mentioned above, I seek to demonstrate that strategic alteration can take place with any discourse. Also, in helping our TAs understand and then utilize emulative selection, we can help demystify—for the purpose of effectively discerning—some of the difficulties they regularly encounter in enacting conventional theories presented in their writing-pedagogy education. I start with the study conducted by Reid, Estrem, and Belcheir, as well as the follow-up study by Estrem and Reid, which are multimodal and multisite, thus allowing for the examination of liminalities among and between cohorts. In discussing these studies, I draw on fundamentals of imitative practice as developed by classical rhetoricians, as well as by modern scholars.

Reid, Estrem, and Belcheir (2012) concisely note liminality between TAs' writing-pedagogy education and their actual teaching practice. Their three-year, two-site surveys and interviews with TAs reveal the TAs were more influenced by personal beliefs and experiences in and out of the classroom prior to their formal training in pedagogy than they were by the training. Less prevalent in the data was the integration of key principles into the development of syllabi, the design of assignments, and the grading of essays, among other facets of teaching. Focusing even more distinctly on two areas of interviews from the original Reid, Estrem, and Belcheir case study, Estrem and Reid (2012) differentiate between what the TAs might say in the presence of their graduate faculty and how their core beliefs and rationales might alternatively manifest in the absence of their faculty. Within these parameters, the liminality between the TAs' writing-pedagogy education and their actual teaching practice persisted into the TAs' second and third years. Somewhat problematic in the findings was the lack of frequency by which TAs mentioned principles pertaining to pedagogy of approach and pedagogy of content.[5] Particularly problematic was the lack of frequency by which TAs mentioned principles pertaining to focus on encouraging students and focus on student learning. The studies observe how rarely the principles have translated into real evidence of the way TAs use imitation for the benefit of their scholarly practice. Offering a remedy, Estrem and Reid suggest that "*all* of our TAs would benefit from more opportunities to name principles, connect them to multiple sources, and reflect on them" (2012, 463). They are calling for TAs to enact more of their formal training and demonstrate, it could be argued, for more evidence of using imitation pedagogy in their teaching and scholarship.

My claim is not that imitation is better than the practices outlined by Estrem and Reid. Rather, my claim is that this kind of teacher education—grounded in learning theory—actually is imitation. In other words, we teach imitation but don't call it that. The specific principles and multiple sources Reid, Estrem, and Belcheir would like to observe between TAs' behavior in the presence and absence of their graduate faculty are examples of the "very close imitative exercises" encouraged in *De Oratore* and *Institutio Oratoria*. Likewise, setting forth as desired outcomes the integration of key principles from established sources into syllabi, assignments, and grading models Cicero's early pedagogical form of showing the student whom to copy. Setting forth these desired outcomes similarly relocates Quintilian's advice to deploy vocabulary, language structures, and compositional methods in ways consistent with worthy authors. TAs would thus benefit by being challenged to first understand imitation as a complex concept and then identify how and when (and why) they will imitate those (and that) whom they admire.

A broader tendency to refrain from the word *imitation* exists in both composition theory and practice. Possible motives for this hesitancy to state imitation as a desired outcome in the practicum classroom or in conversations between mentors and mentees are quite understandable. In many fields of endeavor, professionals refrain from using the word *imitation* because the term is often connoted toward its extremes. John Muckelbauer explains, "According to most accounts, the demise of imitation pedagogy is explicitly linked to the institutional emergence of romantic subjectivity, an ethos that emphasizes creativity, originality, and genius. If imitation is conversely linked to concepts such as repetition, copying, and tradition, it would thus seem to be intrinsically at odds with the inventive emphasis of romanticism" (2003, 62). From a disciplinary standpoint, perhaps one reason rhetoric and composition has not as often engaged this concept is because of the prevalence of another word so very important to our work in the field: *agency*. Perhaps there is a collective sense that imitation compromises agency? As a field, we work to bestow agency on emerging colleagues such as new TAs, and maybe we're inherently suspicious of paradigms that compromise agency.

Despite the hesitancy to engage with the term on a more broadly defined scale, classical and contemporary rhetoricians have examined and enacted the term. The work jointly clarifies the term for its essential qualities and for its more nuanced complexities. Edward P. J. Corbett's *Classical Rhetoric for the Modern Student* (1971a) provides not only "imitation exercises" as resources for new discourse communities and their audiences but also testimonies about the value of imitation from Winston Churchill, Malcolm X, and other leading communicators of the twentieth century. Though Corbett can be read as grousing just a bit when he observes, "The present mood of education theorists is against such structured, fettered training. The emphasis now is on creativity, self-expression, individuality" (1971b, 249), he takes care to allow for circumstance in delineating "analysis" (i.e., close examination) and "genesis" (i.e., actual reproduction or derivation) as the operative components of *imitatio* (1971a, 27). The desire to impart imitation is also sustained in David Bartholomae's classic "Inventing the University." Though his focus is on the first-year undergraduate writer when he advises the need for the student to "crudely mimic the 'distinctive register' of academic discourse before they are prepared to actually and legitimately do the work of the discourse" (1986, 19–20), his sense parallels the call from Reid, Estrem, and Belcheir (2012) to provide TAs with the generative tools and disciplinary vocabulary from which they can draw in their teaching. People are involved in imitative exercises all the time and don't think of them as opposed to innovation; attempting to model a mentor's approach to writing pedagogy is no different than a classical student attempting to model a writer.

The whole question of the relationship between what TAs learn and how they teach is itself a question of imitation. In his Richard Braddock Award-winning essay, Dylan B. Dryer notes liminality similar to and yet distinct from that observed in the studies by Reid, Estrem, and Belcheir (2012). Having conducted interviews with first-year TAs and analyses of their responses to student essays, Dryer finds that, as novice teachers, TAs tend to stray from the dominant academic writing practices established in disciplinary literature and more often project their own anxieties about academic writing. Dryer thus calls for a distinct form of imitation that includes "deroutinizing *practices*" (2012, 441).

Accordingly, practicum would present conventional theories to TAs and offer strategies for enacting the theories; all the while, students would be encouraged to rethink genres, experiment with material or linguistic conditions, and engage in institutional critique (442–43). What might deroutinizing practices more concretely look like? Take into consideration that, in Ohio, Section 3345.45 of the Revised Code calls for a revision of tenure policy for public institutions who want state funding. In addition to the criteria of instruction, research, and service, commercialization should be added as a criterion. In practicum, faculty and TAs can explore the historical trajectory that has led to this mandate to add commercialization. When faculty present TAs with existing syllabi for analysis and discussion, they can consider how the policy might constrain and enable new syllabi and how those contingencies reflect transfer to and from public and private entities beyond the university. The deroutinizing practices Dryer calls for in developing genres, conditions, and critique establish that interpretive judgment must understand essential principles not only in isolation but holistically. With respect to the ability to cultivate individual expression cognizant of properly selected models, his point is reified by Lanham's (1976) call to partition models and then reintegrate them in innovative ways.

When TAs imitate, their writing-pedagogy education integrates the best of what they and their faculty have to offer. Or at least this would be the ideal. The notion of what constitutes best could certainly be contested. It seems natural for novice teachers to think that a majority of what they observe in a mentor would be the best, or at least above average, in teaching. I remember one of my mentors years ago telling me a story of how his mentor introduced a composition class to transcendental meditation. My mentor thought it was really cool and tried making the same introduction when he taught his first composition course—but did not find the pedagogical practice a fit with his background. What my mentor did find fit him was a sense of balance between rigor and flexibility in his work with students, a sense of balance I in turn took away and later incorporated into my teaching philosophy. Maybe this is an example of emulative selection, of differentiating, perhaps with a little trial and error, between exceptional practices in order to decide which to imitate.

As established by the scholars discussed in this section, the absence of imitation suggests novice teachers are not fully implementing their grounding in dominant academic writing practices. This gap leaves not fully realized the work of the CCCC Committee on Preparing Teachers of Writing, as well as the SIG on the Education and Mentoring of TAs and Instructors in Composition. Imitation done deliberately and carefully enhances formalized mentoring goals and clarity on principled teaching, accounts of teaching challenges, and approaches toward those challenges. Writing-pedagogy education that acknowledges imitation and innovation also improves efforts toward validity and reliability in pedagogical practice.

Many TAs bring with them specialized knowledge, including professional writing experience in corporate and nonprofit sectors, as well as prior pedagogical experience, perhaps overseas or in a K–12 setting, a range of experience similar to that observed by Megan Schoettler and Elizabeth Saur in this volume. Hence, writing-pedagogy education that stimulates imitation and innovation helps TAs enact theories presented in practicum in ways that could be replicable, aggregable, data based, and hence more plausibly subject to Dryer's deroutinizing analyses. When TAs are able to take ownership of principles and policies imposed programmatically, writing-pedagogy education becomes more accessible in its ability to effect changes in teachers' goals and practice.

ENCOURAGING STUDENTS' UNCONSCIOUS REPRODUCTION

The time we spend helping TAs recognize imitation and innovation exist along a continuum rather than as a divide (figure 1.3) can inspire more animated teaching and more effective application of their writing-pedagogy education. Moreover, this awareness can help bridge the distance between the practice of teaching and its theoretical underpinnings. While the latter reinforces programmatic structures, it also more fluidly situates writing as teachable for its material and intrinsic value. As invention places its subject matter into question, writing and writing instruction are more than just means to an end. Critical reflective practice can help TAs see their own histories as students and writers in ways more complementary to and less divergent from their writing-pedagogy education. Describing writing-pedagogy education as an emergent area within the field of composition studies, Estrem and Reid (2012) emphasize the growing parallel between the TA seminar and first-year composition. This emphasis encourages exploration of connections between Bartholomae's (1986) efforts to instill generative tools and disciplinary vocabulary in first-year composition and Reid's endeavors to do similarly in the form of establishing standardized "mentoring program's goals" and performance assessment in yearly mentor education (2008, 52). Estrem and Reid (2012) further maintain that writing-pedagogy education extends semesters beyond the TA seminar; this argument beckons

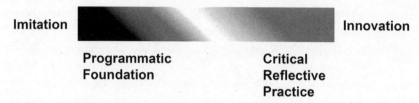

Imitation   **Innovation**

Programmatic   **Critical**
Foundation   **Reflective**
                                Practice

Figure 1.3. Imitation and innovation as continuum

questions concerning the place of composition within the academy. Lisa Ede raises insightful questions. Drawing from personal experience and alternative texts that include cartoons, Ede applies theoretical critique in asserting scholars should attend more carefully to the differences between theory and the practice of theory. In her partitioning, Ede explains "'theory' is an overdetermined term, one whose meaning and consequences vary for different persons and in different situations" (2004, 129). She designates theory as a "situated practice" always open to question. This openness aligns with the critique and reengagement scholars often associate with *imitatio*:

> When we think about the power of ideologies to influence our thoughts and actions and the multiple ways that they can discipline even the most critical, vigilant person, it may be helpful to recognize that, in Burkean terms, we are all "rotten with perfection" ("Definition of Man" 16).
>
> We are all disciplined by ideologies of which we can at best be only partly conscious. And we all at one time or another intentionally and unintentionally contribute to the disciplining of others. (170)

Even Burke's theory of identification/consubstantiation is grounded in imitation. In her statement, Ede asserts that ideology is only partly conscious, though it is from ideology that people often critique and even reprimand others. This commentary reifies Burke's notion of "consubstantiality" and the notion that practitioners sometimes act on underlying principles not always visible in observed practice. Invoking a term originally used in theological circles, Burke distinguishes a sharing of essence or substance that can take on the form of physical aesthetics or deeper cognitive immersion. Burke explains, "Imitation is an essentially dramatistic concept. It makes for consubstantiality by community of ways ('identification'), since [people] can either crudely imitate one another's actions as revealed on the surface, or subtly imitate the *underlying principles* of such actions" (1969, 131). Burke's deeper analysis presents us with the possibility that when new teachers do not appear to mimic their writing-pedagogy education or the examples of their mentors, perhaps there still exists an overlap of underlying principles based on a shared sense of dominant academic writing practices. This possibility suggests the need to not only adjust writing-pedagogy education and/or extend its length but also conduct well-structured synchronous conversations posteducation to discover potential adherence (or a self-assessed perception of adherence) that may not be so visible in observed practice.

Michael Stancliff and Maureen Daly Goggin further complicate the informative and conflictive facets of theorizing TA preparation. Central to this complication is their question, "How can teacher-trainers and mentors best identify and foster sites of ideological conflict and disagreement as a way to model a pedagogical practice of critical reflection?" (2007, 11). Their shared perspective is grounded in their experience as TA mentors. As mentors, Stancliff and Goggin insist on rhetoric as a way of helping students develop a range of possible pedagogies and in the process differentiate their own pedagogical and rhetorical assumptions. The assumptions might be thought of as Burke's underlying principles, and the differentiation can be thought of as Jessica Restaino's (2012, 16) "middle space" of safe experimentation for TAs. Acknowledging TA preparation as a hotly contested area, Stancliff and Goggin model learner-centered principles while affirming goals consistent with the mission of the writing program and the interconnection of theory and practice in the teaching of writing. These goals are similarly articulated by Stephen Wilhoit who, in his *Teaching Assistant's Handbook*, explicates "reflective teaching" by drawing from eleven years' experience as a TA director, years as a TA mentor, personal experience as a TA at three universities, and a survey of literature on TA education:

> Perhaps the most powerful aid to life-long improvement as an instructor is developing the capacity for reflective teaching. Reflective teachers actively and systematically critique their curriculum and pedagogy, identify strengths and weaknesses, explore alternative practices, and make needed changes. Developing your reflective teaching skills is one of the most important steps you can take to ensure you grow as a teacher throughout your career. (2008, 205)

Classical and contemporary scholarship establishes that imitation effectively requires rethinking and experimenting with form and constitution. Consistent with these tenets of imitation, Wilhoit argues that TAs need a wealth of information yet freedom to self-direct their syllabi, assignments, and instructional approach even if it means they sometimes fail as teachers (2008, xix). Maintaining the need for affording TAs a balance of freedom and structure, Wilhoit links imitative teaching and practitioning with the reflective facets of current writing-pedagogy scholarship:

Reflecting-in-action is an individual act performed spontaneously in the classroom and leads to immediate decisions and actions. You usually see the results of those decisions and actions at once—your students' responses help you gauge the success of your decisions. Reflecting-on-action, however, takes place away from students, often long after a class is over. It can be performed at leisure and can involve several instructors collaboratively assessing their curriculum or classroom performance. You usually see the results of this reflection later, when you return to class and teach your students again. (206)

With respect to appropriate models, Wilhoit at the same time recognizes a need for differential training variables not only to the TAs' prior pedagogical and professional experience but also their gender, race, age, intended career trajectory, and type of institution in which they serve. Like Wilhoit and Ede, Stancliff and Goggin believe in the benefit of multiple approaches in the teaching of writing, especially given the range of experiences TAs bring. My first TA had worked as a professional journalist for close to twenty years. This was years before commercialization became a mandate for state-funded higher education, but her role in the course presented a great opportunity to consider transfer in pedagogical development to and from public and private entities beyond the university. Because I believe in the benefit of multiple approaches in the teaching of writing—and am open to new, interdisciplinary principles and vocabulary I might add to my repertoire—it made perfect sense to invite her to lead class on the day students were being taught techniques for conducting interviews.[6]

The potential pedagogical practices offered by Stancliff and Goggin (2007) are in part based on James Berlin's (1988) classification of composition pedagogies, specifically three rhetorics he finds predominant in institutional approaches: cognitive psychology, expressionism, and social-epistemic rhetoric. Among these, Berlin defends social-epistemic rhetoric as placing ideology at the center of classroom practice and affording a mechanism of criticizing—much as Dryer deroutinizes—economic, political, and social arrangements. Here, we have another opportunity to apply fresh perspectives on the liminality of TAships. Recalling that TAs do not always enjoy the same social circumstances and power relations as their faculty, social-epistemic practice helps facilitate careful assessment of the collective benefit of the way TAs draw and disseminate from their specialized fields of expertise. According to Berlin, the social-epistemic perspective recognizes teaching is always political and contingent upon economic and cultural contexts (490). In facilitating personal reflection and autocritique, individualistic ideology informs the improvisation characteristic of expressivist rhetoric. Stancliff and

Goggin (2007) caution that some of their TAs view Berlin himself as politicizing writing instruction in his adamancy that teaching is always influenced by ulterior motives that select from ranging assumptions of what is good, real, possible, and appropriately administered.

Nevertheless, encouraging TAs to consider the concept of unconscious reproduction can help them think about translating respected pedagogical models into their own classroom practice. Imitative technique need not impose restriction upon TAs but rather provide impetus for critical stance, innovation, creativity, and individual expertise. We can accordingly apply the complexities of key principles, disciplinary vocabulary, dominant academic writing practices, the sources from which they are grounded, and the material or linguistic conditions of the local classroom.

We can apply these complexities to measure and account for the objectives and outcomes that attend the various degrees of modeling and other forms of imitative exercise. In their essay in this collection, Lillian Campbell and Jaclyn Fiscus-Cannaday apply such complexities to dissect the use of space for the purpose of modeling a student-centered classroom. Also in this volume, Jennifer K. Johnson discusses modeling as a practice that can help negotiate the competing paradigms of literature and composition, and Kathryn M. Lambrecht offers modeling as an approach to eliciting community and identity in the texts of first-year writing students. Though introducing students to the study of emulative selection is not the only way to foster rhetorical awareness in writing pedagogy education,[7] it is an approach to helping new teachers appreciate programmatic goals, outcomes, and rubrics as more than mechanical or habitual repetition. As this introduction at the same time challenges TAs composite experiences and successes by assuming critical reflection, it offers a means toward encouraging more intricate ways of enacting acquired expertise. Instructing TAs to cultivate emulative selection as unconscious reproduction that brings into consciousness the affinity among teachers, their students, their mentors, and their discipline allows them to perceive, reproduce, and comprehend the variability of the form and function of imitative discovery—a more encouraging possibility compared with resisting this work or reducing it to performance. This emphasis also progresses imitation from textbook exercises to an essential place in the making of knowledge for both teaching and writing. In a way appropriate to particular circumstances, imitation is not set forth as a finite range of categories and features of discourse (sentence types and other syntactical units, for example) but rather as heuristics for expressing ideas in styles that negotiate difference among various discourse communities. Said another way, TAs would learn generative possibilities rather than anticipated shortcomings.

REINVIGORATING IMITATION STUDIES BEYOND THE CLASSROOM

The rhetorical training of first-year composition teachers should, of course, overlap with the research undertaken by scholars of rhetoric and composition. We can envision, experiment, and enact ways of bringing imitation into the practicum classroom. We can help new teachers develop intricate methods of adhering to rules and forms by presenting them with ways to integrate multiple models properly selected for emulation. We can set about enunciating as a discipline the rationale for the necessity of such focus. As I emphasize emulative selection, which is just one facet of imitation, I do not aim to preclude areas of inquiry that represent imitative study as a comprehensive field. Rather, focusing on the training of TAs allows me to offer a purpose imitative study might serve in writing-pedagogy education. Equally important is the purpose writing-pedagogy education can serve in detailing what imitative studies look like. As Vandenberg has observed, an opposing tension exists between imitation and innovation in composition studies: "In large part, this is because those against it see imitation as working against innovation; they see the form constricting and restricting both the content and the individual wishing to express himself" (2011, 125). Integrating imitation—including a mature, comprehensive awareness—can help writing-pedagogy educators comprehend its disciplinary record and relationship with classical and contemporary rhetoric.

Attempting to modernize or refurbish classical insight accepts not only discourse that appears consistent with original essence but also takes into account strategic alteration. Indeed, it is exactly classical rhetoric's treatment of generative performance that can help us direct our TAs toward the relationship between mastery of content and innovative occurrence. Surveying the process of emulative selection among conventional theories and pedagogical models offers deep resources because such selection involves the largely unconscious critical engagement TAs use in their actual classroom practice. I further maintain that attention to emulative selection, and imitation more broadly, can contribute to closing the gap between theory and practice (graduate education in general), as well as between students' formal training and prior professional experience (writing-pedagogy education as a field). Writing-pedagogy education could serve as a central locale that emphasizes imitative features of discourse helpful to practicum coursework and mentoring arrangements, such as those categorized in this volume by Kylee Thacker Maurer, Faith Matzker, and Ronda Leathers Dively. Ultimately, imitative studies in writing-pedagogy education have the potential to elevate not only the rhetorical capacities of our TAs but also our concept of writing-pedagogy education as a field and our ability to inform discussions pertaining to liminality in the academy and the public sphere.

NOTES

1. I extend sincere thanks to editor Bill Macauley and the anonymous reviewers for their detailed feedback and guidance. Many thanks also to Suzanne Wasilewski and all the TAs with whom I have worked.

2. In these cases, TAs sometimes recall having asked themselves as undergraduate students what the assignment had taught them or what they now know from the assignment that they didn't know or understand beforehand. In these recollections, TAs posit that the students their mentors are teaching would not immediately see how the assignment benefits them because they have to finish it in the next class session.

3. Reid (2011) rightly encourages establishing writing-pedagogy education (WPE) as an official subfield to complement existing disciplinary structures, including the CCC Committee on Preparing Teachers of Writing and the SIG on the Education and Mentoring of TAs and Instructors in Composition.

4. Reid, Estrem, and Belcheir (2012) encourage disciplinary colleagues to continue similarly designed cross-sectional research projects that would add to the pool of variables examined at specific points in time. Lauren Obermark, Elizabeth Brewer, and Kay Halasek offer one continuation that reports "demonstrable differences in individuals' senses of preparedness and autonomy" even among second-year TAs (2015, 35). The data from their study informs a professional-development program by which the researchers collaborate with TAs, incorporating their background and perspectives.

5. In Estrem and Reid's (2012) taxonomy, pedagogy of approach includes classroom practices and community engagement; pedagogy of content includes teaching critical reading, teaching writing as a process, and expanding students' understanding of writing.

6. From my TA's experience, I learned to incorporate into the lesson the principle "endure awkward silences." Interview subjects will eventually speak even when they are initially silent in response to a question. I also learned to advise students to specifically ask for anecdotes while interviewing. Anecdotes help provide data with depth and dimension.

7. Exposure to ethos, pathos, and logos would be a textbook example, literally and figuratively, of existing alternative efforts to incorporate rhetorical awareness into the curriculum for first-year TAs.

REFERENCES

Bartholomae, David J. 1986. "Inventing the University." *Journal of Basic Writing* 5 (1): 4–23.
Berlin, James A. 1988. "Rhetoric and Ideology in the Writing Class." *College English* 50 (5): 477–94.
Burke, Kenneth. 1963. "Definition of Man." *Hudson Review* 16 (4): 491–514.

Burke, Kenneth. 1969. *A Rhetoric of Motives*. Berkeley: University of California Press.

Cicero, Marcus Tullius. 1967. *De Oratore, Books I–II*. Translated by Edward William Sutton and Harris Rackham. Cambridge: Harvard University Press.

Corbett, Edward P. J. 1971a. *Classical Rhetoric for the Modern Student*. New York: Oxford University Press.

Corbett, Edward P. J. 1971b. "The Theory and Practice of Imitation in Classical Rhetoric." *College Composition and Communication* 22 (3): 243–50.

Dryer, Dylan B. 2012. "At a Mirror, Darkly: The Imagined Undergraduate Writers of Ten Novice Composition Instructors." *College Composition and Communication* 63 (3): 420–52.

Ede, Lisa S. 2004. *Situating Composition: Composition Studies and the Politics of Location*. Carbondale: Southern Illinois University Press.

Estrem, Heidi, and E. Shelley Reid. 2012. "What New Writing Teachers Talk about When They Talk about Teaching." *Pedagogy: Critical Approaches to Teaching Literature, Language, Composition, and Culture* 12 (3): 449–80.

Foley-Schramm, Ashton, Bridget Fullerton, Eileen M. James, and Jenna Morton-Aiken. 2018. "Preparing Graduate Students for the Field: A Graduate Student Praxis Heuristic for WPA Professionalization and Institutional Politics." *WPA: Writing Program Administration* 41 (2): 89–103.

Lanham, Richard A. 1976. *The Motives of Eloquence: Literary Rhetoric in the Renaissance*. New Haven: Yale University Press.

Muckelbauer, John. 2003. "Imitation and Invention in Antiquity: An Historical-Theoretical Revision." *Rhetorica* 21 (2):61–88.

Obermark, Lauren, Elizabeth Brewer, and Kay Halasek. 2015. "Moving from the One and Done to a Culture of Collaboration: Revising Professional Development for TAs." *WPA: Writing Program Administration* 39 (1): 32–53.

Quintilian, Marcus Fabius. 2001. *The Orator's Education (Institutio Oratoria)*. Translated by Donald A. Russell. Cambridge: Harvard University Press.

Reid, E. Shelley. 2008. "Mentoring Peer Mentors: Mentor Education and Support in the Composition Program." *Composition Studies* 36 (2): 51–79.

Reid, E. Shelley. 2011. "Preparing Writing Teachers: A Case Study in Constructing a More Connected Future for CCCC and NCTE." *College Composition and Communication* 62 (4): 687–703.

Reid, E. Shelley, Heidi Estrem, and Marcia Belcheir. 2012. "The Effects of Writing Pedagogy Education on Graduate Teaching Assistants' Approaches to Teaching Composition." *WPA: Writing Program Administration* 36 (1): 32–73.

Restaino, Jessica. 2012. *First Semester: Graduate Students, Teaching Writing, and the Challenge of Middle Ground*. Carbondale: Southern Illinois University Press.

Stancliff, Michael, and Maureen D. Goggin. 2007. "What's Theorizing Got to Do With It? Teaching Theory as Resourceful Conflict and Reflection in TA Preparation." *WPA: Writing Program Administration* 30 (3): 11–28.

Sullivan, Dale L. 1989. "Attitudes toward Imitation: Classical Culture and the Modern Temper." *Rhetoric Review* 8 (1): 5–21.

Vandenberg, Kathleen M. 2011. "Revisiting Imitation Pedagogies in Composition Studies from a Girardian Perspective." *Contagion: Journal of Violence, Mimesis, and Culture* 18 (1): 111–134.

Wilhoit, Stephen W. 2008. *The Longman Teaching Assistant's Handbook: A Guide for Graduate Instructors of Writing and Literature*. New York: Pearson.

2

MULTIMODAL ANALYSIS AND THE COMPOSITION TASHIP
Exploring Embodied Teaching in the Writing Classroom

Lillian Campbell and Jaclyn Fiscus-Cannaday

Lillian Campbell and Jaclyn Fiscus-Cannaday gathered this research at the University of Washington (UW)—a large public institution in which most undergraduate students identify as STEM—while they were both graduate students in rhetoric and composition at UW. There are two writing programs at UW housed in the English department: the expository writing program (EWP), which is the larger of the two and adopts a writing-across-the-curriculum approach, and the interdisciplinary writing program (IWP), which adopts a writing-in-the-disciplines approach. This research draws on the experiences of first- and second-year TAs tasked with being instructors of record for one of the strains of the EWP first-year writing course.

As composition TA Cleo begins teaching complex arguments, she draws her fingers into a fist. Watching a video of herself later, she laughs: "My crystallization hand motion that I did was really funny. Bring all of the things you want to say together into a big fist." Meanwhile, TA Chris explains how arguments shape an essay's organization by making a dramatic weaving gesture, which he later connects to his scholarship in medieval literature: "Text comes from textus, which is Latin for cloth or to weave, so I mean . . . weaving your concession throughout your argument is an important point." In these moments, new TAs offer complex pedagogical performances of writing concepts, drawing on embodied resources informed by their own writing experiences, teacher education, and disciplinary identities. This chapter calls for composition TAs to pay increased attention to the embodied and performative aspects of their teaching, especially as they navigate the liminal position between burgeoning scholar and first-year writing teacher.

DOI: 10.7330/9781646420896.c002

While scholars have long recognized the complexity of writing TAs' identifications and institutional positions, their classroom performances are an underutilized site for studying processes of identity negotiation. This chapter begins with a review of scholarship on the relationships among TA liminality, performative pedagogy, and embodied writing. We position this research at an intersection between education scholarship on teaching as embodied performance (Enriquez et al. 2015; Freedman and Holmes 2003) and writing studies research on material and embodied writing processes (Gonzales 2015; Haas and Witte 2001; Wolfe 2005). We argue that multimodal discourse analysis has much to offer writing TAs working to understand their complex positioning and unique identifications, providing an analytic framework for attending to how embodied talk "index[es] specific discourses about self, writing, [and] academia" (Lillis 2009, 176).

Next, we introduce data from a case study of four first-year composition TAs—three literature scholars and one composition scholar—all second-year graduate instructors in the same composition program at a large public university. Each teacher was video recorded during a lesson on argument and then interviewed about select moments from that lesson and about their views on writing, disciplinary identity, and pedagogy. The images featured in this chapter are recreations of the TA's gestures in the screenshots that we used for analysis. Unfortunately, the quality of those screenshots was not high enough to include them in publication. Our analysis demonstrates how gestures can index both connection making and tension between disparate areas of disciplinary expertise. TAs also physically enact a range of versions of what constitutes good writing, emphasizing practices like nuancing and close reading. Analysis of how each of these TAs negotiates their unique history and perspectives on the classroom fuels even more questions. How do TAs balance teaching general principles about writing practice with a view of writing as situated and constantly in flux? How do they structure a classroom discussion to support authentic, collaborative discovery of knowledge? How do TAs value student incomes while ensuring they achieve program outcomes? How do they take what they learned in previous classrooms and apply it to new teaching contexts? This proliferation of questions is evidence of the richness and complexity that becomes visible through multimodal analyses of TAs' classroom performances. The approach modeled in this chapter certainly does not promise easy answers. However, it does offer a framework for further understanding the complex layers of personal experience, institutional regulations, and programmatic guidelines that undergird the composition TA position.

In the conclusion, we discuss implications of an embodied view of the composition TAship for TA training, professional development, and future research. Videotaping lessons is already a popular exercise in TA training, but our research points to possible improvements to this practice. We argue that teaching videos can help TAs recognize and evaluate the strategies they use to negotiate a multiplicity of identities in the classroom. We also discuss how future researchers might adopt our methodological framework for projects involving teacher development and embodied identity performance. Overall, this chapter demonstrates that by theorizing and attending to composition TAs' embodied resources in the classroom, writing TAs can better understand the unique affordances and limitations of their liminal position.

EMBODYING LIMINAL TA IDENTITIES

Recent research demonstrates how new TAs negotiate a range of identities—as students, scholars, writers, and teachers—which can support, interfere with, or complicate their teaching experiences. The unique position of graduate students as novice academic writers and teachers who are "themselves still learning disciplinary writing conventions, genres, and ideologies" has the potential to make them effective brokers of field-specific writing norms (Winzenried 2016). At the same time, composition TAs' burgeoning identity as disciplinary scholars, often in fields outside rhetoric and composition, can shape their developing teaching personas and limit their ability to find a comfortable role in the composition classroom (Restaino 2012). For some composition TAs, the split between their scholarly work and their classroom teaching can lead them to see the identities of teacher and scholar as incommensurable: "Their identities as scholars lie outside of composition while their identities as teacher lie within it. By seeing these identities as separate, they are unable to see the relevance of composition scholarship" (Grouling 2015, "Graduate Student-Teacher Identity").

To help new composition TAs navigate the complexities of their various identities, many writing programs require practicum courses, which offer theoretical perspectives and pedagogical insights for teaching writing. As Jennifer Johnson discusses in detail in this collection, these experiences do the work of enculturation: steeping graduate students in the composition theory of their specific writing program's brand. Scholarship on new composition TAs has found general resistance to the theoretical thrust of these practicum courses and demand for emphasizing pragmatic teaching strategies (Grouling 2015; Hesse 1993). In response, a number of scholars have called for more diverse modes of writing practice within the practicum course, arguing that reflective writing activities, journaling, and drafting can lead to better engagement and TA self-understanding (Ebest 2005; Reid 2009). Leah Zuidema and James Fredricksen assert that providing a variety of writing experiences for preservice teachers is vital: "They should experience a depth and breadth of writing opportunities and be guided in reflecting on those experiences to better understand how writing works" (2016, 15). Given the increasing investment in multimodal pedagogy, one could also argue that teachers should have opportunities to practice and reflect on multimedia composing. Indeed, in "Multimodality, Performance, and Teacher Training," Laura Micciche, Hannah Rule, and Liv Stratman (2012) offer examples of multimodal assignments that call TAs' attention to the "extra-linguistic aspects of teaching" ("Updating an Old Standard") and foster critical reflection.

Micciche, Rule, and Stratman's (2012) research has implications that go far beyond multimodal assignments for TA pedagogy courses, however. Their study argues that by conceiving of the composition TAship as embodied, TAs can gain new ways of understanding how their identities are negotiated during a "pedagogical performance." For the authors, teacher identity is always performed and constantly in flux: "Gestures, vocal tendencies, listening practices, and movements, among other things, produce us as teachers" ("Introduction"). This perspective is not new; research on secondary education has long drawn on theories of performance and embodiment to understand teachers' classroom experiences (Enriquez et al. 2015; Freedman and Holmes 2003; Louis 2005). Performative frameworks have often been used in contexts in which the teachers' body is markedly different from the students' in order to understand how these physical differences can be bridged. For example, Elisabeth Johnson's (2013) article explores how an English teacher counters her own white, middle-class identity and reaches her black, working class students through engagement with popular-culture artifacts. Working from a cultural studies framework, this research is primarily focused on understanding how bodies index affiliations with particular groups or identities and how that might impact classroom practices.

Instead of viewing the body primarily as a site of social construction, recent theories of embodiment also emphasize its rhetorical force. As Kristie Fleckenstein explains, "While the body exists as a social construct, reinforced through language and image, embodiment exists as an ongoing creation arising out of an individual's unique incarnate experiences in the world" (2009, 107–8). A focus on embodiment, then, calls attention to situated performances and raises questions about how individuals enact conflicting allegiances and identifications. For example, Pierre Bourdieu's (1980) theory of habitus emphasizes how over time and through participation in different communities and institutions, individuals accrue physical ways of being in the world that are not fully conscious. Meanwhile, T. Kenny Fountain's concept of trained vision draws on these theories to describe how disciplinary expertise is a process of "develop[ing] the skilled capacities necessary to use the discourse and objects, the displays and documents, according to the explicit and tacit rules of that community" (2014, 5). For composition TAs, then, part of the process of developing teaching expertise involves negotiating between movements they have accrued throughout their lives and the new discourse and objects of the classroom—the chalkboard, the attendance sheet, the student desks.

Within rhetoric and composition scholarship, there is growing interest in how student and professional writers embody both the writing process and their views of writing; however, there has been less attention to how teachers do the same. For example, Christina Haas and Stephen Witte (2001) and Joanna Wolfe (2005) both consider how groups of writers (a multidisciplinary engineering team and a group of engineering students respectively) use gesture and movement to negotiate the writing process and distribute knowledge across group members. Meanwhile, Laura Gonzales (2015) and Andrea Olinger (2014) study how students' gestures and movements index their attitudes towards writing. Gonzales's research on video recordings of multilingual-student focus groups describes how their gestures convey their views on the differences between textual and multimodal composing. Meanwhile, Olinger draws on video interviews with three scientific coauthors to demonstrate how they use verbal and gestural metaphors to convey their understandings and values about scientific writing style. These findings showcase how studying embodiment can illuminate writerly and disciplinary identities, and we build off this research to explore the embodied practices of new composition TAs. Given their liminal positioning within multiple identities, our study draws on theories of embodiment to better understand how TAs' pedagogical performances can index disciplinary alignments, teaching identities, and ideologies about what makes good writing.

DATA COLLECTION AND ANALYSIS

The four TAs discussed in this chapter responded to a program-wide email at a large public university, which introduced our study and called for composition TAs in their first or second year to participate.

Upon selection, teachers informed us when they would be introducing argument to their students for the first time so we could observe the class and video record their lesson. Most TAs selected the day they were teaching complex claims, the composition program's term for an argumentative statement in college-level writing. The writing program distinguished *complex claims* from a term students might be more accustomed to from high school: *thesis*. We visited their classrooms on the agreed-upon day, described the project to the class before our observation, and obtained consent from both teachers and students to having their audio and visuals represented in publications. We then video recorded the lesson and later selected clips emblematic of the TAs' performances, focusing on excerpts in which gestures were being used to coordinate classroom activity, communicate information, and embody their conception of argument. About two weeks after we observed their self-selected class, we conducted semistructured interviews with participants, obtaining background information about teaching experience, research interests, and writing beliefs. We also played the selected clips, asking participants to describe their embodied teaching practices and discuss connections to their classroom aims and scholarly positioning.

To analyze our multimodal data, we began by creating screenshots of the teaching clips we had identified prior to our interviews and transcribing the classroom talk from these excerpts. We then transcribed all four participant interviews and open coded the video and interview transcripts with attention to (1) disciplinary positioning, (2) student orientation, and (3) views on writing. We organized our coding into a large spreadsheet. For each instructor, we selected quotes from the interview that had been coded for each of the three categories. We also described key embodied moments in which the TAs' positioning came to the fore. For example, for Chris, under *student orientation*, we had quotes describing the limitations of the composition curriculum, his frustrations with programmatic outcomes, and his focus on "deprogramming" students from their high-school learning. Under *embodied moments*, we noted his tendency to face the board while rewording student contributions and his frequent open-handed stance used to pose rhetorical questions, among others. After organizing quotes and gestures in this way, we collaboratively developed a descriptor that captured the nuances of these perspectives and their embodiments. For Chris' student orientation, we used *untrained informant* to highlight both his emphasis on lack of experience and his authoritative positioning in the classroom. Ultimately, we found that our third category, *views on writing*, overlapped substantially

Table 2.1. Teaching assistants by course, disciplinary positioning, and orientation to students

Participant	FYC Course	Disciplinary Positioning	Orientation to Students
Chris	Literature-based	Expert: expertise in his discipline is fundamental to his self-identity and his role in the classroom	Untrained informant: believes his experience as an academic writer can be a resource for helping "deprogram" students' writing but doesn't buy into programmatic vision or goals
Matt	Literature-based	Flâneur: confident in his disciplinary knowledge but likes to move between disciplines in ways that suit his "weird" interests	Coordinator of chaos: wants students to experience an authentic exploration of ideas. He coordinates conversation to the degree he feels necessary, but is also invested in foregrounding student voices.
Cleo	Stretch version, nonfiction	Pragmatist: disciplinary knowledge informs teaching, and teaching informs disciplinary interests (recursive relationship)	Connection maker: emphasizes the relationship between lessons and students' prior experiences, highlighting the role of their incoming knowledge in learning
Greg	Multilingual, nonfiction	Practitioner: frames research interests and scholarship in relation to his experiences teaching	Activity organizer: spontaneously leverages student and environmental affordances to guide the learning process, drawing on his extensive teaching experience

with the first two, so we only developed descriptors for each participants' disciplinary positioning and student orientation. A full list of descriptors and their definitions can be found in table 2.1 above, along with information about each of the TAs' composition courses. Unpacking these categories and what they can tell us about TAs' pedagogical performances became the basis for the analysis section of this article.

Finally, our transcription approach for this article was informed by Sigrid Norris's (2004) ethnographic research on German women's identity construction. Her framework incorporates both embodied modes (gesture, gaze, posture, etc.) and disembodied modes (music, written/printed text, layout). Norris transcribed talk over screen clips of video data in order to emphasize relationships between movement and discourse. We also selected snapshots to showcase embodied modes, but for ease of readability, we numbered those snapshots and put them alongside the discourse. Ultimately, this method enabled us to draw on both interviews and transcribed video excerpts in our analysis to highlight the various contradictions and connections visible in participants' pedagogical performances. As previously mentioned, we were unable to include the original screenshots in this chapter but have recreated the gestures we analyzed.

BACKGROUND ON PARTICIPANTS

The four TA participants in this project—Chris, Matt, Cleo, and Greg[1]—were pursuing their PhDs from the same English department but had varied academic specialties and teaching backgrounds. They all were in their second year of teaching composition within a writing program that has a WAC approach, uses program-wide outcomes, and gives TAs flexibility in course design. Our research participants had all completed a new TA orientation and taken a practicum course during their first year of teaching. Greg, though a new TA in this context, had over six years of teaching experience internationally through the Peace Corps and in other university contexts. He was teaching a multilingual section of a nonfiction FYC course and studying composition and multilingual pedagogy. Chris and Matt were teaching literature-based first-year composition (FYC) courses and were literature scholars. Finally, Cleo was teaching the first of two courses in a stretch version of FYC for underprepared students. While she was primarily a literature scholar, she was also interested in pedagogical applications of literature for writing studies. After our study, both Cleo and Greg would take on leadership roles as graduate student assistant directors of the first-year writing program, training and supporting new TAs.

Given their range of experiences, each TA has a different perspective on what constitutes good writing and how the composition course can support it. Chris and Matt ground their ideas about writing in their own experience as academic writers. Chris is somewhat resistant to the writing program goals, mainly because he feels teaching composition is outside his area of expertise. He draws on his experiences as an academic writer to inform his pedagogy, ultimately believing good writing is tied to the larger educational goals of developing "nuanced, critical thought." He is willing to align with the composition program's outcomes to the extent that they can foster this complex thinking but also expresses frequent concern that students will be unable to engage flexibly or situationally with the writing practices he is teaching, "that they perhaps become wedded to it." Much like Chris, Matt is invested in complicating student thinking within the classroom and destabilizing assumptions about a text, an object, or the world. For him, good writing facilitates this complex thinking or opportunities for what he describes as a "second look." Rather than carefully structuring his classes to teach complexity, however,

Matt favors an improvisational classroom atmosphere in which students arrive at understandings of writing through dialogue about texts.

In contrast, Cleo and Greg are more inclined to rely on programmatic and teacherly knowledge to shape their understandings of good writing. Cleo structures her course content around the writing program's standardized goals, pedagogical values, and shared jargon. However, her past experiences as an underrepresented college student, coming from the same high school as many of her current students, also make her empathetic to student experience. She endeavors to recognize and value the knowledge her students bring with them into the classroom. Ideal student writing for Cleo, then, leverages previous writing strategies but contextualizes them within the language and goals of the university's composition program. Finally, as someone who has taught a wide variety of students in both local and international contexts, Greg's understanding of good writing is grounded in what he has seen as the biggest challenges for his prior composition students. For example, when discussing argument, Greg notes, "I was seeing a lot of students make a claim that wasn't debatable at all. . . . It was sort of like an accepted truth for their target audience or something so extreme that they would never convince [them]." Thus, his lesson focuses on encouraging students to articulate specific claims and subclaims that warrant debate. While Greg has his own perspective on good writing, student contributions are central to communicating this perspective. In his classroom, Greg relies on experiential knowledge to adjust his lessons responsively to student needs and available class time, space, and resources. To showcase patterns within new TA demographics, the next section of this chapter is organized so TAs with tension between their scholarly interests and teaching are compared to those with scholar identities that work in concert with their teaching identities.

CHRIS AND MATT: NEGOTIATING DIVERGENT DISCIPLINARY AND TEACHING IDENTITIES

For TAs involved in large composition programs, Chris and Matt offer familiar personas. We are well accustomed to the English PhD students whose primary focus in graduate school is the advancement of literary scholarship. They are often grateful for the teaching experience and opportunity to fund their education but less enthusiastic about composition curriculum. These TAs may be visible in practicum courses as resistant voices, the tensions in how they are identifying as scholars and as teachers more immediately apparent than the rhetoric and composition

TAs we discuss in the next section. While Chris and Matt may seem familiar, however, a closer examination of how they embody contradictions in their pedagogical performances can destabilize our assumptions. This analysis provides new perspectives into the challenges literary scholars face as TAs in composition programs, as well as their potential affordances for negotiating this liminal position.

In relation to his field, we label Chris a *disciplinary expert* because his identity as a medieval literature scholar is fundamental to his self-understanding, and much of his knowledge about writing is tied to his disciplinary experiences. Early on in his interview, when asked about his scholarship, Chris provided the longest and most specific explanation of his field: "I work on Anglo-Latin literary culture from 500 to 1100. I specialize particularly in Latin-Latin glosses, Latin-Anglo-Saxon glosses, and Anglo-Saxon pedagogical approaches." This well-developed disciplinary identity continued to manifest in various ways throughout our conversation, from mentioning "a junior colleague of mine at Oxford" to spontaneous literary references. Meanwhile, Chris's clear scholarly identity shapes his understandings of writing. For example, when asked about his incoming knowledge of argument, he gave a lengthy anecdote about his recent experiences with publishing an academic journal article to demonstrate how much one's work changes over time. In the field of medieval literature, Chris experiences writing as highly situational, iterative, and complex, and he hopes to translate this perspective to students in his introductory writing courses as well.

In orienting to his students, Chris also takes on an expert role, but one he attributes to his experiences writing as an academic and not to training in composition; we call this identity the *untrained informant*. Chris described feeling underprepared to teach writing, especially to nonnative English speakers. However, he still imagines a role for himself in "deprogramming" students away from the assumptions they bring from high-school writing experiences that writing is straightforward and formulaic: "That's been so beaten into them as they work towards you know their SATs and things like that and so deprogramming them can be a challenge." For Chris, the primary goal for his courses is to teach students to begin to recognize and appreciate the complexity and nuance of academic writing processes. However, he struggles with teaching the course outcomes in ways that can emphasize this nuance and situational awareness. For example, when asked how he might revise a lesson on complex claims that broke down the component parts of argument one by one, he discussed the possibility of ending the PowerPoint with "talking about the iterative nature of writing and how like this isn't a one-size-fits-all approach . . . at the same time I'm wondering if that might not confuse issues more." Here, he has trouble reconciling his scholarly understanding that writing is iterative and situational with student expectations that they will learn a set of clearly defined writing skills during the course. He wants to complicate their assumptions but also worries about the impact this complication will have on the writing they produce. He fears what he teaches will ultimately be taken up just like their previous writing "rules." Thus, his experiences offer an opportunity for TAs to reflect on how they mitigate the tensions between their own understanding of writing and their views of students' expectations.

As an untrained expert, Chris is in charge in his classroom, standing at the front of the room and using the chalkboard and PowerPoint to communicate information. While he often solicits student participation, their responses are typically used as starting points to arrive at his own insights about writing. As he writes student responses on the board, he usually faces it and records his own version of the comment. In turning to the board, he physically creates an opportunity to reinterpret student answers in line with his aims for the discussion. Another frequent mode of student engagement for Chris is to ask a question with an obvious answer and pose with his arms open (figure 2.1c). This mode allows Chris to solicit student participation while maintaining control over the direction of the class conversation; students are positioned as contributors to an existing line of discussion.

As the expert in the room, Chris's gestures emphasize what he believes to be at the core of successful college-level writing—nuanced, complex thinking. Midway through explaining the component parts of a complex argument, he hit the air three times with his fist: "Nuance, nuance, nuance. Be nuanced in your thinking! That's the most important thing that you're going to take out of this class is nuanced thinking, right?" His lesson on complex claims suggested this nuance could manifest in a number of ways—from getting specific about a text to intertextual engagement. He ties comments about nuance to lessons about how to structure both a complex claim and a paper as a whole, calling for students to integrate ideas and make connections throughout the length of the paper. The following excerpt aligns with figure 2.1a–g.

CHRIS: [2.1a] You see how you start doing that? You start introducing [*makes winding motion with both hands*] other ideas? [2.1b] Now do you just drop it in here and never come back to that? [2.1c] No, you'll want to engage with it at some point and it's oftentimes good

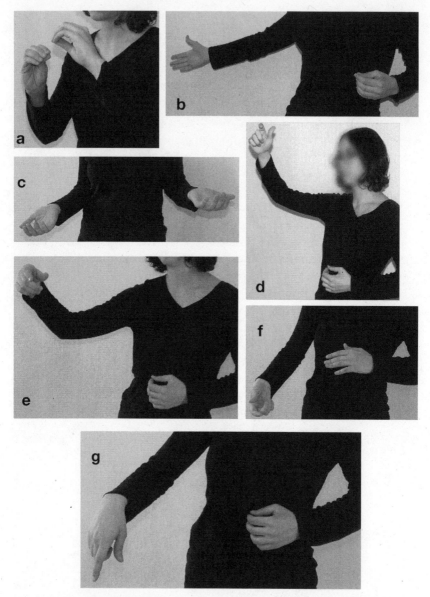

Figure 2.1. Chris's weaving gesture uses his finger to trace the integration of the student's argument at different stages of their paper.

to engage with [2.1d–f] that other idea or that other perspective throughout [*goes back and repeats spiral twice more*] throughout your paper, kind of weaving it in rather than [2.1g] relegating it to a paragraph at the end before the conclusion.

In one sequence he uses weaving as a metaphor to highlight the importance of integrating concessions to other arguments throughout a paper. When we discussed this excerpt during his interview, Chris saw clear connections between his weaving gesture and both his disciplinary background and views of good writing. He explained,

> The reason that we're concerned about these complex claims . . . is that we're looking for something that is more cogent and also compelling and nuanced because I mean like that's the idea behind the liberal arts education. . . . So these little gestures are kind of like "look we're connecting it back to your argument" . . . it's kind of a goofy little, remember connect them back. Similarly the kind of like weaving these, and this is the thing because of course "text" comes from "textus," which is Latin for cloth or to weave, so I mean that weaving that stuff through it is weaving your concession throughout your argument is an important point I feel for them.

Chris went on to discuss how students are prone to relegating a concession to the conclusion, a habit he sees as connected to the many problematic writing incomes they learn for standardized tests or high-school courses. Overall, Chris's gestures and physical positioning in the classroom help illuminate both his disciplinary allegiances and his expert-instructor positioning. His gestures punctuate detailed explanations to students about how to arrive at good, nuanced writing. While students have opportunities for participation (i.e., his rhetorical questions), the conversation is structured around Chris's goals. Meanwhile, the gestures emerge out of Chris's experiences and values with writing and education—from the physical metaphor of weaving to his repeated emphasis on nuance, which reflects Chris's belief that complex thinking is not the cornerstone of just a writing course but also of a liberal arts education.

In contrast, Matt identifies his discipline as "nineteenth-century lit and philosophy of science, I guess," already indicating some ambivalence about the distinct tracks of literary scholarship. We ultimately label Matt the *disciplinary flâneur* in reference to his flexible attitude towards disciplinary expertise and his investment in wandering through different philosophical ideas and perspectives, taking them in with curiosity but also a degree of removal. He described his interests as "a weird blend, it's all this stuff like object studies . . . a lot of philosophy of the subject, but also materialism and epistemology." These disciplinary interests translate to a pedagogical investment in encouraging students to take a "second look," especially at the material world around them and how they react to it. Describing his teaching goals, Matt explained, "A lot of it is actually attention to the ordinary, like really ordinary things that they would typically skip over . . . in the text itself and also in their reactions to it. . . . What in those kind of gut-level first reactions can be productive to formulating a more complicated argument?" Thus, in drawing on his disciplinary interests to teach writing, Matt aims to foster in students a curious disposition much like his own that could guide them through complex texts and writing tasks. Matt's experiences, then, have implications for TAs who begin from the assumption that writing is about thinking and are invested in teaching ways of seeing.

Because he is not interested in communicating specific rules about writing and instead wants to model attitudes and modes of engagement, Matt tries to let student thoughts and questions guide conversation. Describing his ideal classroom environment, he reflected, "I like kind of a chaotic atmosphere," and he emphasized he enjoys teaching first-year students because they tend to have more tolerance for chaos in their writing: "They're not as disciplined yet in their disciplines so they're trying stuff." These aims are reflected in how Matt orients to students in his classroom as well, which we ultimately describe as *coordinator of chaos*. Matt's positioning in the room and gestures highlight student perspectives, using these as the center point in a collaborative investigation into what makes good writing. In the lesson we observed, students discussed excerpts from Nietzche about engaging an opponent to consider how they might inform writing arguments and integrating sources in their papers.

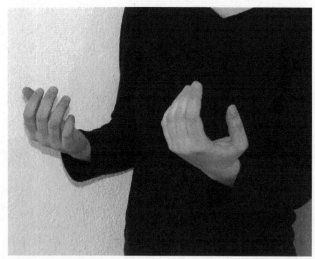

Figure 2.2. Matt leans against the wall with arms casually open to the class.

In order to facilitate coordinated chaos, Matt takes a casual stance in his classroom (as represented in figure 2.2)—typically located in the corner of the room, leaning against the blackboard, with his notebook in one hand and chalk in the other—in the hopes that he will foreground student voices while removing himself from the center of the action. He explained during his interview, "I have this tendency . . . when they're saying stuff I kind of slowly back into the corner and like kind of slouch in the corner while they talk." Other movements similarly emphasize student contributions, including an open-handed gesture to call on students (as represented in figure 2.3c) and detailed transcription of their feedback, which is done at an angle so he avoids facing away from the class (as represented in figure 2.3b). In his interview, Matt described himself as a "transcription fiend like just putting up what they're saying, rather than an organizer," suggesting again his desire to let student voices predominate. At the same time, Matt struggles with this student-centered pedagogy in contexts in which students are less active participants, like the relatively quiet early-morning class Lilly observed. Reflecting on his facilitation style during his interview, Matt commented, "When everything is coming through me and they're not actually talking to each other, I think that can be a difficulty." While Matt's gestures work to foreground student action and remove himself from the center of the classroom, he still finds himself as the coordinator of student responses and is not sure how to engage them in the chaotic dialogue with one another that is his ultimate goal. The following excerpt aligns with figure 2.3a–d.

MATT: What else have we heard about him?

STUDENT: He's pretty sexist.

MATT: [2.3a] Pretty sexist? Yep. [2.3b] [*writes "sexist" on the chalkboard*] Did you notice that anywhere in the reading? [2.3c] Yeah? [*smiles*] Say more.

STUDENT: There was a part in the reading where he talks about like vengeance being the weakness of the woman.

MATT: Mhm. [*writes "vengeance weakness of woman" on the chalkboard*] What'd you think about that?

STUDENT: It was interesting.

MATT: [*smiles, finishes writing, turns to student*] I'm pretty happy you brought that up because you know I've taught this section before and every time I'm like, "So does he say anything about women? [*smiles*] I don't know." [. . .] But it's okay, you know it's okay to say that. He's saying sexist [*underlines "sexist" on the blackboard*] things [2.3d] so um that's part of how, how we would read [*underlines "Nietzche" on the*

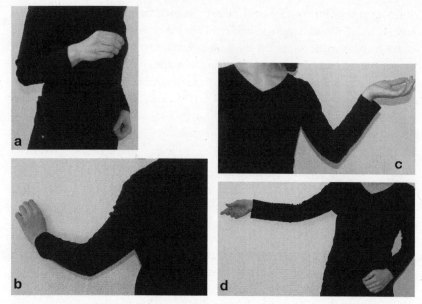

Figure 2.3. Matt models the "second look" for students through his engagement with the class and the white board.

blackboard] his arguments. And part of it's saying what do we do when there's these [*draws a square around "sexist" on the blackboard*] these elements that we don't accept or we want to get rid of and yet there's these other elements that may be helpful for us? How do we take those pieces?

Matt has aims for the class discussion—born from his disciplinary values and views on writing—to practice a specific method of textual engagement and argument. This method questions initial impressions and assumptions about material and digs deeper into implications, teaching for what he calls "a second look." Early on in the class lesson, he models the second look by taking up a student comment about Nietzsche's sexism and writing it verbatim on the board. In this example, Matt uses the comment to emphasize the importance of considering different facets of an author's background and raises a question about how this knowledge impacts engagement with an author's arguments. These questions would guide much of the class conversation on argument, informed by Nietzsche's own claims about how to engage an enemy. Visible in this example are Matt's various embodied strategies for emphasizing the value and even pleasure of the second look. As previously discussed, his gestures highlight student contribution, keeping the student who raised the point actively involved through regular eye contact and open-handed gestures as well as verbatim transcription of her comments. In addition, Matt's smiling throughout this example models for students the pleasure found in digging deeper into Nietzsche's sexism. Meanwhile, his writing on the board serves not only as transcription of student feedback but also as a means of calling students back to a point for that second look. When he underlines and then squares "sexism" and underlines "Nietzsche," it is part of an ongoing investigation into how the understanding of an author must necessarily change as we dig into their sexist values. Thus, Matt's movements in this excerpt—both physically in the room and in relation to the board—demonstrate a negotiation between putting student voices center stage and modeling an exploratory method of engaging with arguments that is fundamental to his views on writing.

Overall, both Chris and Matt mobilize clearly defined and embodied understandings of what constitutes good writing drawn from their own experiences with scholarly academic prose. Yet they differ in how they help students arrive at these understandings, with Chris keeping careful control over classroom discussion and Matt working to facilitate a collaborative process of discovery. Both of them find surprising ways to leverage their own disciplinary experiences to shape their performances, even as they encounter contradictions in aligning their research and teaching backgrounds. For Chris, though his disciplinary identity makes him feel unprepared to teach a composition course, his teacher identity as an untrained informant positions him as an expert on academic writing. Given his divide between scholarly and teacherly identities, Matt also relies on his experiences as a writer. Yet, because Matt resists a strict disciplinary position, he also avoids the expert role, adopting a coordinator of chaos position. Thus, these case studies offer insight into how two seemingly similar new TAs—those who identify as literature experts with some reservations about teaching composition—might manifest their identities in distinct ways, with overlapping but ultimately very different effects.

CLEO AND GREG: DISCIPLINARY IDENTITIES
COMPLEMENT TEACHING IDENTITIES

Cleo and Greg may also be familiar TA personas; as students with interests in writing pedagogy, they are excited about teaching composition and are invested in the writing program's goals. Though Cleo is a literary scholar and Greg is a compositionist, their teacher and scholar identities complement one another. Greg's scholarly pursuits emerge from his teacher experiences while Cleo's identity as a teacher has influenced her scholarly interests and pushed her more towards pedagogical research. Greg's pedagogical performances are informed by past teaching experiences and his training at other institutions, while Cleo relies on her past experiences as a student and her recent training from the writing program. Though the two vary widely in experience level, both are enthusiastic about teaching, interested in composition as a field, and generally aligned with the writing program's objectives.

In explaining her disciplinary positionality, Cleo said, "Super, super generally I'm thinking about applications for teaching American ethnic literature towards goals of both composition work and community engagement." We identify her as a *disciplinary pragmatist* because of the recursive relationship between her disciplinary knowledge and her writing pedagogy. Though she initially went to graduate school because of her interest in American ethnic literature, her interest in pedagogy and community engagement broadened her disciplinary knowledge to include composition, especially basic writing and translingualism.

As a novice compositionist, Cleo places value in the writing program, trusting its programmatic goals and teaching argument using methods prescribed by the program leaders. Her affiliation to the writing program not only influenced when terminology was introduced in the class we observed but also how argument was taught. For example, when asked why she chose to explain argument as three types of claims (claims of fact, value, and policy), Cleo said, "It was in the textbook." Meanwhile, her breakdown of complex claims—including stakes, evidence, roadmap, and counterargument or concession—came from "orientation." This is in contrast to Matt and Chris, who do not reference the writing program in their understanding of argument but focus on their own writing practices.

Though Cleo's teaching of argument is shaped primarily by her understanding of writing program expectations, she also draws on her own experiences as a high-school student growing up in an area similar to the one many of her students grew up in. Therefore, Cleo's case study demonstrates how alignment with a writing program's objectives can become integrated with a TA's previous writing experience through their teaching. For example, though she teaches the five elements of complex claims defined by the composition program's curriculum, she has moved away from teaching students to write those as "the big block" showcased during new-TA orientation. During her interview, she explained this move: "It makes more sense to students because they're so used to working with thesis statements," and she feels the block model "is too constricting for people and too formulaic for students." Thus, while Matt and

Chris rely on their disciplinary writing experiences to help define good writing, Cleo draws on previous experiences as a student writer to shape her curriculum. Since she frequently considers how she might bridge students' prior knowledge with the expectations of the writing program, we categorize her orientation to students as *connection maker.*

During her lesson, Cleo makes connections to previous learning clear to her students, referencing how they have worked with theses before but today they are going to learn explicitly about claims, a word used in the university's composition classes. This kind of explicit reference to the writing program as impetus for her choice of jargon is repeated throughout the lesson and marks Cleo's negotiation between writer incomes and programmatic expectations. Cleo also uses a conversational tone and open-handed gestures, cushioning any jargon with explanation and physically embodied visuals. During the first part of the lesson, she goes over a self-made worksheet with students that bridges things students already know from high school and her class with the current goal of creating arguments. Then, she asks students to tell her elements of good arguments based on what they already know. She follows up with an activity in which students work in groups to create their own claims on topics of their choosing and share out. Her lesson plan follows a typical I do/we do/you do format modeled in new-TA orientation but uses self-made materials rather than the textbook to make her curriculum student friendly.

Throughout the lesson, Cleo's discourse signals she values using what students already know to help them be successful in this college context. She tends to use open gestures to show empathy for her students, trying to be a friendly guide for them as they adjust to college writing expectations. While she teaches, her joy for teaching is visible through her slightly upturned lips and/or use of her eyebrows and dimples to indicate a slight smile as she talks. She also uses a friendly tone and even sounds as if she might laugh while poking fun at the jargon of the word "claim." In the following excerpt, Cleo models for students an ideal relationship to programmatic expectations for good writing. She engages with the jargon, but her smile and teasing tone seem to recognize it overlaps with writing strategies already familiar to her students. The following excerpt aligns with figure 2.4a–e.

> CLEO: When I say claim, I know I've used claim [2.4a] and argument interchangeably [2.4b, *moving hands back and forth, up and down*] all quarter and that's because they're kinda the same thing [*raises eyebrows, as if in amusement*]. Um when we talk about claims in this class and when we talk about claims [2.4c] generally when you're in

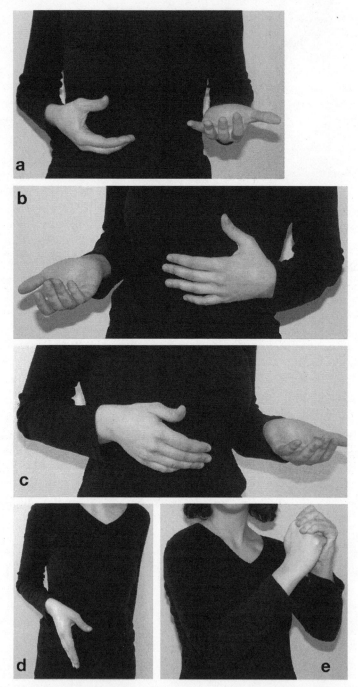

Figure 2.4. Cleo's hand gestures model the crystallization of student ideas into an argument or claim.

composition classes generally at UW, a claim is basically [2.4d] the same as a thesis statement which is what you guys are more familiar with from high school I'm guessing. That kind of distil—that crystallization [2.4e], like what is your argument [*bounces the crystallization symbol for emphasis, with each word*] in one to two sentences that's what we mean by a claim. It's that argument that you're making, the core of your argument.

As she talks, Cleo is in near constant motion. She uses primarily circular gestures with open hands to give an aura of energy and inclusivity. This movement is, in fact, what Cleo noticed most when watching her clips. She reflected, "I try and stay animated . . . I prefer to sit down when I teach because it's, I feel like I am engaging in the conversation with people instead of talking down to people, so to make up for that I feel like I have to do a lot." Because the classroom's layout would make it challenging for students to see her over their computers, however, Cleo stands still and uses constant gesturing in this context. In figure 2.4e, Cleo disrupts her open-handed gestures with a fist, which she moves up and down in rhythm with her voice. As she laughingly explained in her interview, this offers an embodied metaphor for the crystallization of an argument; how students might "bring all the things [they] want to say together into a big fist." Like Chris, Cleo offers a gestural metaphor to capture her perspective on good writing, embodying argument as two hands clasped together and a coming together of ideas into a unified whole. In contrast to Chris, however, this gesture mirrors her understanding of how the writing program defines argument, which was introduced to her in orientation, reified through the explanation in the textbook, and then physically represented to her students. Together, her linguistic and paralinguistic cues show Cleo's empathy for her students, her adherence to programmatic considerations, and her effort to make connections between high-school and college writing expectations. TAs can use her case study to consider how they might productively navigate among competing forces of writing program expectations, past experiences, and teaching personas.

Similar to Cleo, Greg's disciplinary identity is connected to his identity as a teacher. However, for Greg, his experiences as a second-language teacher led him to his scholarly pursuits. As he explained,

Second-language teaching and also language policy [are my areas]. One of the reasons that I wanted to come back to school. I do consider myself primarily a teacher. But being an English teacher in a world where sort of we're at the forefront of a lot of imperial processes I wanted to figure out how can I continue to be an English teacher while not necessarily promoting that sort of hegemony.

Since Greg's dominant identity is his teacherly persona, we identify him as a *disciplinary practitioner*. Although he went back for his PhD because of his interest in the political nature of language teaching, Greg does not explicitly address that topic with his students. Instead, he integrates strategies to best support multilingual students, like speaking slowly and providing multiple modes of communication. When asked about his experiences with the concept argument, Greg referenced prior teaching rather than experiences as a writer, explaining he first came to understand argument in the new-TA training at his first institution in "2009 or 2010." Given that both Cleo and Greg name orientation as influential in their understanding of argument, it seems that new TAs whose teacherly and scholarly identities are aligned may rely more readily on institutionalized understandings of writing. That said, they also may need more prompting to draw on their own experiences as writers as a resource.

As Greg teaches, he reacts to students in the moment, keeping them engaged and fostering learning through discovery. We identify him as an *activity organizer* because he tends to teach students through doing. Rather than offering an isolated explanation of argument, for example, he integrates his commentary on what an argument should entail through a series of activities. In fact, Greg's desk is littered with different possibilities for activities so he can adjust his lesson at any moment in response to the class's pace and interest. Greg does not just ask students to engage in the activity, either; he is also in near-constant motion. Though the smallness of his classroom relegates Greg to the front of the room near the blackboard, he paces and gesticulates to "bring some energy into the classroom." During our interview, when he saw the video of himself teaching, Greg reminisced about one of his first videoed observations in which he noticed he was "swaying." While the swaying was not visible in this demonstration, he still described himself as "a little bit hyperactive perhaps." Greg also tends to touch physical artifacts like the chalk, desk, board, or textbook and use classroom objects as examples when possible. He explained these gestures: "A lot of times what I'm talking about is sort of vague and abstract . . . the more physical, the more present, the more familiar [an object] is then the easier it is to get into it."

Greg's lesson plan to teach argument comes from his past experiences as a teacher; he decides to model possible subclaims of a larger arguable claim for students. Unlike Cleo, who thinks about her own experiences as a college student, or Matt and Chris, who rely on their experiences as writers, Greg uses his teaching experiences to inform his curriculum decisions. He begins his lesson by asking students to workshop a claim through classroom discussion on the chalkboard. He facilitates the activity by questioning students about how the claim could be more arguable, calling on students to hear their suggestions and writing down their specific revisions. Thus, while Greg has clear goals for what he wants students to understand about good arguments, their contributions shape the lesson, and they model the specificity he is after collaboratively.

Afterwards, he glances at the clock, saying, "Yeah I think we'll have time for this," showcasing his teacher experience through both his flexibility and his ability to predict the length of an activity. He introduces a small-group activity in which students work together to put claims in order from easiest to hardest to support. Rather than giving students examples of good arguments, like Chris, Greg asks them to evaluate examples themselves and defend their choices. Once the students confirm they are ready, he asks them to share out, an excerpt of which is included below.

Greg's teaching experience and love for teaching both come through in this short excerpt in which he organizes the students' activity on the board. Like Cleo and Matt, Greg shares his joy with his students by smiling often while he teaches. The "call-and-response" aspect of the activity makes him laugh because "[he's] taught this four or five times but normally it's not so unified," and his students share in his joy, laughing along with him. Greg's hand gestures are somewhat constricted, unlike Cleo's open gestures, because he is holding all the materials he needs to organize this activity: a piece of chalk in one hand and a copy of the worksheet another. During the interview, Greg explained this choice, saying, "I have tried to write out the numbers before but that takes a while" and "doing the projector in this class is difficult because I have to move students out of the way." Greg's solution is to hold the worksheet and write just the numbers on the board, but he regrets turning towards the board because it might make the lesson more difficult for his multilingual students to follow. Overall, Greg relies on interactivity to teach his students, emphasizing his own values for a strong argument—arguable claims being supported by specific subclaims—through touching the board as he facilitates the shareout. The following excerpt aligns with figure 2.5a–d.

Greg: [2.5a] [*looking at the activity worksheet*] And then what next?

Group of Students: Five . . . One

Greg: [2.5b] [*turning away from the class to write the number on the board*] Five or one [2.5c, *rotates back to students, smiling*], so which one, five or one?

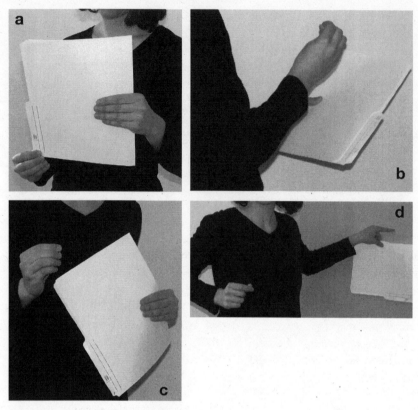

Figure 2.5. Greg acts as an activity organizer at the board, encouraging student suggestions and documenting them.

GROUP OF STUDENTS: [*laughter*] Five

GREG: Okay five then [*writes "five" on the blackboard*]

GROUP OF STUDENTS: [*in unison*] One

GREG: [*writes "one" on the blackboard*] Okay. Does anyone have anything significantly [2.5d] different than this? Okay so let's take a look at this.

Because Cleo and Greg see reciprocal relationships between their identities as teachers and scholars, they rely on their own experiences as students or in other teaching contexts, along with composition training provided by the writing program. One of the strengths of these complementary identities is the TAs' openness to using teaching to inform their scholarly pursuits and scholarship to inform their teaching. Yet, they still struggle with conflicting ideologies about writing. Cleo negotiates her desire to honor students' incomes with her adherence to the writing program's expectations, while Greg works to align various teaching experiences with this current context. Ultimately, embodiment plays a role in mitigating these conflicting perspectives. Cleo clasps her hands together in a fist to show how an argument crystallizes ideas; Greg touches the board to demonstrate how claims are built upon one another. These two case studies offer insight into the productive navigation of competing identities for TAs who attempt to blend past experiences with new writing program demands. They also complicate the notion that new TAs who buy into a writing program are seamlessly negotiating these identities.

CONCLUSION

All of our participants' pedagogical performances showcase their disciplinary identities and their orientation towards the students in their classes. Our participants' beliefs about what constitutes good writing manifest not only in their talk but also in their embodied actions. From punching the air to emphasize "nuance" in writing, then underlining, then squaring a concept on the board to physically enacting a "second look." From a raised eyebrow that pokes fun at programmatic jargon to a collective laugh with the class about their evaluations of different arguments. One thing we learn from examining TAs' lessons, then, is that beliefs about writing *are* embodied and pedagogical performances can be a site for accessing these embodied ideologies and recognizing internal contradictions. Examining these embodied teaching practices does not lead TAs or WPAs to immediate resolutions. However, looking at the pedagogical performances of four TAs who might seem quite familiar in background and orientation does help illuminate the complexity of their experiences and their choices—the layered, multimodal nature of their positioning.

Pedagogical performances are sites of contradiction, where conflicting identities are made visible and negotiated. We see this in Chris's embodiment of the informant role, where he attempts to provide clear directions for writing complex claims even when his own experience demonstrates how argument is always situated, iterative, and complex. Meanwhile, Matt struggles to help students experience a process of collaborative discovery without taking the conversational lead. While he has a clear goal for what students will learn, he wants to let that goal emerge out of chaotic discussion. On the other hand, Cleo's and Greg's reciprocal relationships between their identities as teachers and scholars still necessitate frequent negotiation between past teaching and learning experiences and programmatic goals. Like Chris, Cleo provides clear guidelines for writing a complex claim and is willing to potentially over-simplify similarities between high school and college so she can honor students' already established knowledge. In an effort to be clear, both Chris and Cleo incorporate lecture elements. Chris uses a more struc-tured lecture with a coordinating PowerPoint and gestures of authority, while Cleo does a mini conversational lecture with a shared worksheet and inclusive gestures. Matt and Greg, on the other hand, use student activity to teach, with Greg using a more structured activity and Chris using a more open-ended conversation. Thus, complicated negotiations of teacher practices are visible in the ways new TAs balance lecturing and activity-based instruction.

Our analysis shows how teacher performance can be used as a site for discovery for researchers, writing program administrators, and TAs themselves. At the time we conducted this research, we were graduate students ourselves, and our own embodied experiences were the catalyst for designing a study that used multimodal discourse analysis to analyze TAs' liminal position. We both functioned as new TAs, then assistant directors of the EWP, and later as more experienced TAs—and we knew the importance of how we carried our bodies as TAs and observed oth-ers' teaching performances. We hope more graduate students will use their own embodied expertise to design studies about graduate students and their liminal positionality. As future research is done on liminality, we suggest that those experiencing their liminality might be called upon to design research studies that can shed even more light on intersect-ing identities not explored here, like race, class, sexuality, and so forth. More research can and should be done into how other identities like class, gender, sexuality, and race play a role in the complicated negotia-tion between teacherly and scholarly identities for new TAs. Though the teachers in our case study did vary in their disciplinary identities and their relationship to the writing program, we only represent snapshots into four TAs, three of whom are white men. What we hope is that this research can offer a starting point for recognizing the interactions between the identities of teachers and burgeoning scholars. Continued research into teacher performance, particularly research that adopts multimodal methodologies for analysis, would provide much-needed insight into complicated teacher identities and offer new perspectives on embodied teaching philosophies.

In the meantime, TAs should consider how they might leverage video recordings of their teaching performances to explore and illuminate a range of identities. This could be an important practice of self-efficacy, which Megan Schoettler and Elizabeth Saur argue in this volume is critical to TA development. Our interviews with TAs in this study productively invited them to identify embodied practices and think about their performance as evidence of their teaching and scholarly identities. These conversations worked as reflective moments, and given the richness of these conversations, we suggest all video analysis be reflected upon through a heuristic, an assignment, a conversation, journaling, or some other genre of reflection. In addition, we believe a TA-led initiative of video review and reflection would help TAs develop their pedagogy. As John F. McCullagh (2012) argues, video reflection can be used as a form of professional development to improve TA teaching. We also are proponents of recording class sessions and using these as a prompt for instructor reflection in writing programs with observations. Assignments could be designed to be not only self-reflexive moments of analyzing embodied performance but also exercises in which TAs have the potential to learn from another's performance by doing the observation and videography for another TA in their practicum course. This is beneficial for TAs to gain experience with mentoring fellow graduate students (Henderson 2010). Graduate student observees could reflect upon their embodied performance much as our participants did, while their graduate student observers could provide video services and note the extent to which their colleagues imitate the programmatic goals. Imitation, as Lew Caccia argues in his chapter in this collection, helps students practice identifying composition theory in practice, and this practice could provide a tangible example of how imitation and innovation exist on a continuum rather than in a dichotomy.

Along with incorporating multimodal assignments in which TAs might explore their embodied performances as Micciche, Rule, and Stratman (2012) suggest, we also recommend that TAs find opportunities to read scholarship on teaching performances. This scholarship can educate TAs about how to negotiate tricky relationships between their burgeoning teacher and scholar identities. Liminal positioning is not something graduate students experience only as new TAs. They also have the potential to experience liminality in various roles within their career trajectory: postdoctoral positions, writing program administrators, and other hybrid positions are increasingly popular. To understand how to negotiate their current liminal positioning and their potential future experiences, we see analysis of and reflection upon video recordings to be incredibly important. Ultimately, our research suggests that video-based analysis of teacher performance paired with critical reflection can help TAs attune themselves to critical embodied moments during their teaching and to think comprehensively about how habitual movement patterns are emblematic of larger understandings of writing and teaching. We hope that in doing so, TAs can identify and better understand their liminal positions and develop effective strategies for negotiation both in their current role and in their future ones.

NOTE

1.   All the names used for the TAs are pseudonyms, in accordance with IRB.

REFERENCES

Bourdieu, Pierre. 1980. *The Logic of Practice.* Translated by Richard Nice. Stanford: Stanford University Press.

Ebest, Sally Barr. 2005. *Changing the Way We Teach: Writing and Resistance in the Training of Teaching Assistants.* Carbondale: Southern Illinois University Press.

Enriquez, Grace, Elisabeth Johnson, Stavroula Kontovourki, and Christine A. Mallozzi, eds. 2015. *Literacies, Learning, and the Body: Putting Theory and Research into Pedagogical Practice.* New York: Routledge.

Fleckenstein, Kristie S. 2009. *Vision, Rhetoric, and Social Action in the Composition Classroom.* Carbondale: Southern Illinois University Press.

Fountain, T. Kenny. 2014. *Rhetoric in the Flesh: Trained Vision, Technical Expertise, and the Gross Anatomy Lab.* New York: Routledge.

Freedman, Diane P. and Martha Stoddard Holmes. 2003. *The Teacher's Body, The: Embodiment, Authority, and Identity in the Academy.* Albany: SUNY Press.

Gonzales, Laura. 2015. "Multimodality, Translingualism, and Rhetorical Genre Studies." *Composition Forum* 31 (Spring). https://compositionforum.com/issue/31/multimodality.php.

Grouling, Jennifer. 2015. "Resistance and Identity Formation: The Journey of the Graduate Student-Teacher." *Composition Forum* 32 (Fall). https://compositionforum.com/issue/32/resistance.php.

Haas, Christina, and Stephen P. Witte. 2001. "Writing as an Embodied Practice: The Case of Engineering Standards." *Journal of Business and Technical Communication* 15 (4): 413–57.

Henderson, Barbara. 2010. "Mentorship of Graduate Teaching Assistants: Effects on Instruction and a Space for Preparing to Teach Adults." *Studying Teacher Education* 6 (3): 245–56.

Hesse, Douglas. 1993. "Teachers as Students, Reflecting Resistance." *College Composition and Communication* 44 (2): 224–31.

Johnson, Elisabeth. 2013. "Embodying English: Performing and Positioning the White Teacher in a High School English Class." *English Education* 46 (1): 5–33.

Lillis, Theresa. 2009. "Bringing Writers' Voices to Writing Research." In *Why Writing Matters: Issues of Access and Identity in Writing Research and Pedagogy,* edited by Awena Carter, Theresa Lillis, and Sue Parkin, 169–87. Amsterdam: John Benjamins.

Louis, Ross. 2005. "Performing English, Performing Bodies: A Case for Critical Performative Language Pedagogy." *Text and Performance Quarterly* 25 (4): 334–53.

McCullagh, John F. 2012. "How can video supported reflection enhance teachers' professional development?" *Cultural studies of science education* 7 (1): 137–52.

Micciche, Laura, Hannah Rule, and Liv Stratman. 2012. Multimodality, Performance, and Teacher Training. *Computers and Composition Online.* http://cconlinejournal.org/ccon line_Sp_2012/Multimodality_Rev-2011-12/tdm.html.

Norris, Sigrid. 2004. *Analyzing Multimodal Interaction: A Methodological Framework.* New York: Routledge.

Olinger, Andrea R. 2014. "On the Instability of Disciplinary Style: Common and Conflicting Metaphors and Practices in Text, Talk, and Gesture." *Research in the Teaching of English* 48 (4): 453–78.

Reid, E. Shelley. 2009. "Teaching Writing Teachers Writing: Difficulty, Exploration, and Critical Reflection." *College Composition and Communication* 61 (2): W197–W221.

Restaino, Jessica. 2012. *First Semester: Graduate Students, Teaching Writing, and the Challenge of Middle Ground.* Carbondale: Southern Illinois University Press.

Winzenried, Misty Anne. 2016. "Brokering Disciplinary Writing: TAs and the Teaching of Writing across the Disciplines." *Across the Disciplines* 13 (3): 1.

Wolfe, Joanna. 2005. "Gesture and Collaborative Planning: A Case Study of a Student Writing Group." *Written Communication* 22 (3): 298–332.

Zuidema, Leah, and James Fredricksen. 2016. "Resources Preservice Teachers Use to Think about Student Writing." *Research in the Teaching of English* 51 (1): 12–36.

3

DISCIPLINARITY, ENCULTURATION, AND TEACHING IDENTITIES
How Composition and Literature TAs Respond to TA Training

Jennifer K. Johnson

As any seasoned graduate student can attest, part of pursuing a graduate degree is becoming acculturated to specific disciplinary practices expected of members of an academic community. Adapting to a new disciplinary culture in this way can be challenging, particularly if the new practices are based on unfamiliar assumptions. Many scholars have considered the role enculturation plays in the development and success of graduate students in English. Variously referred to "enculturation" (Dobrin 2005), "acculturation" (Berkenkotter, Huckin and Ackerman 1998), "conversion" (Bishop 1990; Roen, Goggin, and Clary-Lemon 2007; Welch 1993), "indoctrination" (Ackerman, personal communication, March 2006), or "apprenticeship" (North 2000; Sosnoski and Burmester 2006), the notion that there is an expectation that graduate students will adhere to an established set of disciplinary norms can be found throughout the literature pertaining to graduate work in English (North 2000; Sosnoski 1994). James Sosnoski and Beth Burmester (2006) argue that these expectations are so firmly entrenched they have developed into "scripts" to be performed by graduate students and professors alike.

Consider the case of Nate, a first-year graduate student struggling to learn the "conventions and conversations" prevalent in his rhetoric program's discourse community, as these differed from those he had become accustomed to in his undergraduate program. Carol Berkenkotter, Thomas Huckin, and John Ackerman (1998) broadly consider the enculturation process Nate experienced as he grappled with adopting these new disciplinary practices. The study describes Nate's sense of liminality as he strives to acculturate himself to that new community. In her 1993 *College English* article, Nancy Welch chronicles a similar experience she had as a graduate student trying to fit into a program

DOI: 10.7330/9781646420896.c003

that embraced a theoretical construct antithetical to the principles that had been espoused in her previous training. As a means of emphasizing the fervor with which the program faculty attempted to convert her and her fellow graduate students to the theoretical paradigm dominant in the new program, Welch (1993) relies on an extended religious metaphor in her essay, referring to notions of "testimony," "confession," "baptism," and "conversion" (387).

This process of enculturation is especially challenging when a graduate student is occupying a liminal space between two disciplines. Such positionality requires these students to negotiate embracing two different, and perhaps even conflicting, sets of disciplinary paradigms. And because TAs are already navigating student/teacher liminality (see Donegan, this collection), their challenge is even further pronounced.

Although many teaching assistants (TAs) come into composition TA-training programs with composition backgrounds, a large faction hail from literature or other areas of English studies. While it may be assumed all of the subspecialties in English studies (most notably, composition, literature, and creative writing) adhere to the same teaching and learning paradigms, there are significant variations among them. According to Shari Stenberg (2005), "The feature that most distinguishes composition from its disciplinary siblings is its primary focus on pedagogy, and, more specifically, its conception of pedagogy as a mode of knowledge production, not merely a vehicle for knowledge transmission" (130). As a result of these differences, some TAs from English experience more barriers than others in embracing composition's disciplinary practices. This chapter focuses on the specific challenges literature students in particular may face in composition TA-training programs as they are exposed to and encouraged to adopt the ways of thinking and practicing in composition.

TA training is not only an introduction to teaching writing but also a means of enculturating new TAs to composition theory and practice. But because these disciplinary paradigms may be markedly different from those new composition TAs were previously exposed to, these individuals may experience a sense of cognitive dissonance resulting from the liminal position between two disciplines they are inhabiting. As Wendy Bishop (1990) and Christine Farris (1996) note, the process of developing a teaching identity is complex because it requires a negotiation of the perspectives about teaching students bring with them to their graduate study, along with the new ideas and theoretical positions they encounter as they pursue their coursework and move along the path to becoming teachers themselves. As this group of TAs works to develop a cohesive teaching identity that will serve them as instructors in composition while they simultaneously pursue their degrees in literature, they are likely to experience a powerful sense of liminality.

This essay reports on the results of a bounded, explanatory case study that was conducted to identify the ways TAs' pedagogies reflect their TA training and/or the teaching paradigms associated with their disciplines. In this IRB-approved study, two stimulated recall interviews were conducted with five TAs from a literature graduate program and five TAs from a composition graduate program to identify how TAs from the two disciplines responded to the practices and principles espoused in the training. The study was designed to develop an understanding of disciplinary differences, as well as to determine how and to what extent they manifest. Specifically, the study focused on whether TAs from composition and from literature took different practices and principles away from their composition TA-training program, and, if so, to what extent their disciplinary affiliations played a role. The findings revealed that because the literature TAs had to negotiate liminality not only via the teacher-student dichotomy but also within the space between literature and composition teaching paradigms, their experience was particularly challenging.

REVIEW OF LITERATURE

Because this study is focused on teacher preparation and whether TAs' responses to it are impacted by their respective disciplinary backgrounds, the consideration of what it means to be an effective teacher is particularly germane. The process of preparing to teach a writing class—or any class, for that matter—entails making pedagogical decisions. As Margaret Lindgren (2002) argues, "All teachers make choices about how to relate to students and whether and how to involve students in determining course content and processes. These decisions often position TAs on a continuum, with a lecture-based course on one end and a workshop-oriented course at the other" (297). Arguably, TAs might position themselves on that continuum based on their own understanding of what constitutes an effective classroom dynamic, and this perspective is ostensibly informed by their experiences, which are likely born of disciplinary norms and affiliation.

In her study of TAs' attitudes and practices in their first year of teaching, Farris (1996) claims that the process of negotiating the relationship between predispositions and disciplinarity is based largely on TA experiences and understanding of what it means to be a teacher.

Constructing a theory of composition is primarily an interaction among an individual teacher's past, present, and future, his or her students, the program, the textbook, and composition "lore." It is an active, recursive, and critical process. Instructors continually test what they already believe about writing by simultaneously adjusting practice and theory in order to resolve differences between that belief system and what they confront in the student writing, textbook, program guidelines, and graduate experience that constitute their total academic experience. (170)

This already-difficult process is likely made much more so when TAs come from a background with different standards, practices, and paradigms than those they are being exposed to within their training program.

The Role of Disciplinarity

In the modern university, disciplinarity not only functions as a means of organizing departments and specializations but also carries with it the perspectives and values of these departments and the larger disciplinary cultures to which they belong. More specifically, disciplinarity both shapes and reflects how teaching and learning are conceptualized and conducted within these cultures.

Despite the range of classroom approaches adopted by TAs—as well as by experienced teachers—there is some agreement within composition studies as to certain best practices for composition classes, such as adherence to the process model, peer-reviewing activities, workshopping student texts, teaching grammar within the context of student work rather than as a drill, and so forth. While the values of the TA-training program under study here are consistent with those listed above—and thus they may also be familiar to the TAs who are studying composition—not all of these practices may be as commonly accepted by faculty in other subdisciplines of English studies. For example, literature faculty may not share assumptions about effective teaching strategies with composition faculty (Peterson 1995) given the differences between teaching and studying literature and teaching and studying writing, with the former focusing on textual consumption and the latter on textual production (Scholes 1985).

Enculturation

Because graduate students are in the process of acculturating themselves to their discipline, it is not at all surprising they might adopt and perpetuate those paradigms associated with their disciplinary community. Sosnoski (1994) explores the dynamics of the graduate student/

English professor relationship and details the top-down nature of the master/apprentice model of what he refers to as the "Magisterial Curriculum." Stephen North (2000) also discusses at length the magisterial phenomenon and its implications, pointing out that "the *Magister* could demand—and expect to get—a conformity in disciplinary and professional behavior that belied heterogeneities of other kinds" (66; italics in original).

Yet while this process of enculturation may occur throughout graduate studies, it may be particularly prevalent in TA preparation (Dobrin 2005), even if the TA program in question is not adhering to the type of "conversion" model Duane Roen, Maureen Goggin, and Jennifer Clary-Lemon (2007) describe. Sidney Dobrin (2005) posits that the TA practicum can serve as a powerful site of enculturation, arguably even more so than other areas within graduate study. According to Dobrin (2005), the practicum "generally speaking, is not merely a space in which new teachers are 'trained' or even professionalized, but one in which they are enculturated into the cultural ideologies of composition," which "makes the practicum one of the most powerful and important spaces of occupation in composition studies" (21). It stands to reason that the perspectives and theoretical constructs already apparent within graduate programs would only be more evident within the TA practicum, given its role in disseminating theory and in helping graduate students embrace a paradigm that will serve the institution as the TAs move toward teaching FYC.

Stenberg (2005) also considers the notion of enculturation in TA training as she describes the "teacher-as-trainee" model of teacher preparation, in which TAs are viewed as "empty vessels" (64), and thus "the pedagogy of the teacher-training program was not left open to reflection or critique, nor were students positioned as having valid insights and ideas that might work in dialogue with, or even alter those ideas" (65). Roen, Goggin, and Clary-Lemon's (2007) conversion model of TA preparation is closely aligned with this model.

Still, as Farris (1996) makes clear in her study of four new teachers of first-year composition, this conversion is not a simple process given graduate students' varied backgrounds, perspectives, and personal predispositions, all of which play a role in the development of an individual's teaching identity. Bishop's 1990 book *Something Old, Something New* illustrates similar findings, as the TAs in her study "developed their own idiosyncratic versions of the process paradigm [forwarded in their TA practicum], based primarily on their personal teaching histories and their perceived classroom needs" (139).

As these studies suggest, graduate students develop their teaching philosophies through a complex interplay among factors such as their educational experiences, their personal perspectives, and their preconceptions. This negotiation becomes even more complicated when graduate students are placed in a position in which they are being acculturated to competing ideologies, such as may be the case when graduate students from literature participate in a composition TA-training program. Moreover, even though enculturation processes may have shaped their philosophies, graduate students may not be aware of the extent to which they have been affected by their disciplinary affiliations. This shaping can take the form of adherence to a particular philosophy or theoretical frame but can also extend to actual teaching practices within the classroom, as the results of this study demonstrate.

Teaching Paradigms: Teacher as Scholar versus Teacher as Learner

Given graduate students' need to acculturate themselves to their programs' ideologies and approaches, the notion that there are various models of effective teaching and that these models reflect different disciplinary paradigms indicates how and why graduate students from literature and composition might hold disparate assumptions about what it means to teach and learn to teach writing. And given the focus of this study, these models and their origins are worthy of exploration, particularly as they relate to the teaching and learning practices of the two disciplinary areas.

Stenberg's (2005) *Professing and Pedagogy* discusses and critiques four primary models of teaching within English studies: "teacher as scholar," "teacher as owner," "teacher as trainee," and "teacher as learner." While the "teacher-as-trainee" model is discussed above as a reflection of the conversion approach to TA preparation, the "teacher-as-owner" metaphor is useful to consider here as it reflects the idea that "professors are thought to develop in isolation, or in relationship to the scholarship they engage, rather than as a result of collaboration with other teachers" (xxii). The model, then, denies the collaborative nature of teacher development, seeing the process as instead based purely on discipline-specific norms and ideologies. Sosnoski and Burmester (2006) also see this approach as problematic since it reifies the "master/apprentice tradition in education" at the expense of a more collaborative, collegial interaction. Particularly key to this present study however, is the delineation between "teacher as scholar" and "teacher as learner," as Stenberg (2005) suggests these models reflect the disciplinary expectations for professors in literature and in composition, respectively.[1]

Stenberg (2005) further argues that "no metaphor has played a greater role in the professorial enterprise than that of 'teacher as scholar'" (33), in which teaching is the by-product of scholarship, and teacher development is thought to come naturally as one develops as a scholar. Under this model, "good professing has more to do with the relationship one has to knowledge than to students" (12). Similarly, citing Friedrich Nicksen, North (2000) notes that the German philologists who served as the originators of what became US English departments viewed teaching as a natural outgrowth of scholarship: "Teaching, as such, they did not consider at all as an art which could itself be taught, but rather took it for granted that anyone who was himself proficient in a science ought to be able to teach others" (6). Indeed, the notion that teaching is naturally connected to one's scholarship is reflected throughout English studies and academia at large, as many graduate students are provided with little, if any, pedagogical training within their own discipline(s) (Stenberg 2005).

In contrast, composition students, especially those who have been studying at the doctoral level, are immersed in considerations of pedagogy by the very nature of their studies. Presumably, these individuals would be receptive to the composition theory and pedagogy offered in TA preparation, whereas literature students from an English department that does not appear to value close consideration of pedagogical questions might be much less engaged with it (Peterson 1995). Because literature students are in the process of preparing for a career in teaching literature, and they may be coming from a culture in which—according to North's (2000) argument—training in literary studies is all that is necessary to be an effective English teacher, these students would potentially see this same teacher preparation as lacking in value.

Stenberg's (2005) "teacher-as-learner" metaphor enacts a learning-centered model of teaching in which teachers continue to learn and develop throughout their careers, as opposed to achieving "mastery" over teaching at one point and then becoming stagnant, as she argues that those who adhere to the "teacher-as-scholar" model are in danger of doing. She posits that this metaphor is in keeping with James Slevin's (1996) view that the field of composition abides by the original meaning of the word *discipline*, which derives from the Latin word for learner (cited in Stenberg 2005, 129). Bishop (1990) closes her book on TAs' development with a similar observation, which she uses to characterize the manner by which composition teachers are encouraged to relate to their students: "Writing teachers are no longer expected to be at the center of the writing classroom. They are learning instead to stand supportively to the side and offer their students opportunities to grow and learn" (144). Similarly, Donald Finkel's (2000) book *Teaching with Your Mouth Shut* argues that although the idea of the "great teacher" who spouts knowledge and pontificates during class is still entrenched throughout academia, composition's more collaborative approach to teaching and learning is a more effective model.

The literature cited above suggests that the fields of composition and literature subscribe to very different ideas of what it means to be an effective teacher. If this is indeed the case, then these disparate views help explain why the collaborative approach to teaching encouraged in the TA-preparation program at the site of this research might be less appealing to the literature students—and might therefore engender in them a stronger sense of liminality—than it would be to the composition students. It would also explain why activities such as peer reviewing and the scaffolding of assignments, both of which the composition TAs readily embraced, were less appealing to the literature TAs who reported that they had not seen either practice in any of their literature classes. These distinctions have important implications not only for how TA training is conducted but also for how TAs themselves might approach the liminality inherent in encountering an unfamiliar disciplinary paradigm.

TA-Preparation-Program Approaches

Much has been written about the tension between TAs' needs for theory and/or practical information within their training programs. For example, Darin Payne and Theresa Enos (2002) cite the work of Catherine Latterell (1996), Tori Haring-Smith (1985), and Doug Hesse (1993) when they note, "It is still common for TAs to be led through a practical, nuts and bolts 'training course' that enables them to simply get through their very first semester of both graduate school and teaching" (51) without ever establishing a theoretical basis for what they do in the classroom.

Practical preparation courses such as these may appeal to TAs' concerns about teaching FYC for the first time, "yet such TAs often do not gain the theoretical background many deem necessary for adequate instruction in composition, nor are they given the opportunities to understand why their preparation takes the form that it does" (Payne and Enos 2002, 51). While those TAs who are interested primarily in practical classroom concerns may not see such nuts-and-bolts preparation courses as inadequate, scholars such as Robert Scholes (1985) and James Berlin (1996/2003) remind us that pedagogy is inextricably intertwined with theory, and that therefore, TAs who are unacquainted with theoretical principles are at a clear disadvantage as they work toward developing their pedagogies.

One common approach to TA training is what Haring-Smith (1985) refers to as the "integrated approach" between theory and practice, which she claims "is the only one that admits our graduate students to colleagueship. It acknowledges that they need to study composition before teaching it, but it also allows them to investigate the subject from a more sophisticated angle than that which they will present to their students. It treats them as teachers and thinkers, not clones or apprentices" (36). Integrating theory and practice within a TA practicum encourages TAs to balance the two into a cohesive and sustainable pedagogy that reflects their own values and beliefs. This integration may seem intuitive to students who have studied composition in their graduate coursework, whereas for those who have studied literature or other academic disciplines, TA training may be their first introduction to composition theory and pedagogy.

This study considers these disparate ideas about the value of various pedagogical practices and the implications of the perspectives associated with them. It also builds on the work of Stenberg (2005) as it explores the extent to which disciplinary paradigms related to teaching, such as the "teacher-as-scholar" and "teacher-as-learner" models in particular, resonate with TAs from literature and composition.

METHODS

Because this study was focused on a specific TA-preparation program in a particular era, it is a bounded case study (Creswell 1998). And because it was conducted to determine whether there is a relationship between TAs' disciplinary affiliations and the ways they respond to their TA preparation as well as to their experiences with teaching FYC, it is an explanatory case study, which explores causal relationships in a particular phenomenon (Yin 2003). As recommended by Robert Yin (2003) and Janice Lauer and William Asher (1988), several qualitative data-collection methods were utilized including conducting stimulated recall interviews, collecting written artifacts such as teaching-philosophy statements and FYC syllabi (which were used to develop questions for follow-up interviews), and reviewing two TA handbooks provided to the TAs by the composition TA-preparation program and the English (literature) department, respectively.

Specifically, two stimulated-recall interviews were conducted with each of ten former TAs (five of whom were graduate students in literature and five of whom were graduate students in composition). The interviews were designed to elicit information about how the TAs had responded to the TA-preparation program and to discover what they had taken away from it in terms of pedagogical practices and principles, as well as why individual TAs responded to the program in the way(s) they did. In addition, interviewees were asked to submit their teaching philosophies and first-year writing course syllabi. These documents were then analyzed for the purpose of developing individualized questions for the second interview, which focused on participants' current teaching practices. While the first interview gleaned information about interviewees' backgrounds and their memories of—as well as their responses to—their TA-preparation program, the second interview focused on participants' current teaching practices in an effort to determine to what extent these practices were consistent with what was espoused in TA preparation.[2]

TA-Preparation Program's Course Design

The TA-preparation program featured in this study is housed in an independent writing program that provides TA preparation, as well as FYC courses and upper-division writing courses. The program itself is a stand-alone unit in that it—and therefore TA preparation—is separate from both the university's English department and its PhD program in composition, which is held in the university's school of education.[3] At the time this study was conducted, the TA program was comprised primarily of graduate students from English and education, where the university's literature and composition PhD programs are respectively housed. The TA program thus became a place of contact for graduate students from literature and composition—two disciplines often closely associated with one another due to their traditional affiliation with English studies but who in this case might not have otherwise interacted.

Typically, literature, composition, and TA preparation are all components of an English department, and individuals preparing to become composition TAs may not always be firmly affiliated with one discipline over the other. As a result, it can be difficult, if not impossible, at most institutions to get a clear read on disciplinary distinctions in the attitudes of TAs from English departments. Due to the unique situation of the study site in which literature, composition, and TA preparation are all housed in separate departments, this university offers a rare opportunity to isolate and explore potential disciplinary differences in the attitudes of literature and composition students toward their TA-preparation experience and writing instruction in general, as well as to explore how liminality plays a role in TAs' experiences.

This TA-training program utilized the Haring-Smith (1985) "integrated approach" to theory and practice, which is discussed above. The program consisted of a two-quarter sequence, beginning with a graduate seminar in the spring quarter before TAs began teaching and culminating in a practicum during the fall when they were teaching their first course for the program. The seminar activities included readings in composition theory and practice, observations of first-year composition classes, and construction of individual syllabi that the TAs were encouraged to continue developing in the fall and that they would then use in their winter and spring classes. In the summer before the second-quarter practicum course and before the TAs began teaching, they were required to attend a two-day orientation session in order to review policies and touch base with their fellow TAs, as well as their supervisors and the program's director. The practicum in the fall quarter consisted of sharing course materials in addition to reading assigned materials and participating in class discussions about composition theory and research. In these ways, the practicum course built on the work of the seminar by providing a place where TAs would be offered support during their first quarter of teaching.

Although the TA-preparation program evolved tremendously in the ensuing years, during the time the data for this study were gathered, the TA-preparation courses underwent few, if any, changes in terms of curriculum and design. At the time this study was conducted, all the TAs in the seminar course were given a copy of Laurence Behrens and Leonard Rosen's (2002) *Writing and Reading across the Curriculum*, which the writing unit required at that time as the common FYC text for the TAs' first year of teaching. Along with the common text, TAs used a common syllabus their first quarter, although after that they were encouraged to develop their own individual syllabi and assignments.

Participants

Interviewees for this study were selected primarily on the basis of their successful involvement with the TA-preparation course in the years under study, as well as their willingness to participate. Selection criteria also required that they be enrolled in the university's literature graduate program or the composition graduate program and that they be currently teaching or have recently taught FYC in the university. Individuals who were unsuccessful in the TA-preparation program (i.e., those who were not rehired or who resigned from the program) were excluded as participants from this study. This exclusion was established because the purpose of this research was to examine the attitudes of individuals who successfully utilized their preparation to become teachers of composition. Moreover, this exclusion helped ensure the findings were not subject to undue bias, as resistance to the practices and principles espoused in TA preparation was likely to be higher among those TAs who were considered unsuccessful.

At the time the ten participants were initially contacted for this project, four of them had already accepted positions at other institutions. Three others were preparing to leave the university to accept tenure-track positions, and one was leaving to pursue other endeavors before perhaps returning to academia at a later date. The remaining two planned to remain at the university as they completed their dissertations and hoped to continue teaching FYC there. By the time the study was completed, all ten had earned their PhDs.

The interviews were conducted approximately five years after each group of TAs had participated in the TA-preparation program so the participants could reflect on their preparation and consider the extent to which their current teaching practices and principles were or were not related to what they had been exposed to during their preparation courses. An added benefit to interviewing the groups of TAs from literature and composition several years after they had completed the TA-preparation program was that the time that had elapsed made it further possible to identify whether those principles potentially attributed to the interviewees' disciplinary affiliation had endured over time. Conducting these interviews so long after the completion of the program thus provided more concrete answers as to not only what the TAs had taken away from their preparation but also to whether and to what extent there was a relationship between the interviewees' perspectives and their disciplinary affiliation(s).

RESULTS AND DISCUSSION

The study's findings revealed that TAs from the two groups took markedly different teaching principles and practices away from their TA training in manners consistent with their respective disciplinary philosophies and affiliations. Specifically, the data illustrated a disparity in how the TAs from the two disciplines approached the teaching of first-year writing and in how they viewed their FYC students. These disciplinary differences were particularly evident in terms of various teaching paradigms associated with each of the two disciplines and via a schism between the literature TAs' focus on addressing practical matters versus the composition TAs' interest in exploring the theoretical underpinnings of their practice. These findings are elucidated in the sections below.

Teaching FYC

The data revealed a clear difference in how TAs from the two groups approached the teaching of FYC, both philosophically and pedagogically. Philosophically, while the composition TAs were passionate about teaching FYC and viewed it as a source of important work for themselves and their students, the literature TAs were focused more on the professional experience it gave them, which is understandable given most of them were in the process of building their resumes and their teaching repertoires as they looked forward to securing positions as professors of English.

Pedagogically speaking, the TAs from the two groups also embraced different practices from their preparation program, and they approached the teaching of FYC differently. Moreover, these differences seemed to be related to their disciplinary affiliations. For example, the principle takeaway for the literature TAs from the preparation program pertained to the activities and texts they were asked to use in their first quarter of teaching. This finding seems to reflect the literature TAs' stated preference for the practical information offered by the TA-preparation classes over the theoretical information, which was much more heavily embraced by the composition TAs. Also, there was a disparity in how the two groups viewed their FYC classrooms, with the composition TAs subscribing to a student-centered model while the literature TAs seemed to rely on a more traditional—or professorial, as Stenberg (2005) might describe it—approach. This divergence is discussed further below.

All the literature TAs pointed to various practices and principles they felt could be traced back to their TA preparation in the writing unit. For example, when asked if there was anything in her teaching she thought reflected what she learned in the TA program, Diane responded, "Yeah: grading rubrics, setting up the grading, peer review, dividing up the units into sections, writing across the curriculum. All of those things we did in our prep classes." Indeed, while the literature TAs referred to these practices and principles and indicated that some of these continue to be a part of their teaching, this group of literature TAs collectively embraced only two of them: the peer-reviewing activities and the scaffolding of assignments. However, all of the literature TAs referenced their continued use of texts and assignments they had been exposed to or invited to use during their training, suggesting these materials had a more lasting impact on their course design than did the practices or principles they learned about in TA training.

The composition TAs also pointed to several practices and principles they still use and that are consistent with their TA preparation. In addition to their collective adherence to peer reviewing and the scaffolding of assignments, this group also unanimously embraced a process model. Moreover, several of the composition TAs indicated they were committed to focusing on higher-order concerns rather than surface-level issues when responding to and assessing their students' work, as well to using a WAC/WID approach[4] in their classes. Finally, the composition TAs were unanimous in their commitment to developing student-centered classrooms, which they undertook in several different ways, as seen in the following pages.

Positioning of Students

A comparison of the two TA handbooks—developed by the writing program and the English department, respectively—seems indicative of the different teaching paradigms associated with the two disciplines and helps explain why the TAs from the two groups viewed teaching and first-year students so differently. These handbooks reflect disparate notions about what it means to be a teacher and how one should relate to students, both in person and in terms of assessing students' work. While the TA-training handbook for the writing program encourages TAs to connect with students and develop a community with them both in person and through their writing, the English-department TA handbook warns TAs against spending too much time on reading student papers, which it describes as the "most thankless and time-devouring of all TA duties." The English-department TA handbook goes on to urge TAs, "Try to space your grading out so that you don't find yourself with 35 papers to grade in one night, as this can damage healthy brain tissue and reduce life expectancy." While grading thirty-five papers in one night is certainly not advisable, the tone in these passages of the handbook reflects a distinctly negative attitude about reading student work.

Granted, the literature TAs had other graduate student responsibilities totally separate from the teaching of composition, so they were more pressed to potentially corral their teaching responsibilities, whereas for the composition TAs, teaching writing was an extension of their graduate studies. That said, it does seem clear that the two handbooks position students and frame responding to student work very differently, with the writing program TA-training handbook suggesting that responding to student writing is an innately valuable activity, while the English-department handbook encourages TAs to limit their time reading student work in order to maintain time for focusing on other scholarly activities. The disparity between the two handbooks' positions clearly reflects Stenberg's (2005) "teacher-as-learner" and "teacher-as-scholar" paradigms and thus underscores how the literature TAs are set up to wrestle with liminality not only within TA training itself but also when it comes to the grading of their FYC students' work.

The interviews also revealed fundamental differences in how the TAs from composition and from literature viewed students and students' writing, and these differences at times caused tensions to arise between the two groups. Three of the composition TAs—Nick, Jackie, and Piper—indicated they were troubled by the disparaging way some of the literature TAs spoke about their students and their students' writing. In citing one of these instances, Piper recalled thinking to herself, "You're an educated individual; how can you berate your students for having poor grammar skills? Does it need to be fixed? Do we need to work on that? Is that something you want to help them with? Yes. Are we going to sit there and tease them because they misused a certain word? I just felt like the intentions were so different." Piper's frustration here demonstrates the tension over the two groups' disparate teaching paradigms, with the literature TAs again positioning themselves as scholars in the classroom rather than learners (Stenberg 2005).

Embracing Theory versus Practical Information

Another key difference between how the two groups of TAs responded to TA preparation was in relation to their engagement levels with the theory and/or the practical information covered.[5] But as a result of this disparity in engagement, the two sets of TAs wound up taking different pedagogical practices and principles away from the preparation program. For example, while the composition TAs expressed appreciation for theoretical positions such as the importance of empowering students and developing student-centered classrooms, the need for building a community in the classroom, and so forth, by and large the literature TAs expressed their appreciation for the classroom practices and activities they were provided, such as the set curriculum—including various units and assignments—the textbooks they had been required to use, sample syllabi, and so forth.

This finding suggests that because of their focus on practice over theory, the literature TAs developed a limited ability to design their own curriculum given that they lacked the theoretical basis to do so. Nancy, one of the literature TAs, noted she continued to feel she struggled to develop new assignments or to utilize a WAC approach outside the common text the TAs were asked to use: "The one thing that TA training didn't teach me is how to move away from the models and understand what WAC is beyond the way it's set up in the common text." Nancy went on to explain she still had "a hard time seeing WAC outside of the three units [we were exposed to] on cyberspace, obedience to authority, and Hamlet." And while this may be a result of the fact that "[their] first quarter a lot of [them] just stole a syllabus, lesson plan, and units from somebody else," Nancy further explained that she not only appreciated the set curriculum but that she would have liked even more guidelines than she was given: "I wanted somebody to give me the lesson plan and let me implement it." Another literature TA, Diane, made a similar point, noting that when she taught for a local community college, she struggled to design her course without a set curriculum or template to follow.

While it makes sense that TAs from outside composition would be eager to adopt activities and a curriculum for a class they have little to no experience teaching, the fact that many of these TAs did not develop a theoretical basis to go along with their curriculum no doubt limited their future ability to develop units and activities of their own. Indeed, five years after their TA-preparation class, some of the literature TAs still used in their classes many of the same activities and assignments they were exposed to as new TAs. This was much less common with the composition TAs, many of whom came into the TA training program ready to begin designing their own assignments and units based on the theoretical bases they had already begun to develop for themselves. Because the theory presented in the TA-preparation courses did not resonate with the literature students' disciplinary background, they had trouble embracing it, and thus they remained stuck in the liminal space between the disciplinary paradigms.

Teaching Practices

Another fundamental difference in the responses of the two TA groups seemed to be an outgrowth of how they perceived their role in the classroom, which may very likely be a reflection of the modeling the TAs saw in their own experiences as students in the classroom. While all the composition TAs indicated they viewed themselves primarily as guides or coaches in the classroom, several of the literature TAs embraced a more top-down approach. The disparity in pedagogical approaches was evidenced not only by their words but also by the classroom practices they adopted and the activities they used. In particular, these differences manifested in three primary areas: responding to student papers, developing a student-centered classroom, and scaffolding assignments.

Responding to Student Papers

In terms of responding to student work, several of the composition TAs mentioned their commitment to encouraging students to focus on higher-order concerns before issues of grammar and style, a principle several of them traced back to their TA preparation. As Anna explained, "I got the idea that maybe you don't need to worry about every little detail. You know, like maybe you can focus on the bigger picture." However, the TAs from literature had a more pedantic view of grammar usage and instruction. In fact, literature TA Nancy indicated that one of the benefits of having taught FYC was that it made her "a more enthusiastic editor" of her students' papers, a sentiment that reflected her focus on correctness in her students' work.

Developing a Student-Centered Classroom

Another key difference in approaches was seen in the varying levels of commitment to developing student-centered classrooms. All the composition TAs cited their emphasis on developing and maintaining student-centered classrooms through various strategies and activities. Many of the classroom principles the composition TAs brought up in the interviews—such as seeing writing as a mode of inquiry, using student texts in the classroom, promoting collaboration, and working to develop a sense of community in the class—reflected their belief in the importance of creating this type of environment, at least in part as a means of working toward student empowerment. Two of the literature TAs, Amber and Justin, indicated that empowering students was a key component of their teaching philosophy, but neither they nor any of the other literature TAs mentioned any specific principles or practices associated with a student-centered approach.

Scaffolding Assignments

While the TAs from both groups emphasized the scaffolding of assignments and the importance of presenting writing as a process to their students, literature TAs Nancy and Daniel pointed out that these practices were not common in either the undergraduate or graduate literature classes at the university. Because these activities were not modeled within the English department, both Nancy and Daniel found themselves grappling with how best to introduce them into their classrooms. The TA training program was then working to acculturate the literature students to a practice more closely aligned with composition than with literature, again placing the literature students in a liminal position as they worked to negotiate these competing paradigms while also trying to establish their teaching identities and acculturate themselves to their home departments.

CONCLUSION

Question: What's Disciplinarity Got to Do with It? Answer: A Lot.

A key goal of this study was to elicit data that would indicate to what extent the perspectives held by the TAs translated into their actual classroom practice. It is one thing to toe the programmatic line in a TA-preparation class and/or to demonstrate adherence to a particular paradigm as a TA, but when it comes to discussing teaching philosophies, a teacher's classroom persona and materials speak volumes about what they believe about teaching. Lindgren (2002) is recalled here: "All teachers make choices about how to relate to students and whether and how to involve students in determining course content and processes" (297). Moreover, at least to some extent, these choices reflect a teacher's notion of what makes for an effective classroom dynamic, a perspective very likely informed by disciplinary norms and affiliation. Kathleen Blake Yancey (2002) notes that "attention to the TA's identity, both the preconceived identity the TA brought to the experience of development and the new/revised identity developed over time, is critical." Yancey further argues that "such attention includes considerations of questions having to do with the TA's construct of teacher/faculty member. How does the new TA understand the identity of a teacher? A faculty member?" (72).

The data collected for this project indicate that the two groups of TAs in this study indeed viewed the act of teaching writing differently, given the emphasis TAs in each group respectively placed on various approaches. These findings reflect the liminality experienced by the participants from literature and can be better understood by referring to Stenberg's (2005) argument that there are four primary metaphors teachers rely on as they develop their teaching identities: teacher as scholar, teacher as trainee, teacher as owner, and teacher as learner. In this case, it seems that while the composition TAs embraced the "teacher-as-learner" metaphor, the literature TAs were more inclined to adopt the "teacher-as-scholar" metaphor to guide their teaching practices and their interactions with students. Throughout the interviews, the idea of "teacher as scholar" was reflected repeatedly by the literature TAs, many of whom were looking forward to careers as scholars in which teaching would be a secondary activity. But perhaps this should not be surprising given that this group of TAs also reported their graduate professors seemed to adhere to a master/apprentice model (North 2000; Sosnoski 1994), as well as to a "traditional disciplinary dynamic" that positions "the professor as knower and the student as empty vessel" (Stenberg 2005, 136).

The notion of "teacher as learner" can easily be connected to the idea of student-centeredness, an approach that has become almost synonymous with effective composition practice. As Claude Hurlbert (2012) points out, "Student-centeredness is the crucial component of sound composition instruction" (60). The fact that all the composition TAs interviewed for this study expressed their commitment to student-centered classrooms is arguably a reflection of how entrenched this principle is within the discipline.

Finkel (2000), Lindgren (2002), and Stenberg (2005) suggest that the fields of composition and literature may reflect different ideas of what it means to be an effective teacher. The interview data collected for this study substantiate this notion, as the composition participants unanimously expressed that they viewed the philosophies of their graduate program and the writing program as virtually one and the same, while the literature participants indicated that they saw the disciplinary identity common to faculty in the English department as being strikingly different in terms of philosophy about the role of teaching and scholarship. This dynamic ensures the omnipresence of liminality for literature TAs.

Implications

Hopefully, the data revealed in this study provide insights useful to TAs who come from literature or other disciplines outside composition. The study's results demonstrate the importance of being mindful of the disciplinary paradigms that undergird TA-preparation programs, as well as those that inform the perspectives of TAs themselves, even when those paradigms are not immediately apparent. Such mindfulness can enable TAs to develop an explicit awareness of these paradigms, as well as the role they play in shaping individuals' pedagogies, which in turn can help acculturate TAs to the principles and practices associated with composition studies.

Toward this end, new TAs should be encouraged to participate in various activities to help them consider the cultural practices of classrooms/ teachers within their home department and then to analyze their notion of what it means to be a teacher, both within and outside their discipline. Moreover, it would be valuable for them to examine the assumptions they believe these practices are based upon. It might also be useful for TAs to describe their notion of an FYC classroom, including their recollections of their own experiences as students in FYC. And in terms of the development of a teaching persona, it might be beneficial for TAs to consider what kind of student-teacher dynamic they hope to create/engender with their own students—and why.[6] All these activities would provide TAs with opportunities to analyze and learn from their prior knowledge, a strategy that Robertson, Taczak, and Yancey (2012) promote.[7] Activities like these can facilitate TAs' progress as they work to develop a teaching identity that melds their past perceptions and assumptions about pedagogy and praxis with the new ideas they are becoming acquainted with in TA training, a process that should help mitigate liminality.

As TAs better situate themselves, empower themselves, and articulate their subject positions within their training programs, the sense of liminality they experience will likely become less mysterious and less daunting. Indeed, taking on a more deliberately agentive and self-efficacious position in knowing themselves in relation to that TA training can go a long way toward easing frustration, resistance, and, thus, liminality.

Although disciplinarity is so powerfully entrenched within our perspectives that it is difficult, if not impossible, to completely break free from it, the act of interrogating it and its implications can provide TAs with an important opportunity to critically consider how they are approaching the teaching of FYC and examine their underlying assumptions. Engaging in this work supports TAs as they develop their pedagogies and practices and as their teaching identities evolve.

Limitations

The primary limitation of this study is that the composition graduate program at this university is atypical given its placement in a school of education rather than an English department. But while that does suggest the composition graduate students studied here may be especially attuned to issues of pedagogy and praxis, it also enables a comparison between this position and the more literary affiliation evidenced by the graduate student participants from literature.

Another potential limitation is that this study is only documenting the situation at one point in time and at one institution. And, as Bishop (1988) points out, there is great diversity among TAs enrolled in a given TA-preparation program (some are new teachers, some have taught extensively before, etc.). Both these facts compromise generalizability, but as Erlandson et al. (1993) make clear, the intent of a naturalistic study is not to make generalizable statements about the frequency of a particular phenomenon so much as it is to better understand and develop a theory about whether and why the phenomenon occurs, which is the intent of this project.

Suggestions for Further Research

In further research, it could be useful to talk with TAs who were considered unsuccessful in the TA program, in order to get a more accurate read on the reasons for their lack of success. To what extent, for example, did disciplinarity play a role in these cases? And to what extent can these individuals' lack of success be attributed instead to personal predispositions? Did these dispositions change and/or soften over time? Asking and answering these questions could lead to a better understanding of how and why some TAs are less successful than others, which then could translate into a blueprint for how TAs might move through their sense of liminality more effectively.

It would also be useful to collect data about these or other composition and literature TAs' teaching practices further down the road to see how and to what extent their practices evolve after they join other academic institutions as professors. It seems likely that the transition to professorial roles would involve further acculturation, thus yet another instance of having to negotiate liminality.[8]

Finally, further research into the nature of disciplinarity would be particularly beneficial. As the data here show, disciplinarity creates divisions and biases, and yet it is so powerfully entrenched within our perspectives it is hard to break free from, even for the sake of trying to understand it and its implications. It would be advantageous to conduct further research to help elucidate the role disciplinarity plays in how we define ourselves as teachers, scholars, and individuals. A deeper understanding of this phenomenon would enable TAs to better understand and address the liminality many of them experience as they become acculturated to the discipline of composition and as they learn to teach it.

APPENDIX 3.A

INITIAL INTERVIEW GUIDE

BACKGROUND QUESTIONS

What brought you to this university for graduate school?

Did you have a particular career goal you were pursuing?

If yes, what was it?

What kind of work were you doing before coming to graduate school?

What did you study as an undergraduate?

What made you decide to apply to become a TA?

Had you ever taught before?

If yes, what? Where?

If you had taught composition, had you done TA preparation elsewhere?

What were your feelings about TA preparation before you began it?

What were your feelings about teaching writing as a TA for the Writing Program?

How did you feel about teaching writing in general at that point?

TA CLASS QUESTIONS

What do you remember about your TA preparation class?

How would you describe it?

Did you find it useful?

Did you find it interesting or enjoyable?

Here is a syllabus from each of your two TA preparation classes—do these bring up any other memories?

What do you remember about your TA cohort?

What attitudes about the class did your fellow TAs seem to exhibit?

Did the class meet your expectations?

If no, was it better or worse than you expected?

How did you feel about the readings assigned for the class?

Did you find them useful?

Did you find them interesting or enjoyable?

What were your feelings about the composition theory that was presented in the class?

Did you feel as though you got enough practical information from the class in terms of how to fill up class time with your students?

Was there anything you hoped to gain from the class that you didn't gain?

What was the best part of TA preparation, in your opinion?

What was the worst part of TA preparation, in your opinion?

Anything else you'd like to mention?

I'd like to follow up this interview with a brief conversation about your current teaching practices in the next week or so. But in the meantime, if you have a recent statement of teaching philosophy, would you be willing to share that with me?

APPENDIX 3.B

SAMPLE FOLLOW-UP INTERVIEW GUIDE

CURRENT TEACHING PRACTICES

How do you feel about teaching writing these days?

What is the most recent class that you have taught?

Can you think of any principles or practices that you use in your teaching that might be traced back to your TA preparation?

Looking back on it, do you feel that your TA preparation was beneficial to you?

If so, in what ways?

If not, why not?

Is there anything from TA preparation that you have rejected/found unworkable in your current teaching?

Was there anything from your preparation that you initially found unworkable but you now embrace?

Now that you are nearing the completion of your graduate work, what are your professional plans for the future?

Anything else you'd like to mention?

NOTES

1.   This is certainly not to suggest these are the only two models of teaching. However, these two models were indeed most consistent with the perceptions and practices of the two groups of TAs studied here.

2.   A copy of the interview script for the first interview and a sample interview script for the follow-up interview are included in appendixes 3.A and 3.B, respectively.

3.   The fact that the university's graduate program in composition is held in the school of education likely had a strong influence on how its students perceive teaching and learning.

4.   At the time of this study, the writing program adhered to a WAC/WID approach.

5.   And given that the theory espoused within the practicum was decidedly composition oriented, this difference in engagement levels is perhaps not surprising.

6.   Similarly, Kylee Maurer, Faith, Matzker and Ronda Dively (in this collection) refer to Diana Falk's (1995) notion of "preflection," a "reflective session that is held prior to the service experience" (13).

7. Since the conclusion of this study, each of the activities listed in this paragraph have been successfully incorporated into the TA training program that is discussed in this chapter.

8. As William Macauley notes in his introduction to this collection, "It is worth considering the experiences of TAs *during their TAships* as indicators to them of conditions and challenges to come" (7).

REFERENCES

Behrens, Laurence, and Leonard Rosen. 2002. *Writing and Reading Across the Curriculum.* New York: Pearson Longman.

Berkenkotter, Carol, Thomas Huckin, and John Ackerman. 1988. "Conventions, Conversations, and the Writer: A Case Study of a Student in a Rhetoric PhD Program." *Research in the Teaching of English* 22 (1): 9–44.

Berlin, James. (1996) 2003. *Rhetorics, Poetics, and Cultures: Refiguring College English Studies.* West Lafayette, IN: Parlor.

Bishop, Wendy. 1988. "A Microethnography with Case Studies of Teacher Development through a Graduate Training Course in Writing." PhD diss., Indiana University of Pennsylvania.

Bishop, Wendy. 1990. *Something Old, Something New: College Writing Teachers and Classroom Change.* Carbondale: Southern Illinois University Press.

Bishop, Wendy. 1997. "Attitudes and Expectations: How Theory in the Graduate Student (Teacher) Complicates the English Curriculum." In *Teaching Lives*, edited by Wendy Bishop, 192–207. Logan: Utah State University Press.

Creswell, John. 1998. *Qualitative Inquiry and Research Design.* Thousand Oaks: SAGE.

Dobrin, Sidney. 2005. *Don't Call It That: The Composition Practicum.* Urbana, IL: NCTE.

Erlandson, David, Edward L. Harris, Barbara L. Skipper, and Steve D. Allen. 1993. *Doing Naturalistic Inquiry: A Guide to Methods.* Newbury Park, CA: SAGE.

Falk, Diana. 1995. "Preflection: A Strategy for Enhancing Reflection." *Evaluation/Reflection* 22 (Winter): 13.

Farris, Christine. 1996. *Subject to Change: New Composition Instructors' Theory and Practice.* Cresskill, NJ: Hampton.

Finkel, Donald. 2000. *Teaching with Your Mouth Shut.* Portsmouth, NH: Boynton/Cook.

Haring-Smith, Tori. 1985. "The Importance of Theory in the Training of Teaching Assistants." *ADE Bulletin* 8 (Winter): 33–39.

Hesse, Doug. 1993. "Teachers as Students, Reflecting Resistance." *College Composition and Communication* 44 (2): 224–31.

Hurlbert, Claude M. 2012. *National Healing: Race, State, and the Teaching of Composition.* Logan: Utah State University Press.

Latterell, Catherine. 1996. "*The Politics of Teaching Assistant Education in Rhetoric and Composition Studies.*" PhD diss., Michigan Technological University.

Lauer, Janice, and William Asher. 1988. *Composition Research: Empirical Designs.* New York: Oxford University Press.

Lindgren, Margaret. 2002. "The Teaching Portfolio: Practicing What We Teach." In *Preparing College Teachers of Writing*, edited by Betsy Pytlik and Sarah Liggett, 292–302. New York: Oxford University Press.

North, Stephen. 2000. *Refiguring the PhD in English Studies: Writing, Doctoral Education and the Fusion-based Curriculum.* Urbana, IL: NCTE.

Payne, Darin, and Theresa Enos. 2002. "TA Education as Dialogic Response: Furthering the Intellectual Work of the Profession through WPA." In *Preparing College Teachers of Writing*, edited by Betsy Pytlik and Sarah Liggett, 50–59. New York: Oxford University Press.

Peterson, Nancy. 1995. "Passing as, Passing through: Literature-Trained Graduate-Student Writing Teachers and the 'We' of Composition Studies." PhD diss., University of Texas at Austin.

Robertson, Liane, Kara Taczak, and Kathleen Blake Yancey. 2012. "Notes toward a Theory of Prior Knowledge and Its Role in Transfer." *Composition Forum* 26 (Fall). http://compositionforum.com/issue/26/prior-knowledge-transfer.php.

Roen, Duane, Maureen Daly Goggin, and Jennifer Clary-Lemon. 2007. "Teaching of Writing and Writing Teachers Through the Ages." In *Handbook of Research on Writing: History, Society, School, Individual, Text*, edited by Charles Bazerman, 425–47. New York: Lawrence Erlbaum.

Scholes, Robert. 1985. *Textual Power: Literary Theory and the Teaching of English*. New Haven, CT: Yale University Press.

Slevin, James F. 1996. "Disciplining Students: Whom Should Composition Teach and What Should They Know?" In *Composition in the Twenty-First Century: Crisis and Change*, edited by Lynn Z. Bloom, Donald A. Daiker and Edward M. White, 153–65. Carbondale: Southern Illinois University Press.

Sosnoski, James. 1994. *Token Professionals and Master Critics: A Critique of Orthodoxy in Literary Studies*. Albany: SUNY Press.

Sosnoski, James, and Beth Burmester. 2006. "New Scripts for Rhetorical Education." In *Culture Shock and the Practice of Profession: Training the Next Wave in Rhetoric and Composition*, edited by Virginia Anderson and Susan Romano, 325–45. Cresskill, NJ: Hampton.

Stenberg, Shari. 2005. *Professing and Pedagogy: Learning the Teaching of English*. Urbana, IL: NCTE.

Welch, Nancy. 1993. "Resisting the Faith: Conversion, Resistance, and the Training of Teachers." *College English* 55 (4): 387–401.

Yancey, Kathleen Blake. 2002. "The Professionalization of TA Development Programs." In *Preparing College Teachers of Writing*, edited by Betsy Pytlik and Sarah Liggett, 63–74. New York: Oxford University Press.

Yin, Robert. 2003. *Case Study Research Design and Methods*. Thousand Oaks, CA: SAGE.

4

THE GRADUATE TEACHING ASSISTANT AS ASSISTANT WPA
Navigating the Hazards of Liminal Terrain between the Role of Student and the Role of Authority Figure

Kylee Thacker Maurer and Faith Matzker,
with Ronda Leathers Dively

INTRODUCTION

Liminal states can be disconcerting and intimidating spaces, especially when the terrain encompasses threshold concepts that lead to encounters with troublesome knowledge or conceptual difficulties that arise within disciplines as teaching assistants (TAs) perform their duties.[1] Nevertheless, successfully crossing that terrain and learning to navigate those threshold concepts are necessary experiences that allow graduate teaching assistants (TAs) to successfully transition from student to professional, from novice to scholar, and from learner to educator (Meyer, Land, and Flanagan 2016, xvi). Conversely, experiencing liminality without being able to identify or understand it can lead to higher levels of stress and anxiety for TAs, while increasing the sense of imposterhood they may feel. For these reasons, it is important for graduate programs to provide safe and well-supported opportunities for TAs to work through the challenges of identifying and understanding their own liminality and the ways it can positively and negatively impact them.[2] Indeed, it is our contention that the liminal terrain separating graduate student and professor can be a productive space in which TAs can hone their critical-thinking skills, learn how to navigate problematic situations with finesse, and develop more open-minded, creative approaches to their work and academic relationships.

Of course, this transition is challenging for all TAs, but the liminal terrain becomes exponentially more complicated for TAs promoted to administrative-assistant positions because they are then required to maneuver among multiple marginal roles. Such uniquely complex states of being are the focus of this chapter, which explores the experiences of

DOI: 10.7330/9781646420896.c004

two advanced TAs promoted to the position of writing studies assistant (WSA) at Southern Illinois University Carbondale (SIUC). Through our analysis, we hope administrative TAs and those who mentor them might arrive at a more comprehensive understanding of administrative-TA liminality and the benefits of fully engaging with and embracing this liminal space. Moreover, we present this analysis with the assumption that *all* TAs—by virtue of inevitably shared aspects of their liminality—will find it relevant to their respective situations.

With such purposes in mind, the body of this chapter begins with a "Brief but Essential History" by Dr. Ronda Leathers Dively that explains how the university climate acted as a catalyst for the development of this unique WSA position for TAs during her tenure as writing studies director at SIUC. Immediately following Dr. Dively's chronicle, we (Maurer and Matzker), as experienced WSAs, focus on identifying and analyzing the multiple liminal realities we encounter in this role. In spite of any negative stigma attached to liminality, we ultimately argue that TAs should actively identify, confront, and reflect on such spaces—especially those that provide administrative apprenticeship—as they are rich opportunities for gaining essential professional experience and insight.

BRIEF BUT ESSENTIAL HISTORY

A little over a decade ago, when I (Dively) assumed direction of the sizable writing program at SIUC (the program supported approximately ninety graduate teaching assistants and served close to three thousand students per semester), I inherited what felt to be plenty of staff. More specifically, I was fortunate to have a full-time office manager, who oversaw daily logistical operations, and a half-time assistant director—a newly minted rhetoric and composition PhD—who assisted me with undergraduate discipline, teacher preparation, curriculum, and assessment. Furthermore, I was able to rely on a group of five experienced TAs, assigned to my office for half their appointments, who conducted classroom visits with TAs new to the program, advised me relevant to our annual TA-orientation seminar, and helped lead some of the seminar sessions.[3]

Eleven years later, following a steady erosion of that staff under the weight of a growing state budget crisis and declining enrollments, I found myself sharing my office manager with the department chair, wondering how I had lost my assistant director, yet waxing grateful I still enjoyed the support of five experienced TAs. Despite my gratitude for the support I still had, as I transitioned to this new reality, I couldn't help but worry. Given that I was (and had always been) granted only a single course release to run this large program, I feared there wouldn't be enough of me to go around. After all, the person power formerly devoted to office operations had dwindled to half its former status, and I was compelled to take up some of the slack. Even more debilitating, I had lost my administrative right arm, an individual about whom—with his advanced degree in rhetoric and composition, as well as a few years of experience in writing program administration—I was able to assume a certain knowledge base and set of skills. I had been able to rely on this person to address many of the issues that arose on a daily basis without even having to consult me. When consultation was necessary, our common professional backgrounds made for highly efficient exchanges. Having lost my assistant director, then, I was absorbing hours of additional work (hours technically to be reserved for research).

In light of these circumstances, I was forced to reconceive the manner in which I employed the TAs assigned to my office. Of course, the close mentoring of first-year teaching assistants through classroom visits and feedback on instructional practice remained of highest priority. Depending on the size of the incoming TA class, then, I would need to assign two or three of the program's administrative TAs to this particular responsibility. Administrative assistants in this role would come to be known as *instructional mentors* (IMs).

That left me with at least two administrative TA positions every semester that—though unorthodox for our program at that time—could be devoted to duties once held by my former assistant director. Individuals in this role came to be known as *writing studies assistants* (WSAs). Although, as mentioned earlier, administrative duties typically accounted for only half an administrative TA's assistantship (the other half devoted to teaching a writing course), I convinced the department chair at that time that my workload warranted contracting the WSAs to satisfy their assistantships in full within the writing studies program's administrative office. A side benefit of this type of assignment, I reasoned, would be that its relative coherence (in contrast to a half-administrative, half-teaching assignment) would compensate to some degree for the fresh and formidable challenges the WSAs were about to encounter. Moreover, I predicted that such concentrated experience in writing program administration would serve them well on the job market.

With the plan just described in place, I began to feel as if my administrative TAs and I might possibly survive the reduction in writing studies staffing; even so, our survival involved working through some vexing complications. One complication centered on the extent and nature of the training the WSAs would require. Mindful not only of the turnover in TAs through graduations, but also of the department's long-standing desire to provide administrative opportunities for as many TAs as possible, I recognized that—if I adhered to the latter—I would be spending an inordinate amount of time each semester training WSAs.[4] Indeed, they would be stepping into a role they had never closely observed or experienced, and in some cases (though I was able to draft rhetoric and composition PhD candidates from time to time), they were stepping into a role they hadn't even studied. The specter of this revolving door and its impact on my time led me to proposition the chair about keeping the WSAs in their positions for as long as they were on campus and willing to serve.

Happily for me, the chair endorsed this idea, but along with that decision arose another complication. While all assistants in the writing studies program are set apart from their peers in the respect that the director selects them to hold what many regard as coveted positions,[5] those selected to serve in the newly conceived WSA role would be separated in ways even more significant: that is, at least as far as their assistantships were concerned, they would be considered *full-time* administrators. Further, they would be administrators with unique jurisdiction over their peers.[6] For example, the WSAs routinely would be helping to update and revise materials (syllabi, writing assignments, readings) for each course in the writing program's standardized curriculum, materials the other TAs were expected to teach.[7] They would also be leading introductory sessions for their peers new to the responsibility of teaching upper-level composition courses, and they would be contributing heavily to the planning and execution of the annual TA-orientation seminar. In addition, they would be vetting problems for me between TAs and their students, including disputes over grades and attendance failures; purported incidents of disruptive, disturbing, or unethical student behavior; and student complaints about their instructors. They would even be working as liaisons from time to time between the writing program and other offices on campus (e.g., Disability Support Services, Instructional Technology, and the Department of Public Safety).

Of course, I realized these activities would thrust the WSAs into situations that would muddy their professional identity—situations that would abruptly unearth and pull them into an ambiguous and often uncomfortable space between the familiar roles of student or first-year composition instructor and the very different role of departmental authority figure. Even though I anticipated some of the challenges they would face in this murky area (not only with other TAs but also with undergraduates, faculty, and staff), as the years have played out, the terrain of this unique liminal space the WSAs occupy has revealed rises and falls neither I nor they anticipated.

In the remainder of this chapter, two of my former WSAs (Maurer and Matzker) explore this terrain through the lens of a definition of liminality that emphasizes the sociocultural elements of "in-betweenness." Working from Victor Turner's (1967) concept of liminal personae as existing in a "realm of pure possibility [from] whence novel configurations of ideas and relations may arise" (97) and in which they "have physical but not social 'reality'" (98), Kylee Thacker Maurer and Faith Matzker view the administrative assistant's liminal status as navigating between the oppositional identities of a hypersensitive TA and a secure faculty member, all the while engaging in an intellectual milestone (Bell 2008; Elton 1989; Turman 2001; Turner 1974; van Gennep 1960). They focus this sociocultural lens on two types of interactions that largely define their WSA position: relationships with other TAs, whom these administrative assistants are charged with guiding in many capacities, and relationships with faculty and staff, who (perhaps unwittingly) engage them as unwilling participants in power struggles tied to duties associated with their position.

THE WSA AS LIMINAL BEING

As characterized in the introduction to this chapter, the role of WSA at SIUC presents opportunities for profound learning and meaningful reflection that prepare aspiring writing program administrators in ways TAs at many institutions do not have the luxury of experiencing firsthand. In addition, this role promises a competitive edge in the job market and expedites acclimation to administrative positions. Most important, TAs occupying these roles acquire higher levels of professional agency and self-efficacy as they pertain to WPA and teaching writing through WSA's proximity to and inclusion in institutional practices. En route to all these advantages, however, individuals who serve as WSAs spend considerable time embroiled in a quagmire of complicated issues and complex relationships that can potentially prevent them from settling into a clear sense of professional identity. To be sure, the push-and-pull of the ever-changing nature and combinations of variables involved in these issues and relationships makes for unstable footing, denoting a perpetual state of liminality as defined by Turner (1967). Elizabeth Bell (2008), using Turner's description of liminality,[8] writes that limen, "or *the threshold between rooms*, is literally 'betwixt and between.' For ritual initiates . . . they are 'neither here nor there; they are betwixt and between the positions assigned and arrayed by law, custom, convention, and ceremonial'" (Turner quoted in Bell 2008, 133–34). In navigating toward several potential professional thresholds, WSAs are more than simply "betwixt and between" two positions because the position encompasses multiple in-between states, including student, TA, instructor, support staff, and administrator. Inhabiting all these identities at once expands career options to include WPA and managerial positions that may not have been considered otherwise. In other words, WSA positions shift the boundaries and terrain of career trajectories.

The numerous identities we, as WSAs, maintain can sometimes coincide; most times, though, our multiple roles conflict, leading us to "shift [our] limits, or edges," confront our liminal space, and reconstruct and reimagine our identities (Simmons et al. 2013, 9; Talburt 2000, 148), as we are repeatedly called to position and reposition ourselves (Cook-Sather and Alter 2011, 18). This continuous and evolving process leads us toward positive identity transformation, allowing us to more fully comprehend our experiences in this new environment (Simmons et al. 2013, 9). The fluid and dynamic space we occupy as WSAs allows us to gain insight into numerous perspectives and reap first-hand experiences, which, by extension, allows us to more comfortably occupy multiple simultaneous relational groups (Talburt 2000, 145).

Finding ourselves "not fully inside or outside a single community, set of practices, or norms" (Talburt 2000, 165), we relate to, but do not fully belong to, the various communities in our department: other TAs, instructors, faculty, staff, administrators, and students. Though we understood our limits and positions in our prior liminal roles as TAs, we found ourselves in completely unfamiliar territory when we stepped into the WSA position. The liminal position held by TAs often leads them to internalize an us/them dichotomy between TAs and faculty. The "us" is always striving to be "them," and "us" can only successfully cross into the desired dominant space with the assistance of "them"—which creates insecurity and anxiety, to be sure. There is comfort, though, in knowing the role one is navigating has been successfully maneuvered by many who came before. The circumscribed liminal space we occupied as TAs afforded us some stability in that regard, as many TAs have successfully navigated the path to their degrees before us. In our WSA roles, we encounter more fully the type of liminality Susan Talburt (2000) describes as being "produced precisely in the context of the shifting of limits of [the] department, which include new forms of academic production and new forms of social relations, [which] helps to keep those limits in play" (188–89). Indeed, as WSAs, we shift our limits, both academically and socially. Stepping into the WSA position required that we simultaneously step into multiple between existences of a nature few TAs ever have the opportunity to experience.

The initial transition to a hybrid liminal WSA reality from the more familiar liminal space we occupied as TAs exponentially multiplied our feelings of insecurity, inadequacy, and imposterhood. Because of these feelings, we quickly realized our principal liminal challenge rests with our identities—that is, not only how we see ourselves but also how our fellow TAs, faculty members, and other departmental factions perceive us. As Turner (1974) states, the majority of liminals are "highly conscious and self-conscious people" (233), and this accurately describes us. Being graduate students with administrative roles, we are under constant scrutiny from others that deeply affects how we view ourselves—even to the point of identity crises—and how we decipher others' interpretations of our academic identities. Despite all this, navigating the multifarious liminal WSA terrain has resulted in an ability to understand our liminality as a "threshold concept" with great transformative and growth potential (Meyer and Land 2003, 1).

Viewing our liminality as a threshold concept may seem, at first, contradictory. After all, Jan Meyer and Ray Land (2005) distinguish threshold concepts from liminality when they suggest that liminality "appears to be a more 'liquid' space [than threshold concepts], simultaneously transforming and being transformed by the learner as he or she moves through it" (380). Working from this distinction, Nicola Simmons et al. (2013) conclude that thresholds are preceded by an existing pathway to expanded knowledge, and these paths serve to guide us through a liminal terrain (11). Nonetheless, when describing the term "threshold concept," Meyer and Land (2003) write that it

> can be considered as akin to a portal, opening up a new and previously inaccessible way of thinking about something. It represents a transformed way of understanding, or interpreting, or viewing something without which the learner cannot progress. As a consequence of comprehending a threshold concept there may thus be a transformed internal view of subject matter, subject landscape, or even world view. (1)

With this description in mind, we cannot view threshold concepts and our multifaceted liminality as being mutually exclusive when we consider that we could not have progressed in our roles as WSAs without transforming our understanding, interpretation, and views of our identities. Additionally, because we do occupy simultaneous liminal states, there is no single, predetermined path to knowledge; there are multiple paths available at once, and, periodically, we walk more than one at a time. In other words, reflecting on our multiple, simultaneous liminal states has led us to view our novel liminality as a threshold concept that transforms our "internal view of subject matter, subject landscape, [and] even world view" (Meyer and Land 2003, 1).

Even as our liminality has us continually transforming, we are attempting to preserve relationships with each departmental group, especially other liminals (Phillips, Shovlin, and Titus 2014, 58). Edith Turner (2005) explains that liminals unify through the development of communitas, or the "sense of sharing and [the] intimacy that develops among persons who experience liminality as a group. . . . [It is] the gift of togetherness," as liminals endure this crucial rite of passage together (97, 98). It has been our experience that TAs develop communitas during their first year, and this communitas typically continues throughout their time together as graduate students.

Bell has established the normative and existential nature of communitas. Communitas is normative, she writes, in that it is "characterized by 'we' feelings, a loyalty to the group, and a willingness to sacrifice for it. The group is mobilized toward a goal" (2008, 134). Communitas is also existential; statuses shrink and dissipate (134). The individual "self becomes irrelevant. In the group, what is sought and what happens is unity, seamless unity" (E. Turner 2005, 99). While communitas creates harmony, liminality—especially involving a change in position from TA to WSA—can complicate the notion of communitas. Because communitas is mostly created spontaneously, it is a challenge to grasp and is dangerous to depend on (Bell 2008, 135). Turner (1982) states that "[t]he great difficulty is to keep this intuition alive . . . initiation seclusion must sooner or later come to an end. We thus encounter the paradox that the *experience* of communitas becomes the *memory* of communitas" (47). Because liminality is a perpetually fluid state, communitas founded in liminality can dissolve as quickly as it began.

Developing and maintaining a relationship with each other as direct liminals in WSA communitas is as rewarding as it is vital to successfully filling our roles. As we have found, our WSA communitas is a crucial support system while we occupy this administrative position. Kathryn Elton (1989) notes that, when two graduate liminals work closely together, an awareness of equality is present (56). She further states that two graduate students will either unify in their endeavors, or their attempts to collaborate will fail based on the simple fact that they are liminal graduate students (56). We entered the WSA role together in the summer of 2015. At that time, we were both completing PhD coursework.

Similarly situated in this way, our WSA communitas developed out of our simultaneous journey into administrative positions, and between us there is no rivalry, seniority, or sense of superiority. We share roles and responsibilities, we communicate effectively to address gaps in our collective knowledge, and we are aware of our equality as we closely work together as graduate liminals. Thankfully, we have not experienced tension between the two of us, which we attribute to genuinely liking one another and having personalities that seamlessly mesh. Had it been otherwise, we both acknowledge we may not have been able to endure the sense of isolation and alienation that can accompany the WSA title.

Even though we happen to work very well together, the challenges we encounter with our peers, staff, and faculty within the English department and across campus create ambiguous, if not outright paradoxical, situations for us (Phillips, Shovlin, and Titus 2014, 43). For example, we often feel powerless in our position, but TAs view the WSA role as a position of power. Furthermore, frequent role-reversing encounters keep us perpetually off balance, such as when we are called on to advise faculty members. These challenges are most salient in the context of two strands of experience: exchange of information and physical, temporal, and intellectual boundaries.

EXCHANGE OF INFORMATION

Exchanging information with TA peers and faculty is a primary responsibility for a WSA. This exchange can become problematic, however, when TAs and faculty provide us with information or seek counsel with issues beyond our experience and depth; when these instances occur, we feel pressure to provide "correct" answers and feel viewed as incompetent when we cannot. Working through such feelings of professional ineptitude, though, moves us closer to the thresholds separating us from our desired professional goals, as each of these "unexpected and incomprehensible" situations carries us over the threshold into troublesome knowledge, where we reconceptualize meaning and transform our understanding of self and disciplinary subject matter (Meyer, Land, and Flanagan 2016, xi). It is difficult, however, for us to continuously bear in mind that these confrontations with conceptual difficulty are promoting our expertise and professional personas.

Further compounding the levels of conceptual difficulty we face as WSAs is the excessive amount of information we are privy to. As a result, even though we have both grown to be quite knowledgeable about the policies, procedures, and curricula attached to our writing program, we have also come to understand we must find a certain level of "comfort in the discomfort" of simply not knowing the answer to every question (Simmons et al. 2013, 17). However, TAs can often be dismissive of our positions relevant to our professional thresholds, expecting us to have all the answers to their questions. Consequently, we have grown aware of the danger of our TA peers potentially perceiving us as incompetent and untrustworthy if we cannot readily provide an answer to a question or, worse still, if we provide an incorrect answer. Trust issues, whether internalized by us or experienced externally with fellow TAs, can be accelerated by the fact that we frequently recommend other university departments to assist our TAs in addressing any issues that may arise (e.g., Disability Support Services, Instructional Technology, Department of Public Safety, and Counseling Services), and, depending on a TA's previous experience with these services, they may doubt that the avenue we recommend will actually address their concern(s). If a TA is suspicious of the competence of a particular service we recommend, any distrust the individual feels toward that service is often transferred to, and internalized by, us. In these instances, rather than viewing WSAs as dedicated peers committed to the aid and support of the TA communitas, TAs view WSAs as administrative lackeys who are committed to the university.

Our experiences in administration have proven to us that the best interest of the student and the best interest of the department or university are often one and the same, and this viewpoint distinguishes us from many of our TA peers, who tend to look upon university and departmental administration as entities distinct from them and, at times, as entities to be distrusted (we know we sometimes felt this way as TAs). For example, TAs often misconstrue how writing studies policies are generated, assuming they are developed and implemented solely in order to ensure we meet departmental or university policy criteria[9] when, in fact, as we often communicate to them, our policies are advanced with TA interests foremost in mind. During writing studies staff meetings, there is a give-and-take between the director and us. No matter the policy, our director makes sure she does not strap the TAs with additional work or negatively impact their already-limited pedagogical agency in any way. Her goal is to protect our TAs; in doing so, she employs us—as former TAs who have recently been in the trenches of first-year composition—to help create the policies, always keeping the current TAs' workload, well-being, and developing sense of self-efficacy in mind. WSAs, then, act as a bridge, although a tenuous one, between the fluid, liminal space occupied by TAs and the fixed, dominant space occupied by administration. At any time, with one small misstep, our TAs can begin to view us as belonging more to one side than the other. Still, we offer guidance and assistance on university and departmental policies and procedures as best we can, always being careful to use friendly, conversational language that conveys an atmosphere of trust in both the TA and administrative points of view in the hopes we can preserve our foothold in the TA communitas and diminish any skepticism TAs may feel toward those policies.

Despite our best efforts, our peers still sometimes view us as solidly positioned within the administration and therefore may exclude us from the TA communitas. For this reason, we frequently tailor our language in a way that communicates we still identify as TAs. To be sure, we are extremely careful when crafting our emails to TAs and to the department's writing studies listserv. When giving TAs advice and reminders of policies, we tend to draft our emails several times and meticulously reread them, even asking each other to proofread before sending. We make every effort to use a friendly and relaxed tone, and we occasionally delete our professional signature as well so as to not foreground our position. We have found these measures help reinforce the message that we are their colleagues, often allowing us to reenter, or reaffirm our position within, the TA communitas.

We view our TA peers as direct colleagues, despite our disparate liminal states. The term *colleague*, however, is a slippery term when it comes to faculty and WSA relationships. Though some faculty members have embraced WSAs as colleagues, others have not. Most faculty members, having interacted with us only as students in their classrooms, seem hesitant to accept the information we are able to provide and/or to share information with us. We can map our experiences as WSAs directly onto Alison Cook-Sather and Zanny Alter's (2011) discussion of "student consultants," a TA role whose liminality is similar to our own. In discussing the impact the confusing nature of liminal, transitory states can have on TAs (including WSAs) and faculty members alike, they write,

> Because it is located among established roles and responsibilities in a classroom, the student consultants' position immediately raises questions of alignment or allegiance that do not necessarily emerge without the catalyst of someone occupying an in-between position. Is the student consultant aligned with the faculty member? . . . The consistency with which this question is foregrounded for student consultants speaks to the salience of the "in-betweenness" they experience. . . . But even in the context of developing a collegial relationship with a faculty member, student consultants' "expertise" is predicated on their student identity. (16)

When exchanging information with faculty, we often sense that the crux of these conversations is (understandably) grounded in our student identities and couched in questions of our allegiance and alignment as such. When faculty members intersect with our multiple liminal identities, though, they tend to hesitate on both sides of any important exchange of information: they question how much administrative information they can ethically divulge to a member of the TA communitas, and they question the ethos behind university and departmental information relayed through one of their students. Therefore, although ours is a facsimile of the faculty role, faculty members necessarily maintain the boundaries separating us and them, preferring to situate us more firmly in the more familiar—albeit fractured—TA communitas.

Unlike most faculty members, however, our writing studies director shares as much information with us as she deems ethical in her endeavors to more fully prepare us for the roles of WPA or professor of rhetoric and composition, including us in professional, sometimes sensitive,[10] conversations germane to the administration of the program. While we are extremely grateful to be allowed at least some access to all the facets of a WPA's position, we must be careful during social encounters with TAs, as they are sometimes tempted to try to wrest confidential departmental information from us. Of course, we are not privy to some of the information they desire, but we are aware of intimate details surrounding matters that fall under our purview. Therefore, we must remain on guard, as private information simply cannot leave the writing studies office. In other words, being a WSA requires a level of professionalism that extends beyond the office and beyond the established standard for a TA.

Socializing with TA friends outside the office environment is yet another distinction between the ways we navigate toward our professional thresholds, as TAs often confide in us information about their work they expect friends to keep in confidence. For example, our peers might mention to us they let class out early or canceled class altogether, or they may admit they were not fully prepared to teach a particular lesson. On these occasions, our peers fail to recognize that, as WSAs, we are expected to inform the writing studies director when TA problems or potential issues arise, regardless of the atmosphere in which the information is communicated. Our jobs require that we help maintain the well-being of the department's TAs *and* students, and, therefore, we must treat information offered during social events or private conversations in just the same way as information gleaned during working hours. This aspect of our job has occasionally led our TA friends to distrust us, creating an additional fissure in our communitas, and in some instances, those friendships have dissolved.

Still, TAs routinely come to the WSA office to discuss their problems (personal, academic, and professional), as it is presumably more difficult for them to approach the writing studies director with matters they believe can make them appear incompetent. Even if a meeting between a TA and the director is prompted by us, TAs often stop in to talk with us afterward, occasionally revealing additional information that contradicts what was said in their meeting with the director. Of course, when TAs disclose contradictory information, we must report it back to our director, resulting in yet another brand of information sharing that can build tension or awkwardness between WSAs and TAs and further proving that our communitas, much like our liminal states, is in constant flux.

Regardless, all TAs are encouraged to talk with us, to discuss their triumphs and woes and to work with us in figuring out the best method for maneuvering toward and through troublesome knowledge or other aspects of their TA experiences. Some TAs visit us for these purposes fairly regularly. These TAs are able to recognize that we, like them, are betwixt and between and navigating toward similar thresholds. When this occurs, TAs are able to tap into our experience, knowledge base, and resources in a way they might never attempt with our director or any other faculty member. Ideally, they can also communicate their problems and insecurities freely and frequently, and they can diminish the learning curve by reaching out to us with multiple and diverse questions. In other words, we provide "sustained, scaffolded support for composition teachers from all backgrounds so that they can gain familiarity with some composition research" (Wardle 2013, 4) and best pedagogical practices.

However, other TAs—especially new and inexperienced TAs—are hesitant to come to us because they do not want to appear as though they are struggling with teaching, the graduate school load, or their liminality as they are orienting themselves to a different town, school, and professional cohort. As Andrea Williams and Tanya Rodrigue point out in their foreword to this collection, most TAs are full of apprehension, as they are new to teaching, and they are fearful that if they exhibit any signs of weakness, a negative stigma will be attached to their names. This fear can cause a ripple effect that can disrupt their instruction and cause issues in the writing program, such as substandard lesson plans and lack of timely grading. Sometimes TAs even attempt to deflect their classroom authority onto us. For instance, TAs often send their students to us to address concerns such as tardiness or absenteeism. Even though these are matters that fall under our purview in terms of adhering to policy, students are often sent to the WSA office because

TAs are still developing as agentive professionals and may be too timid to address simple disciplinary concerns with their students. As their peers, we do not want to—and strongly feel we should not—assume authority over their students and usurp or damage their classroom credibility; this is simply not our job. Rather, as WSAs we offer pedagogical advice, help monitor program policies and procedures, and guide our TAs through troublesome spaces as they are developing their individual teaching identities. Our TAs are instructors of record, and with this designation comes a level of responsibility they must accept as their own. Consequently, we are aware they can feel as if we are shirking our responsibilities or failing to collaborate within the TA communitas when we communicate to them the necessity of establishing their own classroom authority.

Some TAs tend to forget we are advancing toward our professional thresholds as they are, and they may also make assumptions about our roles based on our presence alongside administrators and faculty. For example, we lead many of the sessions during our orientation seminar, so new TAs have a tendency to draw parallels between us and faculty members, initially assuming we are similarly positioned in the departmental hierarchy. These assumptions are further conflated by our working knowledge of the curriculum and policies, as well as our long-established working relationships with the writing studies director and other faculty members. These experiences are destabilizing for us as we attempt to navigate the TA communitas, multiple simultaneous relational groups (Talburt 2000, 145), and multiple in-between existences, and they make us quick to want to put our peers at their ease in our presence by attempting to dilute the authority that encompasses the WSA title. Despite the fact that we try to be helpful and to remain approachable by reinforcing our position within the TA communitas, some TAs continue to see us solely as authority figures with a perceived higher rank, which further complicates our liminal identity.

While some TAs attempt to deflect their authority onto WSAs, other TAs are covetous of these administrative situations. Rivalries can arise between us and those who want to hold the WSA position, and therefore we can be critiqued more harshly by them. Those who engage in this rivalry willingly disrupt the communitas we have painstakingly attempted to preserve. This rivalry was most salient when we were new to the position, notably with former WSAs, and remains salient regarding the amount of time we have held our positions. The few previous WSAs still in the program dislike the fact that someone who came into the graduate program after they did is now in their prior position.

Nonetheless, while this tension, whatever the cause, between current and former WSAs can be thick, we, as liminals, are aware our position is not permanent, as a liminal's level of power fluctuates (Phillips, Shovlin, and Titus 2014, 52). Cook-Sather and Alter (2011) reinforce the transitory and tentative nature of any liminal situation, writing that "those in a liminal state are never secure: their position is never fixed but instead constantly shifting and vulnerable" (3). Despite the liminally tentative nature of our position, the length of time we have held these positions further fuels this rivalry, as some TAs feel it would be best if there was a higher rate of turnover. Earlier in this chapter, Dr. Dively discusses the logistical issues with a revolving-door approach to the WSA position, and the levels of complexity we have experienced in becoming competent WSAs solidify her convictions. TAs are selected for this position early in their graduate studies so they will have the time and exposure necessary to become knowledgeable and skilled in these roles. If the turnover were, say, yearly, the program would undoubtedly suffer, as learning the WSA role takes significantly longer than some anticipate. After all, we are still learning crucial lessons even though we have held these positions for a few years. Nonetheless, we are well aware that as we walk down the halls of our building, our peers tend to view us either as models holding a position they hope to attain or as rivals battling for a select position.

PHYSICAL, TEMPORAL, AND INTELLECTUAL BOUNDARIES

Despite our unwillingness to let go of our solid footing within the TA communitas, we cannot ignore the reality that we do possess a dual authoritative identity our fellow TAs do not. As WSAs, we have become proficient in the writing studies curricula, and we have developed a sense of authority over university and departmental policies and procedures by being able to explain and administer them. Typically, the type of authority that arises from the accrual of WPA knowledge (our ethos) does not directly impact our TA communitas, but WSA disciplinary authority (as it is commuted through us from our director) can escalate tensions between TAs and WSAs, disrupting our TA identity and communitas. This tension makes us uncomfortable, as we are required to act as disciplinarians within a group we simultaneously identify with. Naturally, this role requires a synchronous association/dissociation within the communitas. Thus, we tend to push against this idea of authority in our position, preferring to perceive ourselves as still belonging to the TA communitas, while we in fact slip in and out of it as we negotiate multiple liminal identities. Our concerns over being excommunicated from our TA communitas have caused us to develop a strong aversion to appearing authoritative, so much so that our director has often had to remind us that WSAs inescapably possess a level of authority and ethos distinct from other TAs in the department.

Due to this struggle, we have found there are simultaneous hierarchies within each group of people to which we marginally belong. For example, as TAs, we can relate to our peers; however, being a WSA and a TA simultaneously gives us a perceived "leg up" on our peers. Knowing this leads us to think of liminality in terms of degree, or scale. Bjørn Thomassen (2013) includes the concept of scale, or the intensity of the liminal experience, when he describes the dimensions of liminality, adding it to the dimensions of subject, space, and time (17). He writes,

> Sometimes, however, liminal experiences become intensified as the personal, group, and societal levels converge in liminality, over extended periods of time, and even within several spatial "coordinates." In other words, most experiences of liminality are circumscribed by some kind of frame, whereas others are closer to "pure liminality," where both spatial and temporal coordinates are in play. (17–18)

Viewing liminality as existing along the type of continuum Thomassen describes here—beginning with liminality circumscribed within a frame and ending in pure liminality—we consider the WSA role as occupying a position at or very near pure liminality, which expands the boundaries of our physical, intellectual, and temporal spaces.

In order to find some footing in this more expansive, fluid WSA liminality, we frequently default to the authority of the writing studies director in order to preserve our TA communitas. We are aware that even when we readily provide correct answers, TAs, instructors, faculty, staff, and students would rather hear directly from the writing studies director, which encourages us to deflect authority onto her. Talinn Phillips, Paul Shovlin, and Megan Titus (2014) explain that "liminals may lack the minimal authority that comes with having the initials PhD behind their names" (53), and this is certainly how we feel. Further, if an occasion demands that we be directive or forceful, we also tend to defer to the authority of our director or a departmental policy in an attempt to avoid acting under any assumed direct administrative authority of our own. When this occurs, we are exceedingly aware of the paradox we are complicit in advancing. On the one side, we are trying to bridge the gap between TAs and the administration, and on the other, we are deferring to the higher authority of administration to mask our alignment with, and enforcement of, administrative policies. This is a poignant example of how we are impacted by (and impact others with) the multiple liminal realities we inhabit. Paradoxes such as this one make it imperative for us to never lose sight of our positions relevant to our professional thresholds.

In visualizing these thresholds, we have created strategies to help us combat the idea of authority figure versus peer. Rather than embracing a perception of ourselves as authorities, we have made resolutions to maintain or create communitas with our fellow TAs through office space and preflection. For example, we have found our office setup can have a direct impact on the ideas of authority that surround our title. This realization came about when a new TA came to the WSA office seeking advice on a minor matter. He entered the office, stopped, looked at us, backed out of the door to look at the office sign beside the door, and then reentered, saying he thought he had inadvertently entered the director's office because ours looks so much like hers and is adjacent to her office. Naturally, like most teachers and administrators, we attempt to make our office as comfortable and accessible as possible. Nevertheless, we are the only graduate students with an office in the bank of administrative offices. Like the similarly situated student consultants Cook-Sather and Alter (2011) analyze, we find we "do not fit into the network of classifications that normally locate states and positions in the cultural space" (8). For the student consultant, this lack of classification affects how they "position themselves—literally (where they sit and why), but also metaphorically (in their relationships to themselves, to their faculty partners, and to other students)—shapes how they experience themselves and how they are experienced by others and informs the perspectives they develop" (8). The initial reaction to our office by the above-mentioned TA provided us with much insight into how our physical space—where we sit and why—shapes our experiences with our peers and how we could be unintentionally advancing a rhetoric of power. We immediately revised that rhetoric as best we could by rearranging our office setup, repositioning where we sit, incorporating a "bottomless" candy dish, and adding lighthearted, whimsical decor. While we did not immediately realize the ramifications of being the only graduate students who have an office in the series of faculty and staff offices, the fact is that since our first day as WSAs, we have been sandwiched between the director of writing studies and the director of graduate studies on one end of the bank and the English department chair and the director of undergraduate studies on the other end. Our efforts to revise our physical space were immediately rewarded, as TA attitudes began to shift and they became more willing to not only stop in for a quick visit (or piece of candy) but to also more frequently communicate their issues and concerns. Even though we have an office in a specific area, we do not view ourselves as possessing the same authoritative power over our peers that the occupants of the offices adjacent to ours do, and we want to communicate that distinction to the TAs through any means at our disposal in order to preserve our place in the TA communitas.

At the same time we are attempting to maintain a foothold within the TA communitas, we are attempting to gain any semblance of footing within the faculty, staff, and administration communitas. While the duties of WSAs and these other factions sometimes coincide, WSAs are feeling the tensions of these career duties for the first time (Elton 1989, 58). Paul Turman (2001) effectively describes the confusing nature of the TA role specifically in relation to faculty, and this description serves to highlight how especially perplexing the hybrid liminal reality of a WSA can be: "One is expected to develop a level of independence as a TA while being dependent on senior faculty . . . A dialectical tension develops which has potential to cause confusion concerning one's role in the department" (266). As WSAs, this dialectical tension is not only heightened but is also omnipresent, as we are having to interact with and carry out the duties of so many constituencies (TAs, instructors, faculty, staff, administrators, and students), which forces us to adeptly and frequently change the hats we wear. As a result, choosing which hat to don in each individual circumstance is one of the greatest challenges we face.

However, in some cases, there is not a hat that meets the challenge. For example, it is not uncommon for some individuals to outright disregard the few physical boundaries we possess and trespass on our office space, sometimes overlooking or completely ignoring our preferences and needs. In these instances, our liminality can be poignantly felt. Specifically, such infringements include individuals entering our locked office without our knowledge, removing items from our office without our consent because they deem them to be unessential to our duties, and even opening our windows or changing our thermostat setting despite our protestations. Additionally, some staff members feel strongly that it is their prerogative to know all the details of the interactions that occur in our office—even those confidential in nature—and they frequently demand we supply them with information we do not feel comfortable communicating. Subjectively, these instances reinforce ideas and feelings of a powerlessness that extends even into our immediate workspace. Our office environment can feel hostile, and our personal space can feel violated.

Objectively, however, these instances signify encounters with trouble-some knowledge (Meyer and Land 2003, 4). We can view these actions as arising from the need for an established hierarchy within the depart-ment, and we can see our presence within the administrative bank of offices threatens previously established hierarchies. Whereas office managers or other administrative assistants may perceive their position as higher on the departmental ladder than the position of a TA, our simultaneous roles as administrative assistants *and* TAs blur the estab-lished hierarchical boundaries in a way that now turns the previous space of administrative staff into a liminal territory. In other words, our liminality spills over into their spaces, and they—perhaps for the first time—encounter a liminal position in which the people they view as subordinate to them are on par with them or, potentially, more influ-ential than they are. Therefore, we can see that the unstable terrain we navigate creates a ripple effect. Moreover, as interns of a sort, direct disciplinary action against us is less likely because we are expected to make occasional errors (major and minor) as we advance toward our thresholds. Our liminality, in other words, frequently insulates us from major reprisals. To be clear, this insulation is not guaranteed, nor do we take liberties with it, but we understand how others, who do have more reason to fear administrative discipline, could struggle with positioning themselves in relation to the WSA role. Additionally, our lack of rigid parameters allows us to question departmental norms. Unlike faculty and staff, whose roles are clearly delineated and circumscribed, we are given more opportunity to critically question the daily operations of our department, a practice that has the potential to negatively influence the daily routines that sustain those in more clearly defined roles.

Even though we face many challenges when interacting with the vari-ous departmental factions, we have found that reflecting on our mul-tiply liminal status allows us to understand and sometimes predict and avoid discrepancies, conflicts, frustrations, and concerns that can arise during these encounters. Moreover, we have learned that occupying multiple liminal identities at once allows us to ultimately be

> comfortable in the discomforting spaces we currently inhabit. While our areas of doubt are almost never resolved, we can develop new, hybrid, mul-tiple, or alternative identities that enable us to integrate [our WSA experi-ences] into our academic lives. By adopting an integrative identity script, we can redefine ourselves so we neither abandon our pre-[WSA] academic identities altogether nor cling to them so closely we miss opportunities for [intrapersonal] dialogue and personal transformation. (Simmons et al. 2013, 17)

The development of these new identities, and the cognitive dissonance that accompanies our identity fluidity, can be rewarding and, indeed, transformative. As we constantly deconstruct, reconstruct, and merge identities, we are developing the capacity to quickly and effectively resolve interpersonal, intrapersonal, and extrapersonal conflicts. Additionally, our academic identities are enriched by the insights we gain through these exchanges. The us/them dichotomy between ourselves and our professors is not totally eradicated—our respect for, and subordination to, them remains intact—but we can more plainly understand and correctly interpret their actions as they guide us down the paths to our thresholds.

This dichotomy was put to the test as we welcomed a new director into the writing studies program in the fall of 2017.[11] Although our new director has extensive knowledge in writing program administration, she has had little experience with the day-to-day operations of our particular model of first-year composition. As a result, we find ourselves in the unusual role of being an authority on matters our new director may not yet be. We are often called on to advise her in matters of policy, curriculum, and logistics. At times, this position feels untenable, as we look upon our director with respect and admiration in her multiply dominant roles in writing program administration and as a professor within our department. Being, in some ways, an authority on matters involving our authority figure can make us feel anxious and uncomfortable. We agonize over how to word emails in order to be certain the new director has all the information required to navigate particular situations but simultaneously avoid sounding pedantic and directive. On the other hand, an awareness of WSA liminality serves us well at these times because we are able to reflect on the progress we have made toward transitioning into the spaces we hope to one day occupy. We are able to fully embrace the primary requirement of our title—assisting the writing studies director—and to recall that most people holding positions of authority rely on teams of specialized advisors to assist them in performing their duties. Our recent experiences with the new director have shown we have acquired levels of competency, agency, and self-efficacy necessary to confidently and successfully cross over our professional thresholds that are, by extension, coming into sharper focus. This, of course, has been our department's goal all along—to produce qualified, competent professionals. Nevertheless, though we are drawing ever nearer to our professional thresholds, we remain cognizant of the fact that we are still "betwixt and between" (Turner 1967, 98) and, subsequently, subordinate to our administrators and faculty members. The liminal terrains where WSAs dwell are "comprised of shifting boundaries and spaces [and] may be an enactment of a questioning of fixed place and location" (Talburt 2000, 145). Being "betwixt and between," then, requires us to constantly question our positions relevant to the fixed places of our authority figures and our professional thresholds as they shift quickly, sometimes with each passing moment. In other words, at the same time our WSA title can require us to act as conduits for faculty authority we must avoid projecting a sense of equality during encounters with faculty.

Because of our growing ability to understand the paths to our thresholds, we have finely honed our abilities to reflect and establish our multiple professional identities. One tool we particularly utilize is "preflection," which Diana Falk (1995) defines as "a reflective session that is held prior to the service experience." Because we are often navigating unstable terrain, we engage in preflection before almost every interaction we have with students, TAs, faculty, staff, and administration. We preflect about the various outcomes that may arise depending on what identity or identities we choose to inhabit during a particular interaction. If we respond as a student would, as a TA would, as a staff member would, as a faculty member would, or as an administrator would, what will be the result(s)? This continuous exercise allows us to imagine the various outcomes, and later we can reflect on our preservice opinions and examine them against our lived experience (Falk). The recursive nature of this practice leads us to meaningful reflection that furthers our understanding of WPA, rhetoric and composition, and ourselves as professionals. Preflection also allows us to imagine creative and innovative resolutions to issues, and knowing our role is in part that of a "Critical Organic Catalyst" because we are able to adopt the persona of an administrator while retaining the fluidity of the liminal TA (Talburt 2000, 164), we can put our imagined, innovative solutions into practice and then reflect on the outcomes without fear of reprimand. Again, we find our multiple liminal realities offer us a certain degree of protection, insulation, and creative license since those who hold positions of authority understand we are exploring and learning the professional terrain.

CONCLUSION

As WSAs, we are striving to form identities that are under continuous construction and that consist of surface-apposing roles—students and teachers and administrators. The many internal and external conflicts that arise within the multiple liminal realities of the WSA space necessitate that we alternate between often paradoxical identities (Simmons et al. 2013, 10). However, through the use of strategies we have developed and employed to traverse this liminal terrain, we are attempting to find resolutions to these paradoxes. Simmons et al. (2013) describe this attempt at reconciliation via social identity theory:

> Social identity theory reconciles . . . two positions by suggesting that identity is formed through a dynamic, contextually responsive process of mentally assigning ourselves to social groups depending on which categorization best supports positive self-concept and self-esteem. According to this theory, we hold multiple social identities and will identify with that which is most salient at any given time. (10–11)

However, we see that, in some cases, one identity is not more salient than another. In fact, we believe the combination of our identities can prove more useful than one identity, as shown through the successful strategies we use. As WSAs navigating a liminal space, we should not worry about which hat is better to wear in certain instances; we should embrace all we are and all we will be, and we should use our liminal positions to play up our strengths.

Liminals spend far too much time focusing on what they cannot do. As evidenced above, we have been guilty of doing just that. However, after a thorough examination of our liminality, we see how we can use it to our benefit, both now and in the future. Liminality does not have to be a constraint but can be, if viewed properly, a time of liberation to discover all the facets of our skillsets before we emerge as professionals in the field of writing. To become liberated, we must change the way we think about liminality. Indeed, Phillips, Shovlin, and Titus (2014) assert that "liminal WPAs might more productively navigate their roles through a strategy [called] *thinking liminally* or exploiting the constraints of liminality to further their professionalization and strengthen their programs" (44). Through thinking liminally, we can understand how and where we fit into the world of academia; the temporary and invisible nature of our liminal position can indeed be advantageous to the institution (55, 48). This revolutionary way of thinking about our academic identity shows us the importance of our liminal journey and advances our transformations from neophytes to experts (Simmons et al. 2013, 16–17). To confidently cross the thresholds we encounter, to continue growing in the field we are committed to, we must be willing to embrace and value liminality.

We have found that with a positive mindset toward our liminal, threshold states, the destabilizing nature of the WSA role actually allows us to deeply reflect on our liminality and to understand how it informs and advances our growing academic identities (Simmons et al. 2013, 10). This knowledge allows our multifaceted liminal position to be transformed from a seemingly powerless and ambiguous station to a temporary space from which we have a better vantage point to observe, absorb, apply, or reject the characteristics of those who reside in the dominant spaces that surround us (Shortt 2014, 633). From this standpoint, we can more objectively examine our liminal identities, allowing us to transform them from subversive, subordinate roles into meaningful—though transitory—work spaces. Our multiply liminal existences have allowed us to closely participate in writing program administration, and we have had unlimited opportunities to model ourselves on our director; to navigate difficult student, TA, staff, and faculty situations; and to polish our professional personas. As such, the professional thresholds we are soon to cross have come into clearer focus.

NOTES

1. We are working with two distinct types of thresholds in this piece. The first—and most prevalent—is the one that marks the border between TA liminality and the career space that lies beyond graduate school. The second threshold derives from threshold concept theory, and it is the threshold we cross once our understanding is transformed through engagement with conceptual difficulties or troublesome knowledge; this threshold emerges within our disciplines as we reconceptualize our "meaning frames" due to encounters with "unexpected and incomprehensible problem[s]" (Meyer, Land, and Flanagan 2016, xi). This is a boundary we frequently encounter and negotiate during our tenure as TAs.

2. This statement is made with our personal encounters with TAs in mind, although the many texts that exist with a view toward assisting TAs to identify and understand their liminal states implicitly argue for a need to openly address and discuss the liminal nature of graduate school with the newly indoctrinated in order to ensure they are aware of the in-between space they occupy. In "Examining Writing Center Director-Assistant Director Relationships," Kevin Dvorak and Ben Rafoth (2012) identify the dangers TAs face when they are not able to openly recognize or understand their liminality. These dangers include becoming disenchanted with their work and distancing themselves from their positions.

3. The director of the writing studies program has and continues to be responsible for the selection of TAs for administrative posts within the program. Selection is based on the following criteria: reputation as an instructor, performance in English 502 (a graduate seminar on college composition pedagogy), enthusiasm for writing theory and practice, dependability, and trustworthiness.

4. Of course, the IMs did not present the same problem since all of them had been observed by a TA mentor when they joined the program, and thus they were familiar with the role.

5. Though, given their focus of study, rhetoric and composition students often seemed best prepared for these positions, literature and creative writing students have regularly contributed to the program as administrative assistants. Even the literature and creative writing students recognize that their experiences as TAs in the

writing studies program enhance their marketability. When administrative duties in the program are added to the teaching experience, the impact is exponential.

6. While, historically, TAs who performed classroom visits were "separate" in their own way, the distance was not nearly as profound as it would be for WSAs given that TAs' visits were purposefully characterized as opportunities for *conversations about* teaching as opposed to *evaluations of* teaching.

7. For detailed reflection on the experience of standardizing a program curriculum and the perceived impact of standardization on various writing program constituents, particularly TAs, see "Standardizing English 101 at Southern Illinois University Carbondale: Reflections on the Promise of Improved GTA Preparation and More Effective Writing Instruction" (Dively 2015).

8. Turner's (1967) definition of liminality expands upon Arnold van Gennep's (1960) definition (Bell 2008, 133).

9. TA liminality fosters an atmosphere in which TAs feel their needs or concerns are often overlooked and their voices are not heard. Even though TAs are hugely influential to the success of any university, it is a rare instance when they experience any control over what they teach, when they teach, what material they cover, or—on a larger scale—university practices. From our perspective as WSAs, we have come to realize that what TAs see as an organization structure based on top-down control (e.g., standardized syllabuses, preselected course materials, required platform usage, and assessment-data collection) is actually a bottom-up structure that frees up TAs' time that would otherwise be devoted to developing curriculum, constructing classroom shells on digital platforms, and logging more extensive information for assessment purposes. Instead, this time can be utilized to further develop their teaching philosophies or to do their own coursework and research. This type of seemingly heavy-handed direction also ensures freshman composition students are being provided sufficient, consistent instruction.

10. When I (Dively) served as an Assistant to the WPA in the context of my doctoral studies, I was "protected" from what might be considered sensitive information. While admittedly my role was more in line with that of an IM at SIUC as opposed to a WSA, and while I certainly understand the inclination of a WPA to shield graduate students from politically sticky situations, I've often wished, given my desire to become a WPA, that I had been shielded a little less so I could have felt more fully prepared to address all aspects of the position, especially those involving personnel management. That being said, as I've worked with WSAs over the past few years, I've found myself thinking carefully about effecting an appropriate balance, hoping to provide them a well-rounded administrative apprenticeship while also guarding them from situations that invite undue conflict, particularly with faculty.

11. After nine years in the role of writing studies director, Dr. Dively decided it was time to focus her professional energies elsewhere.

REFERENCES

Bell, Elizabeth. 2008. *Theories of Performance*. Los Angeles: SAGE.

Cook-Sather, Alison, and Zanny Alter. 2011. "What Is and What Can Be: How a Liminal Position Can Change Learning and Teaching in Higher Education." *Scholarship, Research, and Creative Work at Bryn Mawr College*, 1–36. http://repository.brynmawr.edu /edu_pubs/3.

Dively, Ronda Leathers. 2015. "Standardizing English 101 at Southern Illinois University Carbondale: Reflections on the Promise of Improved GTA Preparation and More Effective Writing Instruction." In *Ecologies of Writing Programs: Program Profiles in Context*, edited by Mary Jo Reiff, Anis Bawarshi, Michelle Ballif, and Christian Weisser, 41–67. Anderson, SC: Parlor.

Dvorak, Kevin, and Ben Rafoth. 2006. "Examining Writing Center Director-Assistant Director Relationships." In *The Writing Center Director's Resource Book*, edited by Christina Murphy and Byron Stay, 179–86. New York: Routledge.

Elton, Kathryn. 1989. "Second among Equals: The Graduate Student Perspective." *National Forensic Journal* 7 (1): 53–62.

Falk, Diana. 1995. "Preflection: A Strategy for Enhancing Reflection." *Evaluation/Reflection* 22: https://digitalcommons.unomaha.edu/slceeval/22.

Meyer, Jan H. F., and Ray Land. 2003. "Threshold Concepts and Troublesome Knowledge: Linkages to Ways of Thinking and Practicing Within the Disciplines." Enhancing Teaching-Learning Project (Occasional Report 4). Edinburgh: University of Edinburgh, Higher Community Education, School of Education.

Meyer, Jan H. F., and Ray Land. 2005. "Threshold Concepts and Troublesome Knowledge (2): Epistemological Considerations and a Conceptual Framework for Teaching and Learning." *Higher Education* 49 (3): 373–88.

Meyer, Jan H. F., Ray Land, and Michael T. Flanagan. 2016. Preface to *Threshold Concepts in Practice*, xi–xxxiv. Rotterdam: Sense.

Phillips, Talinn, Paul Shovlin, and Megan Titus. 2014. "Thinking Liminally: Exploring the (com)Promising Positions of the Liminal WPA." *WPA: Writing Program Administration* 38 (1): 42–64.

Shortt, Harriet. 2014. "Liminality, Space and the Importance of 'Transitory Dwelling Places' at Work." *Human Relations* 68 (4): 633–58.

Simmons, Nicola, Earle Abrahamson, Jessica M. Deshler, Barbara Kensington-Miller, Karen Manarin, Sue Morón-García, Carolyn Oliver, and Joanna Renc-Roe. 2013. "Conflicts and Configurations in a Liminal Space: SoTL Scholars' Identity Development." *Teaching and Learning Inquiry: The ISSOTL Journal* 1 (2): 9-21.

Talburt, Susan. 2000. *Subject to Identity: Knowledge, Sexuality, and Academic Practices in Higher Education*. Albany: SUNY Press.

Thomassen, Bjørn. 2009. "The Uses and Meanings of Liminality." *International Political Anthropology* 2 (1): 5–27.

Turman, Paul D. 2001. " 'Learn to Play the Game': Recommendations for Being Successful as a Graduate Teaching Assistant." *Communication Studies* 52 (4): 266–71.

Turner, Edith. 2005. "Rites of Communitas." In *Encyclopedia of Religious Rites, Rituals, and Festivals*, edited by Frank A. Salamone, 97–101. New York: Routledge.

Turner, Victor. 1967. *The Forest of Symbols: Aspects of Ndembu Ritual*. Ithaca, NY: Cornell University Press.

Turner, Victor. 1974. *Drama, Fields, and Metaphors: Symbolic Action in Human Society*. Ithaca, NY: Cornell University Press.

Turner, Victor. 1982. *From Ritual to Theatre: The Human Seriousness of Play*. New York: Performing Arts Journal Publications.

van Gennep, Arnold. 1960. *The Rites of Passage*. Chicago: University of Chicago Press.

Wardle, Elizabeth. 2013. "Intractable Writing Program Problems, *Kairos*, and Writing about Writing: A Profile of the University of Central Florida's First-Year Composition Program." *Composition Forum* 27 (Spring). http://compositionforum.com/issue/26/prior-knowledge-transfer.php.

5

THE INVISIBLE TA
Disclosure, Liminality, and Repositioning Disability within TA Programs

Rachel Donegan

Disability is not an exclusively undergraduate experience. Conservative measures place disabled students as somewhere between 6 percent and 10 percent of university populations. Should this same percentage of disabled students hold for graduate student populations, upwards of 174,000 graduate students have some form of disability (Damiani and Harbour 2015, 400). But the truth is we do not have a clear picture—at all—of how many disabled graduate students there are, what kinds of programs they enter, or even which universities contain more disabled graduate students than others. The research gap is even worse where graduate teaching assistants are concerned. Two research studies on disabled TAs exist, and only one of these—published within the last year—focuses on TAs within writing studies programs. Casie J. Fedukovich and Tracy Ann Morse's (2017) "Failures to Accommodate: GTA Preparation as a Site for a Transformative Culture of Access" focuses on the ways TA programs and expectations can be inaccessible for disabled graduate students. Though this useful study offers an important assessment of inaccessibility in TA programs, the authors argue much more research is needed about disabled TAs, the access challenges they face, the factors that contribute to programmatic inaccessibility, and what WPAs can do to increase access.

Fedukovich and Morse's study aside, a similar level of invisibility exists within composition research as well. Many texts focus on a TA's transition from graduate school to academic professional, but none of these address the ways the presence of disability impacts, complicates, or enriches this shift. Within statistics and composition and rhetoric scholarship, TAs with disabilities don't exist. But we do exist. As Brenda Brueggmann et al. (2001) note in "Becoming Visible: Lessons in Disability," "Many of us 'pass' for able-bodied—we appear before you

DOI: 10.7330/9781646420896.c005

unclearly marked, fuzzily apparent, our disabilities *not* hanging out all over the place. We are sitting next to you. No, we are you" (369). There may not be any hard data at present about how many TAs with disabilities work in rhetoric and composition programs, but trust me, we're there, learning and teaching and navigating our way through.

Though disability-related composition and rhetoric research has grown exponentially over the last ten years, most, if not all, of the research deals with either student experiences or faculty experiences with disability. Given the procedural and, often, political differences between student accommodations and faculty accommodations, these experiences have been dealt with separately. Works such as Amy Vidali's (2015) "Disabling Writing Program Administration" and Margaret Price's (2011) *Mad at School: Rhetorics of Mental Disability and Academic Life* expose the variety of ways disability intersects with fundamental aspects of being a writing program administrator and working in higher education, respectively. However, neither of these texts include the experiences of disabled TAs. Some research studies have interviewed and documented the experiences of faculty with disabilities, and to date only one large-scale research study on disabled faculty, led by Margaret Price and Stephanie Kershbaum, has even been conducted.[1] None of these studies have included the experiences of graduate teaching assistants with disabilities, presumably because of the uniqueness of their liminal status and their ephemerality. Graduate teaching assistants are not permanent fixtures in universities; by their very nature they frequently and systematically enter and exit programs. There is no one set way to classify graduate teaching assistants within a university, and this consistent inconsistency leads to their getting lost in the shuffle. The strange, exclusional liminality of the TA position—a faculty member, but not a "real" faculty member; a student, but often with stricter academic and professional requirements than other graduate students—demands new, dedicated research to how disabled TAs navigate these pathways.

METHODS

With little direct scholarship or statistics to draw from, I evaluated my local context, my own graduate teaching assistant program, to better understand how the presence of disability impacts the student-teacher liminality that exists for all TAs.[2] Middle Tennessee State University is a regionally accredited comprehensive university located forty miles southeast of Nashville. It is one of the largest public universities in Tennessee, with a total enrollment of over 22,000 students for the fall 2017 semester

(Middle Tennessee State University 2017). The English department is mostly comprised of literature faculty, with the exception of two linguistics professors and five composition and rhetoric professors, two of which serve as co-WPAs and co-TA coordinators.[3] The writing program has two graduate students serving as graduate WPAs; I am one of them. In keeping with the department's demographics, most of the TAs have literature-related focuses; however, there are a few composition-focused TAs among them. TAs, whether they are MA or PhD level, must have completed eighteen graduate hours in order to teach; additionally, they must complete the department's Teaching Composition Seminar. Master's level students have the opportunity to teach both courses in the first-year composition sequence during their time as TAs; PhD students are able to teach these courses and sophomore-level literature courses, pending additional qualifications and department need.

I restricted my study to a maximum of eighteen participants: those who had worked as graduate teaching assistants in the TA program during the 2016–2017 academic year. I made no assumptions about who might qualify for the study and sent my recruitment email to all eighteen TAs. This study has received IRB approval,[4] and to date, five graduate teaching assistants have agreed to be interviewed and have their experiences recorded for use in this chapter. Over the course of their interviews, participants were asked a variety of questions about how and whether disability impacted various aspects of being a TA, including specific questions relating to disclosing to faculty and students. I did not limit participants to discussing their experiences in our current program; if they had been a TA in a previous program, they were encouraged to speak to those experiences as well.

All participants have been given pseudonyms and have had other identifying information removed to protect their anonymity. They were very eager to have their stories told publicly, to have their experiences known. In keeping with disability studies views on diagnoses, power, and economic privilege, I did not require participants to provide medical documentation that corroborated their disability status.[5] I gave participants the option to classify their disabilities in more generalized and categorical terms, but all decided to further disclose and provide additional descriptive information about their individual diagnoses for the sake of clarity. My study participants include:

- Paige, a fourth-year PhD student with generalized anxiety disorder, panic disorder with agoraphobia, and major depressive disorder;
- Josey, a third-year PhD student with autism spectrum disorder, ADHD, anxiety, depression, and an unspecified learning disability;

- Jamie, a first-year PhD student with multiple sclerosis and anxiety;
- Ruth, a third-year PhD student with ADHD, major depressive disorder, generalized anxiety disorder, and an unspecified learning disability;
- Lance, a first-year PhD student with type II bipolar disorder.

All the disabilities the participants mentioned are invisible, meaning they do not present visual markers and cannot be discerned based solely on external visual characteristics. Additionally, I chose to include my own experiences with mental illness and being a TA alongside those of my participants.[6] This choice was not an easy one for me to make; unlike my participants, I could not remain anonymous, and, as these case studies reveal, disclosure has its risks. However, I integrated my own experience not so I could allocate less space for my peers' case studies but so I could tell their stories better by being honest about my own. Disability experiences can vary widely from person to person, even among those who share similar diagnoses, and including my own experiences with these case studies is a way to provide a more rounded picture of the range of disabled experiences that can exist within a TA Program.

In this chapter, I work to reposition disability within the composition and rhetoric TAship, to apply a disability studies lens to highlight the access gaps that exist within these liminal spaces, and to note the impact on TA teaching practices. I incorporate disability and composition scholarship alongside case studies of these disabled TAs to offer insights about how disability disclosures affect this liminality and offer practical suggestions for improvement. The foundations of theory and the realities of praxis equally inform these suggestions. Fundamental to my work in this chapter are these questions: What happens to the graduate teaching programs once issues of disability are removed from the margins and are openly articulated and addressed? How can addressing these access gaps improve the quality of composition and rhetoric TA programs for all TAs? By centering disability within the TAship, TAs, TA coordinators, and graduate professors alike gain a better understanding of the multifaceted nature of the TA position and an increased awareness of the ways disability impacts and enriches the work TAs do.

THE POTENTIAL THORNINESS OF DISCLOSURE

The rhetorical complexities of disclosure pop up frequently in disability studies scholarship,[7] and for good reason: the circumstances behind a person's choice to disclose or not are both individual and generalized, based in previous experiences and in the often tenuous exchange of informational power. As individualized as these disclosures were for my participants, they all contained an element of unease, ranging from awkwardness to abject terror, depending on the situations and rhetors present. Stephanie L. Kershbaum (2014) notes these moments of disclosure happen frequently and sometimes unexpectedly in academic spaces, popping up in "hallway encounters, conference presentations, classrooms, email listservs, scholarly conversations." Disclosure moments become, for academics with disabilities, "the culmination of recurring processes in which past experiences are brought to bear on a present moment as individuals recognize opportune moments for action" (63). Disabled academics bring all their past experiences, good and bad, to each disclosing act, in the same way students in a first-year writing course bring all their past writing experiences with them on the first day.

However, I argue that the act of disclosure is far more unstable and uncertain for TAs than for other faculty members, primarily because of the student/teacher liminality TAs occupy. In many graduate programs, TAs are not situated as ordinary graduate students, often due to their institutional role as a teacher-student and the restrictions and guidelines graduate programs place upon them. Most programs construct TAs as the cream of the crop, the stellar scholars and promising teachers-in-training who have earned competitive funding, and who, as a result of said funding and subsequent time on campus, know more faculty members and more about their departments than other graduate students do. The pressure they face is greater. The stakes are higher. This is certainly true in my local context, where PhD TAs are required to take courses year round and, until recently, all TAs were expected to have a higher GPA than those not on assistantships. Such delineations between graduate teaching assistants and all other graduate students in a program seem to be standard.

As graduate students hoping to snag a job in an increasingly competitive hiring market, TAs are also keenly aware that good teaching alone isn't enough to get hired once they graduate; top candidates must present, publish, and network as much as possible. In these circumstances, a graduate student is not in a position of power. There is much more at stake for the student than for the faculty member. A lot of these professional doors can be opened if you impress the right graduate professors and academics at the right time. This universal pressure to be seen, as Paige aptly put it, "as one of the people who gets shit done" can be enormous, and there are usually few, if any, indicators of how those in power will react to a graduate student's disability disclosures. Though we should never be forcing or even compelling students to disclose their disability status, we should be creating enough space for disabled TAs to safely disclose if they choose or feel the need to do so.

For many disabled TAs, the potential risks involved in a negative disclosure experience with a professor—denial of the disability's existence, departmental gossip, exclusion, loss of mentorships, residual awkwardness, and shame—are just too high to merit mentioning disability. To this end, Kershbaum (2014) adds,

> No matter how skillful, no matter how familiar the context, disability self-disclosures do not always accomplish desired effects. Claiming an identity is not a singular accomplishment; it is a mutual accomplishment performed by speakers *and* audiences. Claiming a particular disability identity requires not only that speakers and writers assert it in interactional space, but also that other interlocutors and audiences acknowledge that identity. (62)

These tensions between the acknowledged and unacknowledged disability identity are increased when the disability is not visible or easily discernible. Often, invisibly disabled persons are further marginalized as a "result of a convergence of complicated cultural discourses regarding independence, fraud, malingering, and entitlement; the form it takes almost always involves a perceived discontinuity between appearance, behavior, and identity" (Samuels 2017, 353). Many professors still view granting student accommodations as providing unfair advantages and reducing the rigor of graduate school rather than being a legally protected right and a bare-minimum exercise in equity. However, the true disadvantage is for graduate students with disabilities to be forced to inhabit academic spaces not made for them (Womack 2017, 522).

CASE STUDIES: RECIPROCAL DISCLOSURES

When and if a disabled instructor chooses to disclose their needs in the classroom, accessibility can seem less abstract and more comprehensible for students. These voluntary disclosures can be valuable, as most students (especially nondisabled students) in first-year writing classes may be unfamiliar with disability and how it can impact their classroom experience. Price elaborates on the pedagogical opportunities of disclosure in *Mad at School*, detailing her own experience of disclosing her access needs to her students on the first day of class when going over her syllabus:

> My practice is to read aloud and then elaborate on my syllabus's accommodation statement, giving examples of my own needs as a learner in order to emphasize that such needs are not a question of needing

"more" support, but needing different kinds of support. One of the first things I tell students is that I have difficulty processing aural information; therefore, a question I can't respond to immediately should be written in a note, communicated via email, or they should make sure I write it down. (91)

By discussing her own access needs and the ways she has self-accommodated within the classroom, Price not only destigmatizes the idea of needing different learning support but also provides concrete examples of what this support looks like. In this example, Price also provides a range of strategies for students to meet her access needs: students wanting an answer to a non-immediate question should preserve their question in a visual format for her to return to later. These strategies are also context transferrable, meaning students can adopt them for use in other classroom environments. Providing access strategies like this shows students it's okay—and even encourages them—to be reflective and creative about their own learning needs and processes.

All five of the invisibly disabled TAs I interviewed connected their personal experiences with being students with disabilities to their instructional roles. In these interviews, some participants were more conversational than others, but all spoke to the ways their disability influenced how they taught and moved in their various liminalities. When referencing these past experiences, participants discussed a level of unease with disclosing and providing accommodation documents to professors. Depending on the participant, these feelings ranged from dreading a potentially awkward conversation to fearing retribution if they challenged a professor who would not accommodate them. However, all of them commented on how these same issues and tensions concerning disclosure informed their teaching practices, in particular their dealings with disabled students in their classes. Most participants noted the associated risks with disclosing their invisible disabilities in front of a class (namely, the fear of someone using their disability as the basis of a complaint or a grade challenge), but they had all disclosed to students on specific occasions. In the same way disability often varies from person to person, no two disclosures are identical.

Paige's motivations for disclosing to her students are informed by her own experiences with being a disabled student, particularly her self-described "mental health journey." When I asked about her process of getting official student accommodations, Paige mentioned only getting registered with the campus Disability and Access Center after struggling to pass her PhD examinations, exams students are required to pass before they can start their dissertations.[8] At the time, she viewed accommodations as an available tool to help her pass the exam, but in retrospect she noted that while she had the same anxiety-related struggles while taking graduate courses, she didn't want to believe her mental health issues were severe enough to warrant the additional support. More important, she noted, she feared her professors would see her accommodations and view her as weak or less-than, as if the presence of accommodations was proof enough she didn't deserve to be in the program.

Paige's fears and discomfort over how her professors might perceive or interpret her accommodations are not unique; in fact, M. Remi Yergeau (2013) speaks to the tensions of being a disabled graduate student in the "Reason" section of the powerful "Multimodality in Motion: Disability and Kairotic Spaces." In her portion of the webtext, Yergeau speaks of a professor who refused to incorporate her accommodation of "a more orderly face-to-face system for class discussions," such as raising hands, because he feared "it interrupted the *natural* flow of conversation." Not only did the professor's refusal to accommodate actively exclude her from the class, but it left her feeling "terrible about [herself—as if she] was somehow asking for unreasonable changes to a reasonable curriculum" (Yergeau). The act of providing a professor with an accommodation letter is an indirect and vague act of disclosure and can be an anxiety-ridden prospect—the professor may not know your particular diagnosis, but by virtue of receiving the form, they become aware that you have a disability. However, Paige put those feelings aside and acquired accommodations for her PhD examinations after her second failed exam attempt[9] that granted her additional testing time and the ability to take her test in a low-distraction environment. Soon after, she passed her final exam and advanced to candidacy.

Looking back on her time as a graduate student, Paige noted a shift in her mindset on disclosure. While she was struggling with taking her exams, professors asked how she felt about her upcoming test, and she mentioned having anxiety and securing testing accommodations. Paige attributed this openness with her gradual acceptance of her mental health status, a process in which she grew increasingly comfortable with her identity as a disabled TA. When she told faculty members about her accommodations, they were supportive and positive, which both surprised and reassured Paige. She connected this disclosure experience to her own instructional role: "I only realized after it kind of came out that way that I was missing out on an opportunity to hear if they'd had similar experiences. Because I wouldn't share unless a student shared. So why wouldn't I try to put it out more often?"

As an instructor, Paige looks for cues in her students' writing and comments they make during conferences before disclosing to them. Such disclosures, she pointed out, happen individually rather than collectively. She chooses her moments carefully, looking for phrases like "I have anxieties about . . ." and "I'm worried about . . ." as opportunities for her to share her own experiences with anxiety, to suggest strategies for dealing with anxiety as a student, and to inform them about various resources available to them on and off campus. Breaking down stigmas is also a priority for Paige, chiefly because of her past worries over how professors would view her, and she views sharing her own experiences with disability as a way to inform students that mental health issues are far more common than they may realize.

Out of all the TAs I interviewed, Lance expressed the greatest level of anxiety over disclosing to professors or TA supervisors, something he has not done since starting in MTSU's PhD program. For Lance, the risks involved with this level of openness are simply too great to justify disclosure until he becomes more comfortable with the program: "If it's someone I feel is in a position of authority over me or who may not understand, in my mind—it doesn't matter if they actually will or not, but if in my mind I . . . feel like they're going to look down on me or I'm going to get judged harshly . . . then I will just have to avoid it altogether." Lance's views on disability disclosure are in line with Fedukovich and Morse's (2017) findings with their disabled TAs; they note that "the culture of graduate school was so pervasively threatening to [the TAs] that they chose to work off the institutional grid and solve their disability needs themselves" (40). Lance emphasized how a professor's negative reaction to a disclosure, given their institutional power, has the potential to exacerbate his illness and jeopardize his position in the department, thus making disclosing a risk he is not willing to make.

Though Lance expressed considerable anxiety about disclosing to someone above him on the academic food chain, he remarked about the rhetorical possibilities involved in deciding to disclose: "I think disclosure—whether to peers, or to students—in any scenario—disclosure can be used strategically for benefits that would not come from choosing not to disclose." When I asked him to elaborate on this idea of strategic disclosure, Lance talked about the ways he has used disclosure as a TA. With peers, he has only disclosed after discerning whether or not they would be sympathetic or whether they had been diagnosed with a disability. Immediately after saying this, he laughed, noting it "sounds a lot more methodical than it is." These disclosures, he added, were his way of trying to build a sense of community in the midst of a rigorous, stressful environment.

Lance's strategic disclosures are not limited to his graduate student role but stretch across the liminal boundaries to his instructional identity as well. As an instructor, Lance has used disclosure on a strictly individual, case-by-case basis, chiefly out of concerns for his own privacy. However, he did detail a particular instance in which, like Paige, he divulged his own experiences with mental illness in an attempt to destigmatize the experience and encourage a visibly anxious student to consult campus resources. During a conference with one of his disabled students, Lance used disclosure in order to create a rhetorical and pedagogical middle ground, one where his accommodation needs as an instructor intersected with those of his student. He mentioned how some conversations might be as simple as a brief relational comparison. Lance then modeled such an exchange with me: "You have issues that you feel interfere with your learning process; I have to deal with that as well; therefore, let's work together to meet your needs as I always try to meet my needs." Near the end of our interview he marveled that after a year into this program, he was still hesitant about who he could and couldn't disclose to but hoped he could feel more open about doing so in the future. Even though he had positive disclosure experiences, this tension still remained, echoing Kershbaum's (2014) argument on the recursive nature of such disclosures.

The three TAs who were the most open about others knowing their disability status were Josey, Jamie, and Ruth. Though these GTAs expressed a level of comfort in disclosing to their students, their approaches for doing so varied. For Jamie, incorporating disclosure into her teaching practices serves as a way to increase understanding of disability and to promote personal well-being. When I asked her about her experiences disclosing to faculty, Jamie spoke of how past instructors' reactions to her course accommodations frustrated her and revealed a profound misunderstanding of why she needed them. As part of her accommodations, Jamie has authorization to record the classes she takes. Since she cannot control when she is symptomatic and when she is not, Jamie records every class meeting in case she needs to review it later. As a courtesy, she normally talks to her professors on or after the first day of class to make sure they are informed about her accommodations.[10] Their reactions have not always been supportive. In the past, Jamie's professors have made awkward jokes like "Oh, you're going to record me? I'm going to have to be on my game!" upon learning they would be recorded.

Jamie viewed these seemingly harmless jokes as irritating rather than comforting, as they exposed her professors' fundamental misunderstanding about why she needs to record her lectures in the first place. There is a tremendous rhetorical and social difference between a person of authority expressing genuine interest about how an accommodation works and facilitates learning and a disabled student being forced to defend and justify its worthiness in order to secure it.[11] To illustrate the significance of this accommodation, Jamie spoke about her first hospitalization with MS, which happened during her junior year of college. Her experience was so severe she has no memories of her time in the hospital, and her memory issues lingered once she returned to college.[12] Having the ability to record her classes provides a measure of relief and a safeguard for her in the event of a similar relapse during graduate school. The suggestion that she would ever use her class recordings to judge her professors is an insulting one because, as Jamie pointed out, if she had a relapse and couldn't record her courses, "How [is she] supposed to get through it?"

These experiences have motivated Jamie to use her experience as a disabled TA in order to better empathize with and relate to her students. In discussions with her students, Jamie supplies them with strategies for how to manage their stress levels and have difficult conversations with professors, knowledge she had to acquire on her own and provides in the hopes that their college experiences are easier than hers were. Such conversations, in Jamie's view, are mutually beneficial—students receive additional guidance for how to navigate college, and she humanizes herself at the same time. She explained what she says when speaking to her students at the start of each semester:

> I try and identify with my students, so I tell them, "I've been doing this longer than you have, so I know more than you do, but I'm willing to share it with you and give you the same tools that I have, so that your experience in college is easier than what I was going through."

She approaches these conversations from a wellness perspective, including discussions about stress and best practices for speaking to instructors about these issues. For Jamie, speaking about the self-accommodation skills she has learned firsthand has two intersecting purposes. By speaking to her own experiences as a disabled undergraduate and graduate student, Jamie hopes to humanize herself as an instructor while providing her students with additional support as they transition from high school to college. Though Jamie's disclosure efforts are very well intentioned, they could easily be perceived differently by her students. Jamie's disclosure strategy, though intended to bridge a gap between herself and her students, could have the opposite effect. Her strategy for establishing herself as a credible figure on disability and self-advocacy—"I've been doing this longer than you have, so I know more than you do"—can easily be interpreted as her erecting an additional barrier between her and her students, or as her offering guidance but doing so conditionally.

Josey, a PhD student with autism spectrum disorder and ADHD, spoke of how she discloses her disability status to her students on the first day of the class, as her disabilities intersect with much of the social, interpersonal aspect of teaching. She noted that since she "doesn't people well," these disclosures are intended to help her students understand the various ways she moves rhetorically in the classroom. "I like people to know *why* I'm weird," she said. "There's a reason behind it." Her disclosure is also a practical measure, as she explains to her students that because of her ADHD, "it's really easy to get [her] off task, so try not to." However, Josey also acknowledged how this information could be used negatively, as she pointed out how occasionally her classes contain "that one student who enjoys getting [me] off track . . . I tend to fall for that."

Like Price, Josey advises her students how to react in instances in which her rapid speech and ADHD impact the classroom environment. However, her advice lacks the context transference Price's has. In instances like these, Josey prefers that her students interrupt and politely notify her about her speech during class ("If you need to stop me, stop me!"), which allows her to correct her course in the moment. Though this frank and direct approach could work, this strategy is slightly worrying, as Josey asks her students to do the work of accommodating instead of her sharing what specific strategies she uses to monitor her pacing and speech patterns in university environments. Her directive to students to openly interrupt a lesson in progress also contains some hiccups, especially given her concern about students who might distract her intentionally. Other concerns exist as well. Given the somewhat inescapable power dynamics of the student/teacher relationship, many students may not feel comfortable interrupting their instructor in this way, regardless of the reason or intentions behind it.

I do not want to vilify Josey, Jamie, or their experiences in disclosing to their students. Certainly there is no perfect way to discuss disability, especially an instructor's personal connections to it, in a classroom environment. Disclosure is, like all communicative acts, something we are not born doing but learn, and learning to disclose effectively becomes even more difficult when what is being disclosed is not something openly discussed in academic environments. For many, it is an anxiety-riddled prospect, one fraught with many negative possible implications.

But the thorniness of their disclosures underscores the importance of listening and speaking to disabled experiences, both in university environments and classroom spaces.

Like Jamie and Josey, Ruth is open about her disability status with both her peers and faculty members, primarily out of a desire to destigmatize mental disability and those seeking mental health treatment. Ever aware of the potentially negative social consequences for such openness, she argued, "Has it ever been used against me? Probably. But I don't give a fuck because those people are awful." Ruth noted that on her more symptomatic days when she told other faculty members about how her anxiety made teaching difficult, her concerns were dismissed as her being uninterested in teaching altogether. She commented, "At first, a lot of the professors in my department were just like, 'Well, you don't really like teaching, so maybe you should think about some other career paths.'" Ruth added that fortunately for her, these professors became more understanding over time, eventually encouraging her to try to find a way to treat her anxiety and keep teaching in the program.

However, some of Ruth's intended disclosures were silenced before she had a chance to speak due to the power dynamics present in graduate courses. Ruth uses her laptop in her graduate course as a preferred way to take notes, as typing serves as a way for her to channel her focus and pay closer attention during lectures and discussions. Because of its benefit to her learning, Ruth's ability to use a laptop in class is listed as one of her official student accommodations. In her interview, Ruth spoke of an instance in which she was using her laptop to take notes on the first day of class and her professor told her to put it away, referring to himself as a Luddite who did not want his students using any technology in his courses. Ruth had planned to give the professor her accommodation letter at the end of the first class, but after this interaction, she decided against it, as she was intimidated by the professor and did not want to be labeled as confrontational or a problem student, the same sense of fear Yergeau (2013) speaks to in "Reason." Additionally, Ruth knew that, given the course's subject matter and her clear interest in it, she would likely need recommendation letters from the professor in the future and did not want to risk harming her chances of obtaining them. In that moment Ruth felt torn between her immediate success in the course and her potential for the future. Since securing mentorships with senior faculty is so critical to a graduate student's success, it is understandable that a disabled graduate student would feel forced to forgo their accommodations rather than risk angering a potential mentor or recommender.

Ruth drew clear lines connecting her own mixed experiences with disclosing as a student to how she discusses disability with her students. Though she is not comfortable with disclosing to the entire class as Josey does, she frequently mentions her mental health status in individual conversations and in conferences. The response has been largely positive: "When I've talked about it with students in the past, they respond really well. I don't talk about this to all of my students, but to the ones who tell me that they're having a hard time with depression or whatever, it makes inroads and maybe will encourage them to reach out and get some help." In varying degrees, all the TAs I interviewed mentioned using their own disability and their authority as an instructor to combat the presence of stigma in their courses, presenting a fascinating trend that cries out for further research and critical evaluation.

I've been one of the lucky ones in terms of disability disclosures—nearly all my self-disclosures to my graduate professors have been positive. However, my first experience with disclosing to a professor was terrifying. In my first semester of my master's degree program, I had a massive depressive relapse two-thirds of the way into the semester. This was not my first time in dealing with depression (and wasn't my last), but the stress of starting graduate school exacerbated it considerably. The change in my demeanor, behavior, and work quality was obvious. Coming to class and participating in seminar discussions felt excruciating, as the depression drained my natural extroversion from me. Making eye contact with professors and peers felt physically painful. All my social instincts felt wrong, and the act of speaking felt so inconsequential, so futile. My ability to concentrate was shot; I could only read a few pages at a time before I needed to take a break, which made keeping up with course readings and assignments impossible. I knew I needed to talk to my professor—I feared he would think I didn't care about my work, or that I was a lazy student, or that letting me into the program was a huge mistake—and it took time to summon the courage. These fears were magnified by the fact that my professor was graduate program director at the time.

I remember this disclosure so clearly: emailing him and asking to make an appointment to talk, trembling with fear and shame outside his office, crying halfway through the conversation. At the time I knew next to nothing about the Americans with Disabilities Act or what accommodations I could obtain from our campus's Disability and Access Office; I thought my professor was going to tell me that struggling with coursework meant I had to drop out of the program.[13] I walked into the meeting preparing to plead for my future. But the reaction I received—one of genuine compassion and concern—both shocked and relieved me. My professor said he could tell something was wrong, and we both agreed my staying in the program and his class was less disruptive and therefore the best choice for my overall well-being. More important, he offered to give me as much time as I needed to complete my assignments without requiring any official documentation. He knew the process of getting accommodations is not always a quick or simple one. As the conversation ended, I could feel some of the intense pressure I felt start to slowly dissipate. I left that meeting with a plan to register for student accommodations, an overwhelming sense of relief, and a degree of confidence in my ability to survive and advance in graduate school.[14]

Though my initial academic disclosure was positive, I have never forgotten about the intense fear and worry I felt leading up to it. What made me so terrified to talk about my disability? I felt afraid because I had no departmental cues that I could be taken seriously while disabled. No one told me before I disclosed that I could be a strong student and have official student accommodations; this was a truth I had to discover for myself. No one mentioned that the department wouldn't discriminate against me or that professors would still be willing to work with me. Few professors discussed anything disability related in their courses aside from referencing the university-sanctioned disability statement, and many professors skipped this step altogether. Limiting our disability discussions to boilerplate statements designed to prevent lawsuits, as I previously mentioned, shifts all focus away from departmental policies and procedures and places the sole burden of responsibility on the student. When we refuse to center disability, to incorporate it in meaningful and public ways, the gap left leaves more than enough room for inaccessibility and ableist assumptions to infiltrate programs and flourish.

The following year I started teaching as a TA, and I made a conscious effort to let these experiences inform my teaching and how I talked to my students about disability. I didn't want my students with disabilities to share my deep-seated fear and shame, but I had no idea how to actually accomplish this. This effort has evolved significantly over the years, ranging from adding a timid "If you have questions about getting registered for accommodations, let me know!" to the required boilerplate disability syllabus statement, to talking more openly about how to register for student accommodations in conferences with struggling students, to adding an access statement to my course documents.[15] Figuring out if or how I should include disclosure has been a lengthy process, a journey that mirrors my own comfort and confidence level as a TA.

This process on one occasion involved a generalized disability disclosure to my entire class. In my most recent first-year composition course,

I talked with my students about the eight habits of mind listed in the Council of Writing Program Administrators' "Framework for Success in Postsecondary Writing" (2014). I asked them to pick one attribute they considered to be a personal strength and one they'd like to work on during their time in the class. To illustrate this idea for them, I chose persistence as my strength and briefly mentioned getting sick my first semester of graduate school, having to get student accommodations from the Disability and Access Center, but still finishing my master's degree on schedule.[16] Even though I intentionally chose to mention my disability without including specific details, I was still nervous before-hand. But I wanted to try, even in my own small way, to normalize disabil-ity, to chip away at the deeply ingrained social stigmas that often impede mental health treatment. The response from my students was positive. My willingness to disclose, even in vague terms, led one of my students to disclose his depression and how he was struggling to keep up in my course. We talked about what strategies and resources were available to help him pass the course, which he did.

REPOSITIONING DISABILITY

These case studies expose a variety of access issues, some with more immediate solutions than others. One practical and immediately achiev-able solution is to explicitly include disability-informed composition and rhetoric scholarship in pedagogy courses. Hearing these accounts of how these TAs' experiences as disabled students have informed their teaching underscores the value of disability-themed rhetoric and com-position scholarship and the importance of including said scholarship in pedagogy courses. At the end of her interview, Paige suggested includ-ing such scholarship, noting that "just even the briefest exposure to the disability perspective . . . could save a lot of people," undergraduate stu-dents and TAs alike. For disabled TAs, having this scholarship included in pedagogy courses validates their experiences as disabled students and provides additional support for how their personal experiences can inform their teaching.

Disability scholarship is relevant to all TAs, whether they realize it or not. More and more students with disabilities are entering college class-rooms, *and this is a good thing.* Given that, at best, nondisabled people are temporarily able bodied, our concerns and insider knowledge about disability are relevant and beneficial for everyone. TAs with disabilities are skilled at applying their own experiences to their dealings with students and often have developed their own strategies for navigating educational environments not created for them. To this end, Corbett Joan O'Toole (2013) adds,

> Certain, and often very important, information resides within networks of people with shared relationships to disabilities such as strategies for successfully handling discrimination barriers; locating disability-positive professional services; identifying effective resources; finding support; and sharing culture. The depth of these resources is rarely apparent to people outside the community but is openly shared with people who identify their relationships with that impairment community.

As the disability studies field has grown, more and more of this previously privatized knowledge has been theorized and incorporated into research. Additionally, given the highly interdisciplinary nature of disability studies, this knowledge is starting to surface in rhetoric, composition, and writing studies scholarship as well.

However, including disability scholarship in pedagogy courses has the greatest potential benefit for nondisabled TAs and for faculty who are new to this field. Given that nondisabled TAs and faculty do not have firsthand experiences of disability, including disability-themed articles can provide a prime opportunity for scholarship to inform teaching practices instead of the pervasive and damaging disability myths that still exist in higher education. Disability myths in academia take many forms. They construct disability as an inconvenience students can easily overcome if they would only try hard enough, something much too personal to ever discuss openly. Disability becomes a negative character trait or a personality flaw, a deficiency, or even an ambiguous, amorphous presence that can disrupt business as usual in classroom environments.[17] These disability myths are often accompanied with anecdotal, incomplete stories of students and linger in a variety of places, including informal conversations with colleagues, articles in higher education publications, and even, occasionally, within composition scholarship itself (Kershbaum 2014; Wood, Meyer, and Bose 2017). These myths shift blame away from educational environments that fail to provide access and toward students who struggle to learn within environments not made with them in mind. In an article aptly titled "Why We Dread the Disability Myths," Tara Wood, Craig Meyer, and Dev Bose (2017) assert,

> Disability is not something to dread. It just is. We, too, should recognize, value, and (automatically) validate the experiential knowledge of students. If we take this stance as faculty members, we come to realize that anyone with any difference provides another perspective from which to learn and approach a problem from another direction.

Wood, Meyer, and Bose position disability as a difference and a product of diversity, not as a deficiency, a repositioning that affords graduate professors a pedagogical opportunity to reconfigure how they present disability to their students. By viewing disability as a form of diversity, TA coordinators and pedagogy professors can easily include disability alongside other intersectional social issues such as race, class, gender, and identity, issues already likely to appear in their syllabi. Such pairings can help new TAs understand the connections among these issues and the gaps present in the scholarship, which can enhance new TAs' knowledge of disability and possibly lead to future research and writing projects. Pairing readings this way reinforces the idea that disability is far from a fringe social issue—it impacts issues of identity and forces us to question assumptions about who our students and fellow instructors are. This repositioning also creates space to discuss disability myths in an academic setting, a prospect sorely lacking in many academic conversations. The hope is by introducing disability-centered composition scholarship to new TAs at the start of their teaching careers, we have an opportunity to impede these disability myths before they have the chance to infiltrate TAs' attitudes and pedagogy.

Including disability scholarship in TA-training course also offers praxis-related benefits for all new TAs, as well as theoretical and conceptual ones. Numerous disability-related composition pieces focus on accessible course design, which can be invaluable to new TAs. Many of these disability-related composition works[18] uphold universal design as pedagogical framing; by providing students with multiple ways to engage with course material, representing key concepts in multiple ways and modes, and allowing students to express their understanding in multiple formats and outlets, instructors can increase the likelihood that the course is accessible for more students. Approaching course construction from a universal-design model not only decreases the need for accommodations (as many of these concerns are incorporated into the course as a whole) but also enhances the learning of all students, disabled or nondisabled.

Additionally, the mere presence of disability-related scholarship on a pedagogy syllabus communicates to new TAs the significance of that perspective, both academically and pedagogically. Shelley Reid's (2017) "On Learning to Teach: Letter to a New GTA" reinforces this idea, although perhaps unintentionally where disability is concerned. In her letter, Reid encourages incoming TAs to take advantage of their "metacognitive double vision," their ability to watch the various rhetorical and pedagogical moves professors make and to discern information about teaching practices as a result (136). This idea of metacognitive double vision invites new TAs to examine not only the teaching practices of their instructors but also the various texts included in the course, the way the course is constructed, and the variety of voices and perspectives represented in it. The point of this exercise, Reid stresses, is not to encourage new TAs to harshly criticize their professors but to help them build empathy towards their future students who are new to college writing classrooms and are green to the ways colleges operate. Disability-related research, which focuses on creating access, questioning innate assumptions, expanding previously defined concepts,.and valuing interdependence over independence, reinforces this goal.

IMPLICATIONS: FIRST-RATE MADNESS

Making the choice to include disability scholarship in our courses is relatively easy. The real work of changing, or at least rethinking, the culture of graduate programs is much harder. It's not something that can or will change overnight. Given the continuous liminality of TA experiences, and given the depth of the disability concerns at play for disabled TAs, we cannot discuss TA programs and graduate programs separately. For better or for worse, they are two sides of the same coin, inseparable aspects of the TA experience. And as these case studies illustrate, how disability is treated at the graduate level certainly affects how disabled TAs address it in the classes they teach. We must make it clear in our TA programs that disability is not a subject we can afford to avoid. Disability scholarship emphasizes that *disability* is not a bad word, that issues and concerns of disability, including access, are relevant to everyone, disabled or not. But unless disability is explicitly named, this is not what graduate programs teach us. When our only conversations about disability are limited to the legalese of syllabus accommodation statements, we ignore all disability studies has to offer, silencing crucial conversations before they have the chance to start. These rhetorical silences have real consequences for disabled TAs. As a result, often TAs with disabilities feel the need to minimize their concerns, to conceal and self-protect rather than risk being open about illnesses and the realities they cause.

Though disability myths might suggest otherwise, disabled TAs can be valuable assets to their programs. Perhaps the concept of first-rate madness can be helpful in understanding this. In *A First-Rate Madness: Uncovering the Links Between Leadership and Mental Illness*, Nassir Ghaemi (2011) argues that people with mental illnesses are often more creative, resilient, empathetic, and realistic than those without mental illnesses.

The presence of these qualities, Ghaemi adds, aligns well with leadership, especially in the midst of difficult circumstances. Ghaemi does not perpetuate the "supercrip" trope, that the mere presence of disability magically imbues individuals with exceptional, supernatural gifts, but instead suggests these characteristics are forged from personal experiences. Because they have traversed their own crises time and time again, people with mental illnesses often possess a depth of experience nondisabled people simply don't have. This perspective was something Ruth pointed out at the end of her interview: "We have a lot to offer the world. And sometimes I think, not because of our disabilities but the way in which we've had to compensate for those things, we actually work harder and have some insights that other people would not [have]." The challenge for TA programs and graduate programs becomes how to create space, both literal and metaphorical, for TAs and graduate students to speak to their experiences. There are many ways to accomplish this: accessible and anonymous surveys about access needs within individual courses and in programs, workshops on pedagogy, design, and ableism, and forums that center disabled experiences within graduate and TA programs. We must find ways for disabled TAs to speak to their experiences without fear of exclusion, retribution, or discrimination. Neither graduate programs nor TA programs can hope to remedy chronic inaccessibility without actively including disabled TAs or their experiences in the process.

At the same time, we must be careful about how these conversations are crafted and consider whether they serve to break down or exacerbate notions of stigma. Well-meaning efforts to disrupt the social stigma surrounding disability, particularly mental health outreach efforts, can easily have the opposite results. If our conversations surrounding mental disability only consist of "Everyone gets depressed sometimes in graduate school!" or "Testing makes most people anxious!," we can unknowingly expand the boundaries of disability so much that the experiences of disabled people get lost in the noise. Equating these very different experiences can fuel misinformation and stereotypes even more. There is a tremendous difference between feeling situationally sad and being clinically depressed. Feeling nervous about upcoming graduate exams is not the same as having a panic attack. Though equating these ideas may be linguistically and socially comfortable, it can result in further isolation and misunderstanding of the real effects of disability on TAs.

Though the case studies I incorporate are specific to my local context, the implications and access gaps they raise are not. If anything, they expose the depth of what we do not know—namely, how many disabled TAs there, where they are geographically, and what access issues they experience in their programs. We badly need more research, both qualitative and quantitative, where TAs with disabilities are concerned. We need more research that does not idealize or soften the harsh edges of TA liminality for disabled GTAs. Some of this research may involve revisiting previous scholarship about TAs and discerning what theoretical concepts should change or be adjusted in light of disability. How do notions of TA resistance, for example, change in light of disability? When is resistance simply inaccessibility? What kinds of engagement do we privilege in professional-development environments, like TA orientations? What aspects of liminality negatively impact disabled GTAs more than nondisabled GTAs? Are there additional places or spaces where disabled GTAs can lean into the liminality without sustaining undue stress or harm? To be certain, these are hard questions to ask, and, depending on the results, may be hard truths to realize about ourselves and our field. But asking these questions and integrating accessible solutions will be a great benefit to everyone—all TAs, disabled or not, coordinators, and especially the students TAs will eventually teach. Accessible solutions benefit everyone, especially those living within the space between student and instructor.

NOTES

1. Price and Kershbaum (along with Mark S. Salzer and Amber O'Shea) recently published these preliminary findings in the Spring 2017 issue of *Disability Studies Quarterly*, an open-access, interdisciplinary journal. This study is currently in the interview phase.

2. Another, albeit minor, reason for evaluating my local context is financial. As a PhD candidate with limited funds at her disposal, my ability to travel and secure funds for external research is quite limited.

3. MA students in the graduate program have several degree-track options: literary studies, language and writing studies, teaching writing and literature, popular culture and cultural studies, or an open degree plan. This is a recent change for the program. PhD students may only earn a PhD in English. Their degree is more generalized, with eighteen hours of required coursework in English and American literature, literary research methods, and literary criticism. The remainder of the degree coursework, however, is open (Graduate Student Handbook 2017, 9–12).

4. This research (Protocol #17-2253) was approved by the MTSU IRB on June 1, 2017.

5. Diagnoses are often incorrect or changed based on a variety of factors; additionally, being able to get a diagnosis and treatment requires being able to consistently afford the necessary medical care. Our program does not provide health insurance for GTAs.

6. In earlier drafts of this chapter, I was dead set against including my own experiences as a part of the product, but this changed after I read Stephanie Kershbaum's (2013) "On Rhetorical Agency and Disclosing Disability in Academic Writing."

7. See Tobin Siebers's "Disability as Masquerade" (2004), Ellen Samuels's "My Body, My Closet: Invisible Disability and the Limits of Coming-out Discourse" (2003), and others. Price, Salzer, O'Shea, and Kershbaum (2017) also offer a more detailed treatment of disclosure in their article.

8. As of this writing, the stakes for this set of exams are exceptionally high. At the end of their graduate coursework, PhD students select two English-related subareas (out of a list of fourteen possible areas, including rhetoric and composition) in which to test. Each subarea has a list of primary and secondary works students should know; the works on this list are determined by the English department and are not adjustable. Each test consists of a written exam for which students complete a timed, on-demand essay consisting of two or three questions to answer over the course of four hours. Students are required to take both tests in the same semester on subsequent Fridays. If a student passes the written exam, they proceed to the oral exam, where they must defend their answers on the written exam in front of the same faculty who graded their written exam. The content of the oral exam is not limited to the scope of material covered on the written exam; in the oral-exam stage, examiners are free to ask the student about anything related to the content area. A student has only passed the test in a content area if they have successfully passed the written and oral stages of the exam. If a student passes the written stage but fails the oral stage, the process begins again. If a student fails any exam twice, they are kicked out of the program and are awarded a second master's degree.

9. In order to be allowed a third chance at her graduate exam, Paige had to go through a lengthy appeal process with the department and the College of Graduate Studies. Part of this process involved faculty writing letters in support of Paige's getting a third attempt.

10. Recently, our university switched to an email-only system of delivering accommodations. Registered students log into a digital interface at the start of each semester to confirm their accommodations and have them sent to their instructors. This is a dramatic shift from the previous accommodation system, in which registered students received a letter via email detailing their accommodations. Students then could then print the letters, give them to their professors, and have a conversation about their access needs.

11. M. Remi Yergeau (2013) also writes of her experiences of professors questioning her accommodations in her portion of "Multimodality in Motions: Disability and Kairotic Spaces."

12. Upon returning to classes, Jamie found most of her professors were very willing to work with her and let her complete course requirements. However, one faculty member refused to budge over the number of classes Jamie had missed because of her hospitalization, and, as a result, Jamie had to medically withdraw from all her courses and repeat them the following semester.

13. Once again, my fearing I would have to quit the program echoes Yergeau's (2014) comments about unreasonable/reasonable accommodations and expectations in graduate programs.

14. To Dr. Kevin Donovan—I have not forgotten (and will never forget) your kindness in the midst of an exceptionally difficult time in my life. Thank you.

15. You can find more information about access statements (including examples) at accessiblesyllabus.com.

16. For those who are curious, I chose flexibility as the habit I wanted to improve.

17. For a more comprehensive list of disability myths, see Jay Dolmage's (2014) *Disability Rhetoric*, 31–62.

18. Some examples of excellent resources to include would be any of the chapters from Margaret Price's *Mad at School* (2011), Anne-Marie Womack's "Teaching Is Accommodation: Universally Designing Composition Classrooms and Syllabi" (2016), M. Remi Yergeau et al.'s "Multimodality in Motion: Disability and Kairotic Spaces" (2013), and Jay Dolmage's (2015) "Universal Design: Places to Start." This very brief list is in no way comprehensive or complete.

REFERENCES

Brueggmann, Brenda, Linda Feldmeier White, Patricia A. Dunn, Barbara A. Heifferon, and Johnson Cheu. 2001. *College Composition and Communication* 52 (31): 368–98.

Damiani, Michelle L., and Wendy S. Harbour. 2015. "Being the Wizard behind the Curtain: Teaching Experiences of Graduate Teaching Assistants with Disabilities at U.S. Universities." *Innovative Higher Education* 40 (5): 399–413.

Dolmage, Jay. 2014. *Disability Rhetoric.* Syracuse: Syracuse University Press.

Dolmage, Jay. 2015. "Universal Design: Places to Start." *Disability Studies Quarterly* 35 (2). http://dx.doi.org/10.18061/dsq.v35i2.4632.

Fedukovich, Casie J., and Tracy Ann Morse. 2017. "Failures to Accommodate: GTA Preparation as a Site for a Transformative Culture of Access." *Writing Program Administration* 3: 39–60.

"Framework for Success in Postsecondary Writing." 2014. *Council of Writing Program Administrators.* Last updated 2014. http://wpacouncil.org/framework.

Ghaemi, Nassir. 2011. *A First-Rate Madness: Uncovering the Links between Leadership and Mental Illness.* New York: Penguin.

"Graduate Student Handbook." 2017. *Department of English, Middle Tennessee State University.* Last updated August 2017. https://www.mtsu.edu/graduate_english/docs/Graduate _handbook_2017.pdf.

Jamie. 2017. Interview with the author. June 23, 2017. Transcript.

Josey. 2017. Interview with the author. June 12, 2017. Audio recording.

Kershbaum, Stephanie. 2014. "Anecdotal Relations: On Orienting to Disability in Composition Classrooms." *Composition Forum* 32. http://compositionforum.com/issue/32 /anecdotal-relations.php.

Kershbaum, Stephanie. 2013. "On Rhetorical Agency and Disclosing in Academic Writing." *Rhetoric Review* 33 (1): 55–71.

Lance. 2017. Interview with the author. July 19, 2017. Audio recording.

"Middle Tennessee State University." 2017. *US News and World Reports,* last updated 2017. https://www.usnews.com/best-colleges/middle-tennessee-state-university-3510.

O'Toole, Corbett Joan. 2013. "Disclosing Our Relationship to Disabilities: An Invitation for Disability Studies Scholars." *Disability Studies Quarterly* 33 (2): http://dx.doi.org/10 .18061/dsq.v33i2.3708.

Paige. 2017. Interview with the author. June 8, 2017. Transcript.

Price, Margaret, Mark S. Salzer, Amber O'Shea, and Stephanie Kershbaum. 2017. "Disclosure of Mental Disability by College and University Professors: The Negotiation of Accommodations, Supports, and Barriers." *Disability Studies Quarterly* 37 (2): http://dx .doi.org/10.18061/dsq.v37i2.5487.

Price, Margaret. 2011. *Mad at School: Rhetorics of Mental Disability and Academic Life.* Ann Arbor: Michigan University Press.

Reid, E. Shelley. 2017. "On Learning to Teach: Letter to a New GTA." *Writing Program Administration* 40 (2): 129–45.

Ruth. 2017a. Interview with the author. June 26, 2017. Transcript.

Ruth. 2017b. Interview with the author. August 8, 2017. Audio Recording.

Samuels, Ellen. 2017. "My Body, My Closet: Invisible Disability and the Limits of Coming Out." Reprinted in *The Disability Studies Reader,* 5th ed., edited by Lennard J. Davis, 343–359. New York: Routledge.

Vidali, Amy. 2015. "Disabling Writing Program Administration." *Writing Program Administration* 38 (2): 32–55.

Wood, Tara, Craig A. Meyer, and Dev Bose. 2017. "Why We Dread the Disability Myths." *Chronicle of Higher Education,* May 24, 2017. www.chronicle.com/article/why-we-dread -disability-myths/.

Womack, Anne-Marie. 2017. "Teaching Is Accommodation: Universally Designing Composition Classrooms and Syllabi." *College Composition and Communication* 63 (3): 494–525.

Yergeau, M. Remi, Elizabeth Brewer, Stephanie Kershbaum, Sushil K. Oswal, Margaret Price, Cynthia L. Selfe, Michael J. Salvo, and Franny Howes. 2013. "Multimodality in Motion: Disability and Kairotic Spaces." *Kairos* 18 (1): http://kairos.technorhetoric .net/18.1/coverweb/yergeau-et-al/pages/authors.html.

Yergeau, M. Remi. "Reason." "Multimodality in Motion: Disability and Kairotic Spaces." *Kairos* 18 (1): http://kairos.technorhetoric.net/18.1/coverweb/yergeau-et-al/pages /authors.html.

6

FROM IMPOSTER TO "DOUBLE AGENT"
Leveraging Liminality as Expertise

Kathryn M. Lambrecht

INTRODUCTION

In the fall of 2011, I found myself occupying a seat at the sturdy, room-length table at the center of the Department of English graduate-seminar room. A short time earlier, I had completed my undergraduate majors in linguistics and political science and entered grad school secure that, surely, I could handle my new slate of (just) two graduate-level courses in rhetoric and composition. This confidence, of course, did not last long. Over the course of the semester, while I remained physically bound to my chair (seeking invisibility), my mental journeys were boundless, occasionally aimless, and almost always informed by a sense of dread. While these thoughts varied in scope and, admittedly, level of reason, they all centered around the classroom, regardless of whether I was on the teaching or learning side. If questioning whether or not I was cut out for grad school wasn't enough, adding in teaching escalated these concerns ten-fold. Because I sometimes felt like a fraud in my own academic life, I was unsure how I could reasonably succeed in helping my students with the development of theirs.

Over the course of my time as a graduate student, many things changed: I became more confident in my ability to engage with material as a student and more comfortable that I could then deliver that knowledge to others as a teacher. There was no way to expedite this level of comfort; the reality of simultaneous learning and teaching started to feel normal only through practice. It was a game of in and through more than around. One thing that didn't seem to change over time was the feeling that I did not fully belong—that I might not ever *excel* in the academy, even if I was growing more confident I could *survive* in it. From the moment we start graduate course work, we are in over our heads, almost by definition. In the academic world, knowledge and inquiry

DOI: 10.7330/9781646420896.c006

are understood to be boundless, yet also somehow obtainable—with enough planning, enough thinking, and *surely* enough reading, we can work through the problems of our field by following the bread crumbs previous scholars have left for us, all within the span of a few years. Accordingly, graduate school is an experience of urgent learning and adapting in which we rarely give much thought to the natural limits of knowledge and function that come along with being human—we forget, or at least don't always have the time to remember, that as students and teachers, we can only expect so much from ourselves.

As students, teachers, and teacher-students, we think a lot about how we will help our students learn. We build book-length scholarship to determine what sorts of knowledge students need, how they will obtain it and carry it with them (indeed, our focus on transfer is one iteration of this concern), and how we can best deliver the goods. In writing, we often think about the type of agency we want students to have over their own work, the sorts of tools they will need to achieve academic access, and the ways we can help them become better critical thinkers. In a sea of things we do think about, I posit that there are at least two things we don't: (1) we tend not to think of the ways issues of agency have consequences for how we, ourselves, learn, and (2) we tend not to apply the same sorts of frameworks to ourselves as we do to our students. A result is that we don't always approach our own learning with the same patience and care we give our students in working through issues related to academic identity and growth.

Because much of graduate student identity is focused around filling a deficit and gaining expertise we do not yet have, we may not often consider the ways being a developing expert might actually be an *asset*. It is easier to view the in-between of graduate school as a condition in which we have not yet achieved rather than one in which we are in process, growing, and, ultimately, still very much in touch with what it feels like to be in the same messy state of learning as our students. In this paper, I argue for a retheorizing of TA liminality that sees developing expertise not as a deficit but as a potential source of agency that can be used to enhance teaching. Using Anis Bawarshi's term "double agent" to describe the dynamic role of the TA, I suggest that the source of issues like imposter syndrome can be the same source that generates a unique type of agency cultivated from liminality itself if it is seen as a strength rather than a weakness, a source of solidarity with students rather than an absent marker of institutional expertise. This argument relies on two threads of theory heavily woven into this collection: liminality and agency. In order to connect to these threads, I first discuss the ways liminality might be seen as a condition that generates its own form of expertise. Then I discuss how we might pivot from feeling like an imposter to embodying a form of situated agency linked to the positionality of being a graduate student. Finally, I offer suggestions for how approaching the graduate student TA experience in this light can enhance learning for both TAs and their students.

LIMINALITY AS EXPERTISE

Whether it is for a career, for oneself, or for posterity, graduate work is associated with a higher level of expertise than is an undergraduate education. Generally, we call on our most decorated experts within the academy in order to facilitate the creation of new experts through the process of school. However, as scholars such as Edward Said (1994) and Cheryl Geisler (1994) have argued, expertise alone can lead to problems in conveying knowledge, as it can create a divide between expert and layperson. Largely, this has to do with the processes and consequences of acquiring expertise and subject mastery.

In their book *How Learning Works*, Ambrose et al. (2010) attempt to bridge the gap between research and teaching by discussing student issues and how to overcome them. In their chapter entitled "How Do Students Develop Mastery?," these authors discuss Jo Sprague and Douglas Stuart's (2000) model of the stages of mastery: "unconscious incompetence," "conscious incompetence," "conscious competence," and "unconscious competence" (97). In the stage of unconscious incompetence, an individual is *unaware* of their ignorance; in conscious incompetence, they are *aware* of their ignorance; in conscious competence, they are *aware* of their knowledge; and in unconscious competence, they are *unaware* of their knowledge (96–97). Although learning is likely quite a bit more messy than this heuristic presents, the model is useful for helping teachers think through where they are in comparison to their students on the spectrum of knowledge and how that position might impact learning. Without giving this spectrum consideration, teachers risk losing their students because their own expertise is so embedded and so normalized it becomes difficult to bridge the gaps in knowledge their students are working through. If a teacher is so expert they forget the steps it took to get there, it can be difficult to lead students down the same path. It is here that graduate student liminality can intervene in ways rich with pedagogical value.

Liminality is a term used to describe dwelling in the in-between (Bell 2008; Cody and Lawlor 2011). To be in a liminal state suggests an individual is neither entirely one thing nor the other but rather in some sort of a middle space that is often more contingent and less stable. If we map the graduate student experience onto Sprague and Stuart's model of the stages of mastery, it is likely their relationship to expertise exists in the liminal spaces between the various levels, toggling in and out of the stages depending on context and company (or even day of the week, in my experience). All this movement between feeling like an expert (and then feeling decidedly not like an expert) can be exhausting and difficult; however, this mobility can also be seen as a great advantage. For the graduate TA, the barrier that separates expert instructors from their nonexpert students may not be as high—rather, the role of a TA allows TAs to have access to expertise without being defined by it, to understand the process of learning content they are themselves seeking to learn. While this process can be a struggle, it is one that is shared: whether at the undergraduate or graduate level, the student journey of learning is never linear. Because graduate students are still students, their liminal status grants them the opportunity to harness the in-betweenness of their experience and leverage it to help their students learn. In this way, the experience of feeling liminal in regards to academic expertise offers graduate TAs a *different* type of expertise: they are experts in what it is like to be a student, sometimes struggling and sometimes succeeding, taking steps forward and steps back, learning and growing from moment to moment. Seen this way, graduate student TA liminality becomes a powerful source of solidarity and understanding with those they are teaching.

MOVING FROM IMPOSTER TO DOUBLE AGENT

Harnessing the potential of liminality to serve as common ground with our students is one step towards reconfiguring, or at least expanding, what we consider expert to mean. The goal in doing so is to open a space for graduate students to appreciate the unique capacity they have and feel like a participant, rather than an incomplete player, in the academic world. Although many factors go into the reframing of the graduate TA experience, *agency* and *imposter syndrome* are two terms important to contend with on the way to imagining how graduate students might act as productive "double agents" (Bawarshi 2003) of the university.

In Search of Agency and Efficacy

The term *agency* has had a persistent presence in the discourse of the academy across disciplines and contexts: what we mean by agency, what factors signal agency, and what expectations come along with its production can vary widely. While the conversation originated in the field of psychology, questions about agency have become central to all forms of teaching, and every discipline has its own version of how agency functions (often several versions, in fact). Minimally, to have agency is to understand humans are "contributors to their life circumstances, not just products of them" (Bandura 2006, 164). We would like our students to have agency; we need agency to teach our students; and, we hope implicitly, that our students leave with more agency than they brought in with them. In their work "Teaching for Agency: From Appreciating Linguistic Diversity to Empowering Student Writers," Shawna Shapiro et al. (2016) suggest that part of teaching includes creating the conditions for our students to express agency. As instructors, they argue, we "must recognize the constraints that students must inevitably work under, while also expanding opportunities for students to shape the contexts in which they write and act" (34). For the graduate student TA, there is a double task involved with engaging agency: while we consider the conditions we could create for our students to express agency, we also must consider the constraints and conditions shaping our own.

In pursuit of understanding student agency, and agency more broadly, scholars have gained a more nuanced understanding of the way agency functions as a product not of human capacity alone but also of the environment and social dynamics inherent in the construction of the agent. Whereas the early work on agency focused on the human as the nexus of all agentic production, since the turn of the century, more and more work has traveled deeper into the layers of human consciousness to determine what motivates agency (Bandura 2006; Cooper 2011; Freeman 2000). Given agency's relationship to consciousness and conditions, it is no surprise these conversations have become central in the field of rhetoric and composition in considering the agency of the writer. Definitions in rhetoric and composition often share a focus on embodiment: Sonja Foss (2006) sees agency as a relationship between human and structure, S. Scott Graham (2009) sees agency as occupying an authoritative position, Carolyn Miller (2007) sees agency as kinetic energy, and John Trimbur (2000) sees agency as a way of living out a historical moment. All these definitions, to one degree or another, rely on embodied practice, on the relationship humans have with their thoughts, their practices, and, ultimately, their actions. For this reason, considering the embodied experience of the graduate TA is an essential part of reframing their relationship to liminality. One example of this comes from Lillian Campbell and Jaclyn Fiscus-Cannaday, who explore this relationship more extensively in this collection.

A key to understanding agency, arguably, lies with Albert Bandura (2006), who has studied agency since the late 70s and has continued to refine the theory of agency and its uses across the span of many decades. For Bandura, an agent is one who can "influence intentionally one's functioning and life circumstances" (93). While this can take any number of forms, when we think about agency in composition, we might imagine it as the ability for students to see themselves as active in their own writing processes and performances. But what is our role in shaping the agency of students, or even of ourselves? *Can* we make students more agentic during our time as their instructors? Working to *give* students agency may seem a difficult task, especially for TAs who are working to gather their own. While students might only be able to *acquire* their own agency, what teachers can help with is showing students their actions do meaningful and important work in the world. This role could be especially resonant for TAs given their experiences and circumstances.

Bandura (2006) identifies efficacy as a foundational concept in creating agency: "Unless people believe they can produce desired effects by their actions, they have little incentive to act, or to persevere in the face of difficulties" (170). When students are self-efficacious, they are not only agents but intentional agents who know their actions matter. A pedagogical shift towards encouraging efficacy, rather than generating agency, could mean more effective use of our teaching energies, as well as an increase in students' ability to trust in their own processes as they continue along in their education. Perhaps even more important, *efficacy* can become a boundary term that links the experiences of graduate TAs and their students, both of whom are working to acquire knowledge and expertise. In this space, self-efficacy might be seen as a force that is generative/disruptive rather than high/low, as Megan Schoettler and Elizabeth Saur advocate for in their chapter in this collection. A shift from *giving* students agency to focusing on how we can encourage the development of students' *self-efficacy* may be a more attainable goal since it is something both sets of students experience on some level.

For cognitive scientist Walter Freeman (2000), the roots of agency begin with the functioning of the human mind and the relationship we have to assimilating new ways of being. If this is the case, in what ways does language help us assimilate new academic identities? According to Freeman,

> This analysis in terms of neurodynamics can help to explain why the notion of free will remains elusive. A voluntary action is clearly intentional, but it must proceed with awareness. Yet when a person has chosen an action, he or she may not be the first to become aware of the choice. Instead, observers of the action may be the first to become aware of it and attribute agency to the actor. (137)

In other words, it could be the case that we don't choose agency so much as agency chooses us. The link to language is clear: we don't always know the ways our actions or words will be interpreted by others, especially when those actions are interpreted through language. Freeman indicates that an important role of language is that it gives us a way to play out scenarios before we act on them (147). This is especially relevant to the type of efficacy that occurs when students write in the academy. They may deploy linguistic and rhetorical resources available to them, but ultimately it is up to others to determine whether or not the students' work actually did its job. Any time we ask students to prewrite, produce drafts, or create outlines, we are essentially offering them the opportunity to work through options before they settle on a final version.

While Bandura (2006) might say language is what gives us agency, Freeman (2000) and others might complicate the situation by saying we have an incomplete picture of what is happening with language. Though these larger questions about the brain and agency are likely to be studied for a very long time, there remains a tension between language and intentionality for students who are in the process of creating an academic identity for themselves, especially through their writing. Writing is concrete and "on record" as a tangible marker of entrance (or nonentrance) into the academy. Where verbal exchanges seem to count as practice for students that are formative, writing seems to count as summative assessment, creating an air of finality. In this way, the act of writing and the consequences for one's identity seem rather fixed, further complicating both graduate and undergraduate student concern about what the written word will say about who they are or where they belong.

The Roadblock of Imposter Syndrome

While most of Freeman's (2000) book outlines the neurological, ethical, and causal issues associated with how humans make decisions, underlying his work is a central theme in agency and efficacy and their relationships to the way our brains process and act on information. For example, he suggests that central to our decision-making process is the ability to make those choices from a place of understanding that we have control over our processes, actions, and consequences. Without this control, humans tend to falter in becoming realized, causal agents: "We tend to be paralyzed when we lose belief in the efficacy of our own actions, especially when we compound the loss by seeing ourselves as corks bobbing on a stormy sea" (131). The analogy Freeman presents does seem to be a fitting one for those working in the academy who feel like they don't belong—like they are imposters. While it seems student life and instructor life might be easy to separate, problems emanating from one may begin to impact the other. One definition of imposter syndrome comes from Tonia Caselman, Patricia Self, and Angela Self (2006): "Those experiencing IP [imposter phenomenon] attribute success and achievement to external sources such as luck, charm, good social contacts, and hard work rather than to internal qualities of intelligence and ability" (396). While this feeling persists among those striving in the academy, the work of Pauline Rose Clance (1985)—one of the foundational scholars writing about imposter syndrome—reveals an even deeper level of struggle relating to this issue: an increase in success becomes the enemy of feeling capable.

Imposter syndrome, and feeling out of place or a lack of belonging more generally, should be of great concern to the functioning of the educational system. In their study, Christiane Brems et al. (1994) found that a teacher's relationship to imposter syndrome had significant impacts on their relationships with students. After investigating imposter syndrome and feelings of inadequacy within a faculty population, the researchers found that "personal and professional goals and self-assurance about personal competence correlated positively with better teaching evaluations and more numerous and comfortable academic relationships" (183). For a TA, relationships with students and relationships with other academic professionals are absolutely key to success. Any TA who has awaited their first set of student evaluations or has had meaningful relationships with faculty members knows this to be true. In addition, the relationship between teacher and student that is a hallmark of successful undergraduate education can be compromised if graduate instructors do not feel efficacious in their roles as educators. Any barrier that would put these two academic priorities at risk deserves more attention in the literature than it is currently given.

Furthermore, confidence in relationships both in teaching and the larger academic world influence each other in cyclical ways. The better a graduate student feels about their relationship to those in their field, likely the better they will feel about teaching students in a meaningful way as a representative of that community. In his work on self-efficacy, Cevdet Yilmaz (2011) conducted a study of teachers who were teaching a foreign language for the first time in an international setting (in this case, he was looking at teaching English in Turkey). Yilmaz found teacher self-efficacy correlated directly with how much they knew about the subject they were teaching. In other words, if teachers didn't have command over both languages, they were less likely to be confident in the teaching of their students. The relationship to liminality, in this case, is one that causes concern for graduate students. Here we see that, in addition to academic relationships, the better a graduate student feels about mastery over content, the more likely the success in teaching, especially in terms of making students comfortable in approaching the teacher with concerns. The oscillations among teacher and student agency, confidence, and comfort have a real impact on the ways graduate TAs both teach and learn.

The literature on imposter syndrome in and out of the academy has mostly centered on adult learners and professionals. However, Caselman, Self, and Self's 2006 study asked whether adolescents experience imposter syndrome. The researchers responded with a resounding "yes": "Mean scores on the Harvey IP Scale support previous research that IP exists among adolescents at about the same rate as in adult populations" (402). Given this study, it is clear feeling like an imposter happens at multiple levels for different types of students. For the first-year writing classroom, this means graduate student teachers are not alone in their feelings of stress and anxiety about succeeding in college (even if everyone in the room is, indeed, very well equipped to succeed). College classrooms around the country face having students and new teachers looking at each other through imposter-colored glasses while trying to complete their work each semester. This creates an interesting new obstacle on the complicated terrain of teaching first-year writing: two groups of students are trying to achieve similar goals, with similar anxieties, but one group is in charge of the other, operating on behalf of the institution to which they are all trying to gain access. While this scenario may seem to complicate the learning equation, it could instead be seen as an opportunity.

Embodying Double Agency

Because new graduate student teachers play multiple roles, oscillating among teacher, student, and scholar (often learning the norms of each simultaneously), they are an interesting population to consider in terms of what agencies become enacted, in which ways, and at what times. New TAs are engaged in learning a number of new academic registers given that language and its proper use are tools of the trade for participating in seminars, contributing to the field, and teaching academic writing. Typically, these TAs are also in charge of introducing students to the discourse community of the university through instruction in first-year writing courses. In this way, graduate teaching assistants exist at the crossroads of agency, negotiating the expectations of agency as students themselves and setting expectations for and relationships to academic agency for their students.

In his discussion of agency and genre, Anis Bawarshi (2003) suggests the term "double agency" for those who exist in this sort of oscillating identity paradigm. The "double agent," he claims, is "one who is both an agent *of* his or her own desires and actions and an agent *on behalf of* already existing desires and actions" (50). While Bawarshi uses the term to discuss how multiple genres and agencies are at play each time a writer sits down to write, the term *double agency* provides an accurate description of TAs entering the academy as teacher-students. In many ways, graduate students have a foot in each camp, negotiating roles as both professional and amateur, expert and novice, simultaneously.

Graduate students, via their roles as teacher-students, represent both agents of the university as teachers *and* agents who are acted upon by the university as students. While TAs carry out the mission of the university, we are simultaneously having the mission of the university carried out upon us. Sometimes we feel the weight of this when we are faced with situations in which the advice we give is against that of the institution we serve. In office hours, we hear this tension manifesting in many different conversations: "I know that you have to follow a strict schedule to graduate in four years, but have you thought of taking an elective in something you are truly interested in?" "I know that you will make more money in *x* career, but is this what will make you happy?" Maybe most complicated of all, "If what you really want to do is *x* and it doesn't require a degree, have you thought about other options for doing that besides college?" The tension between keeping students' interests at heart and keeping the health of the institution in mind can be difficult to resolve, and navigating the institutional waters surrounding issues like this takes time (perhaps more time than some of the very short programs we enter as graduate students allow). The priority becomes helping students learn to advocate for themselves, to find their own sense of agency in navigating the expectations of the institution, and typically we do this by helping them find ways to express their agency and use their voice.

Reimagining our role as graduate student TAs who function as double agents using liminality to relate across academic boundaries carves out a role for TAs that could displace feeling like an imposter in the academy. For students working in a first-year composition classroom, having an instructor who is also a student can create a sense of solidarity that encourages greater honesty about where a student stands in relation to their studies and the class. If students know they are talking to someone whose academic identity is still in flux, they may be more likely to discuss the burdens of being in flux themselves. When presenting students with strategies for how academics cope with this struggle, they can see the ability to cope arises from shared experience. Because new instructors are not yet established in their field, their advice and experiences might be more believable for students and can generate avenues of trust that might only be available to those occupying a role somewhere between student and scholar. This is not to say that once a TA stops being a student they can no longer relate to students—indeed, teachers in all stages of their careers develop strong bonds with students. However, it is to say that in the liminal space of the TA, it helps to envision the in-between stage as a benefit.

ACTING AS DOUBLE AGENT: MASTERY, EXPERTISE, AND SHARED EXPERIENCE

During my time as a graduate TA, my relationship with feeling like an imposter tended to be cyclic. Each semester, I felt the shift in agentic roles: I came in so worried about my own efficacy that I wasn't very in touch with whether or not my students felt the same way. As time went on, I started recognizing my students' positionalities more and more and feeling my own less and less. After three years of teaching first-year composition, I realized the scale is probably pretty balanced—that my students and I both have a relationship to this phenomenon in some way. Still, it has taken six semesters of teaching to achieve some semblance of balance and recognition that this process has been occurring, and it has required much reflection and energy, some of which was productive and some not.

As composition instructors, key to our pedagogical foundation is the way we think about students and their abilities to act in the world through the use of rhetoric and writing. In her article on rhetorical agency, Marilyn Cooper (2011) suggests that "we need to help students understand that writing and speaking (rhetoric) are always serious actions. The meanings they create in their rhetoric arise from and feed back into the construction of their own dispositions, their own ethos. What they write or argue, as with all other actions they perform, makes them who they are" (443). When we tell our students (and ourselves) that sense of self is connected to writing, there is potential for them to become trepidatious, particularly if they feel neither set in their academic identities nor confident in their abilities to communicate through writing. Surely, if students feel their writing is subpar, getting them to believe they *are* their writing could lead to unintended consequences. Graduate TAs sometimes feel this same sort of pressure because their academic identities are similarly in flux. Given the various commitments we have to our students, our field, and ourselves as graduate students, are there ways we can assist our students and ourselves in gaining access to academic agency through writing?

I suggest that, although agency is shaped based on individual background, there are ways we can help our students work through these issues of academic identity in our composition classrooms and challenge ourselves to do the same. These possibilities revolve around language, experience sharing, and community, and they can be developed by and for students within a classroom setting in such a way that they can help students build an efficacious academic identity, even when (or especially when) operating from liminal spaces.

Language

One of the first ways efficacy can be developed in the learning process is through exposure to, practice with, and discussion about language norms and how they construct discourse communities. In their work, Shapiro et al. (2016) show that teaching language diversity not only validates what students bring to the classroom but also helps them increase awareness for how and when to express their agency through writing. Rather than making writing feel like a monolithic skill students either have or don't have, making explicit the patterns of language used to engage in scholarly conversation can help students gain confidence in using those patterns. For example, breaking readings into component parts, studying the structure of readings and example texts at multiple levels, and giving students the opportunity to try out different structures (individually and in groups) can serve the dual purpose of helping students point out structural differences while encouraging them to be creative in the ways they employ different structures in their writing. When I was in grad school, I found that teaching new structures I was learning in my own coursework not only allowed me to concretize the new structure in my own writing toolbox but enabled my students to see I was excited about it. The fact that the majority of my students took up the structure, played around with the newness of a writing tool, and turned in works they were proud of, while acknowledging they felt out of their wheelhouse, attests to this fact. Taking risks is the stuff of learning how to write, and the graduate TA, being from a liminal space of expertise, is well situated to encourage that kind of growth from students, given that the TA may have just experienced it themselves.

During my time as a graduate student TA, I found that thinking about language and practicing effective language use through the lens of different agentic modes was helpful in making sure I worked through my efficacy issues related to writing. Specifically, seeking out opportunities to engage in the collective mode of agency was helpful in overcoming feelings of imposter syndrome (Bandura 2006, 165). Projects that involved grant writing, panel descriptions, and other collaborative work allowed me to see that my belief that writing was easy for everyone but me was a myth, and that, despite this, we could get there together. Admittedly, it took a few years of graduate work before I forced myself to engage in this collectivity, but it helped greatly in becoming a more self-efficacious writer. It can be difficult to remember that being a graduate student doesn't require that you have all the answers at once, or that everything you write is perfect. Working with other graduate students as a collective first can sometimes make it more comfortable to then start to share individual work, crossing between modes of agency in order to strengthen efficacy among various learning and writing environments. This might be an example of what Kylee Thacker Maurer and Faith Matzker with Ronda Leathers Dively discuss in their chapter in this collection as communitas. As often as I can, I share my participation in these collective writing endeavors with my students, both to encourage them to do the same and to chip away at their perception that teachers know everything and are not subject to the same sorts of writing needs.

Experience Sharing

The second group of activities that can be helpful for encouraging students' sense of efficacy involves the open sharing of experiences about writing. The Caselman, Self, and Self (2006) study suggests that "the experience of genuinely expressing thoughts and feelings has the effect then of moving one into a place of greater confidence and assurance" (402). If students know their experiences are not singular, they may have an easier time moving past their insecurities. This reality is at theheart of many ways to help students feel more self-efficacious: the more students know about other students having similar struggles, the more likely they are to feel a sense of solidarity with their peers. This need for common ground is something that is important at all stages of learning.

As for the role of the graduate instructor, there seem to be mixed views in terms of how much should be shared with students. While Caselman, Self, and Self's (2006) study suggests sharing can be effective, Brems et al.'s (1994) study of imposter syndrome and teaching evaluations found that students of teachers with higher levels of self-efficacy were more comfortable with approaching their teachers. In regards to highly efficacious instructors, "Students believed they increased their own knowledge more in courses taught by such instructors. If these instructors also showed little evidence of imposter feelings, their overall instructor ratings and ratings of their ability to encourage questions were even higher" (190). If we follow Brems et al.'s advice, openly communicating feelings of imposter syndrome can lead students to lose confidence in their instructors and have lower expectations. Where the line is drawn in terms of what is too much or not enough to share with students largely depends upon the instructor, and many graduate teachers wonder what to let their students know and what to guard. In my experience, letting my students know I am a student created a sense of solidarity and relatability, but I separated my shared experiences as a student from my experiences as a teacher. While I am perfectly happy to discuss with them the stress of finals and share my anxieties about my term papers, I would not, for example, discuss with them how stressed out I am about grading their papers, creating lesson plans, or encountering student behavioral issues.

While I think it is important to be cautious about sharing efficacy concerns with students, I have found the opposite has been true in sharing with my peers. Early on in my graduate experience, I was too nervous to speak up in seminars and burdened by what impact my words might have on others' perceptions of me as a student. In my third semester, I realized the more honest I was about my struggles to understand material, the more it helped other people feel comfortable about their anxieties. In a densely theoretical class I had that semester, I filled the silences with guesses at what the material meant and then amended those claims as class went along. I was honest when I was lost; I openly celebrated when I had a light-bulb moment, even though it meant admitting the light had not been on in the first place. I learned this from the students who were ahead of me—once I saw that my peers who were further along than I was were having similar struggles, my comfort level increased and my lack of understanding felt justified. This was incredibly liberating: that I could be in grad school, be confused, admit it, and not be ashamed felt like tremendous growth, even if it felt counterintuitive on the surface. Either way, it seems as if the sharing of experience can be really productive in exposing that no one can be an imposter if *everyone* is.

Community

Strongly connected with the idea of sharing experience is the building of a community in which people feel comfortable discussing their experiences of efficacy. In many ways, encouraging students to share their experiences can have a lasting effect on the way they interact in a classroom environment, whether our students communicate that to us or not. In their study to discover the predictors of imposter syndrome in adolescents, Caselman, Self, and Self (2006) found that, more than anything, having a friend to share mutual experiences with made the biggest difference in helping students assuage their low self-efficacy feelings. "When normal imposter feelings arise from new or challenging tasks," they found, "if one has a close friend with whom to discuss these and discover that the other, too, has faced such thoughts and feelings, a sense of connection and authenticity takes place" (402). In other words, even if we experience a sense of displacement in our liminal spaces, recognizing others share that liminal space matters to us.

At all levels, learning is a social act. Although the transition to college encourages students to see themselves as adults, the fact remains that most of our incoming freshmen are still acting from an adolescent state, and many are seeking social connections to help supplement distance from family members or other support structures they once had. Although instructors cannot force social relationships among their students, there are ways instructors can create opportunities for social learning to take place and for the potential of friendships or at least solidarity to develop among students attending class together. Opportunities for collaborative learning and meaningful group work in class, even asking students to find another student in class to email in case of an absence, can set the tone for sociality. Allowing students to find the balance between personal and academic concerns in the classroom through informal discussions and activities can help build a foundation of trust in other students. One of the other ways for instructors to create this environment of collegiality is to model this collaborative behavior. Discussing with students the ways graduate students depend on each other, create writing or working groups, or spend time together outside school can help students create expectations that learning is not something that must be merely independent—that isolation can impact learning in negative ways.

CONCLUSIONS AND FUTURE DIRECTIONS

Because undergraduate students and graduate student teachers occupy similar roles as *student*, they also have shared experiences in life circumstances from which to draw. Both populations are learning to fill agentic roles in their liminal environments and, because both are experiencing something new, there could be a lot of overlap when it comes to efficacy. In this way, going from being a student to being a graduate student represents a different chapter in the same book about the journey to acquire academic identity. However, the shift in power dynamic often creates a barrier that prevents graduate students from seeing it this way since viewing themselves as students in a teacher identity leads to some cognitive dissonance. How is it possible to occupy both these identities in a productive way, especially in a world where graduate student teachers feel responsible for helping bring their students agency? In an effort to avoid feeling as if we compromise our sense of expertise as teachers, we give up seeing ourselves as students, and our concern grows that we are not strong in either of these identities, even if it just as likely we are growing and improving in both.

Part of the solution might be that we shouldn't really think of ourselves as people who give agency—we probably don't. What we give students is access. What we give them are tools. And this is no different from how our advisors work with us as grad students. One of the risks of negotiating this dynamic role is that some things get lost in translation or unevenly applied: we *know*, as students, that our agency comes from within; we *hope*, as teachers, that we can help generate agency for our students. We must realize in our roles as experts what we *feel* on an everyday basis as students, and only then will we access the real strength of our liminal positions—positions we will only be lucky enough to occupy in the blink of an eye before moving on to different negotiated roles. This is not to say we can't do anything for our students—far from it. I argue that what we can do is give our students access and methods of increasing efficacy, and the best way we can do that is by teaching them how to use language, and how to see their writing and ideas as belonging. The fact that we are negotiating all these same learning processes makes us very capable teachers because we are so close to them. And while we are teaching our students about how to express agency through writing, we should be teaching ourselves the same—if we believe strongly that our students' voices matter, we should at least entertain the idea that we should be as generous with our own voices. In this way, developing a pedagogy with a realistic vision of agency, learning, and the limits and possibilities of both can be an important first step in convincing ourselves that our feelings of imposter syndrome can be converted to a more stable identity of a double agent.

When I began my graduate career, I struggled with confidence. I still do. I never believed my work was smart and, even when praised, I thought I needed to deflect the positivity away from myself lest the people praising me might discover I had somehow pulled the wool over their eyes. I worried they would be extra disappointed when the next project I did revealed me as a fake. Or even worse, the project after that. Or even *worse*, the project after *that*. In terms of teaching, this insecurity worked largely the same way, except the projects turned into units I was teaching. In both cases, it makes sense that I (and others) would feel anxiety about keeping up with expectations: the stakes keep getting higher and higher. In rhetoric and composition, first it's a term paper, then a conference proposal, then a publication, then a dissertation, and after I graduate it will be something else. Whatever it is, the stakes will always be on the rise. And they should be, because that is how we know we are improving, teaching, learning, and growing. Existing in the in-between spaces of learning is the very proof we are progressing, and inviting our own students to do the same can reframe what it means to be a student in ways that celebrate the messiness of learning and writing.

REFERENCES

Ambrose, Susan A., Michael W. Bridges, Marsha C. Lovett, Michele DiPietro, and Marie K. Norman. 2010. *How Learning Works*. San Francisco: Jossey-Bass.

Bandura, Albert. 2006. "Toward a Psychology of Human Agency." *Perspectives on Psychological Science* 1 (2): 164–80.

Bawarshi, Anis. 2003. *Genre and the Invention of the Writer: Reconsidering the Place of Invention in Composition*. Logan: Utah State University.

Bell, Elizabeth. 2008. *Theories of Performance*. Los Angeles: SAGE.

Brems, Christiane, Michael R. Baldwin, Lisa Davis, and Lorraine Namyniuk. 1994. "The Imposter Syndrome as Related to Teaching Evaluations and Advising Relationships of University Faculty Members." *Journal of Higher Education* 65 (2): 183–93.

Caselman, Tonia D., Patricia A. Self, and Angela L. Self. 2006. "Adolescent Attributes Contributing to the Imposter Phenomenon." *Journal of Adolescence* 29 (3): 395–405.

Clance, Pauline Rose. 1985. *The Imposter Phenomenon: When Success Makes You Feel Like a Fake*. Atlanta: Peachtree.

Cody, Kevina, and Katrina Lawlor. 2011. "On the Borderline: Exploring Liminal Consumption and the Negotiation of Threshold Selves." *Marketing Theory* 11 (2): 207–28.

Cooper, Marilyn. 2011. "Rhetorical Agency as Emergent and Enacted." *College Composition and Communication* 62 (3): 420–49.

Foss, Sonja. 2006. "Interdisciplinary Perspectives on Rhetorical Criticism: Rhetorical Criticism as Synecdoche for Agency." *Rhetoric Review* 25 (4): 375–79.

Freeman, Walter J. 2000. *How Brains Make Up Their Minds*. New York: Columbia University Press.

Geisler, Cheryl. 1994. *Academic Literacy and the Nature of Expertise: Reading, Writing, and Knowing in Academic Philosophy*. Hillsdale, NJ: Erlbaum.

Graham, S. Scott. 2009. "Agency and the Rhetoric of Medicine: Biomedical Brain Scans and the Ontology of Fibromyalgia." *Technical Communication Quarterly* 18 (4): 376–404.

Miller, Carolyn. 2007. "What Can Automation Tell Us about Agency?" *Rhetoric Society Quarterly* 37 (2): 137–57.

Said, Edward. 1994. *Representations of the Intellectual*. New York: Vintage Books.

Shapiro, Shawna, Michelle Cox, Gail Shuck, and Emily Simnitt. 2016. "Teaching for Agency: From Appreciating Linguistic Diversity to Empowering Student Writers." *Composition Studies* 44 (1): 31–52.

Sprague, Jo and Douglas Stuart. *The speaker's handbook*. Fort Worth: Harcourt College Publishers.

Trimbur, John. 2000. "Agency and the Death of the Author: A Partial Defense of Modernism." *JAC* 20 (2): 283–98.

Yilmaz, Cevdet. 2011. "Teachers' Perceptions of Self-Efficacy, English Proficiency, and Instructional Strategy." *Social Behavior and Personality* 39 (1): 91–100.

7

BEYOND "GOOD TEACHER" / "BAD TEACHER"
Generative Self-Efficacy and the Composition and Rhetoric TAship

Megan Schoettler and Elizabeth Saur

In early August 2015, at a research university in the Midwest, we began a three-week pedagogy seminar designed to help new graduate teaching assistants develop and refine their pedagogical approaches to the composition classroom. Domestic and international students were accepted into the literature, creative writing, and composition and rhetoric masters and PhD programs and automatically enrolled in this course; thus the TAs came to this space with a wide variety of perspectives, experiences, emotions, and beliefs. It was in this environment that we, the coauthors, first met. Megan was beginning as a student and TA in the master's program in composition and rhetoric, and Beth was coteaching the course as a third-year doctoral student in composition and rhetoric in her role as an assistant director of composition.

Thinking about the early days of that seminar experience, we remember how it felt to be in that space. When Megan met her cohort and new mentors in the TA program, she was elated and energized but also worried about how she could apply her training and experience working with high-school students to her process of teaching first-year composition. When Beth met the new cohort, this time as their teacher and mentor, she couldn't help but recall her own feelings two years previously and suspected these new TAs were navigating a wide range of emotions—anxiety, excitement, hope, dread—all intermingled with various degrees of doubt and confidence. As the seminar progressed, and as we got the chance to know one another and work together, we both realized we shared a similar language to talk about experiences and development as teachers; in other words, our pedagogical approaches seemed to "click" with one another. Just as Megan's interest in theories of self-efficacy enabled her to recognize her own attitudes and dispositions

DOI: 10.7330/9781646420896.c007

about herself as a teacher in a way that was generative for her, so too did Beth's research into instructor affect allow her to understand how her emotions and feelings about teaching could be reframed as generative and empowering. As we explored these theoretical understandings of our teaching in relation to one another, we were able to see how they intersected and aligned in such a way as to foster our perceptions of ourselves as capable and effective composition instructors—in ways we did not necessarily see happening for everyone in the teaching practicum.

In this chapter, we argue that TAs can be empowered with the framework of generative self-efficacy to develop a greater sense of awareness of their own abilities in the classroom and within the field as a whole. This awareness becomes especially relevant when we consider the liminality of the space new TAs occupy: you may be a student, an instructor, or perhaps situated among a variety of academic and nonacademic communities. In what follows, we first establish the definitional understandings at the foundation of our exploration into self-efficacy. Furthering the discussion introduced by Kathryn M. Lambrecht in this collection, and drawing from the work of Albert Bandura, we explain where the broader concept of self-efficacy originates and how research in various disciplines has applied this theory of disposition to the notion of teacher self-efficacy—specifically calling attention to quantitative studies that seek to identify how instructors perceive their own abilities to perform their roles of teachers. While such research has been useful in exploring the potential of self-efficacy as a framework for understanding teachers' levels of confidence and behaviors, we emphasize how these studies rely on problematic designations of high and low self-efficacy, as well as notions of positive and negative affect. Adopting language from previous research conducted on student learning dispositions (Bronfenbrenner and Morris 2006; Driscoll and Wells 2015), we suggest that envisioning teacher self-efficacy as generative and/or disruptive instead can be a more productive framework for TAs to employ as they seek to understand their role in the composition classroom. Following these distinctions, we turn to the results of a qualitative case study of new composition and rhetoric instructors. The interviews with these TAs demonstrate the potential of a generative teacher self-efficacy, especially within an affective framework. We consider these conversations, as well as our own experiences, to demonstrate how such attention to teacher self-efficacy can be productive for TAs in composition and rhetoric.

Before we offer an exploration of the concept of self-efficacy and how it has previously been addressed in relation to teaching, we want to take a moment to make clear the stakes of this discussion. As Susan McLeod points out in the final chapter of her book *Notes on the Heart*, when discussing teacher self-efficacy, we are exploring "not just the power of positive thinking." Rather, "teachers' sense of efficacy will determine the amount of effort they put into their teaching, their task choices, their degree of persistence when confronted with difficulties, their motivation to continue" (1997, 117). When considering the wide variety of challenges you will face in the classroom as a new composition instructor, it is important that you have a sense of your own capacity to help your students in a productive manner. The lived experiences of the new TAs we share throughout our discussion serve to demonstrate this point: as they grapple with feelings of shame, negotiate their roles within academic communities, and reframe the concept of failure, they illuminate the potential for personal and professional development such an understanding of self-efficacy within an affective framework can yield. We aim to show how a framework of generative self-efficacy can help TAs gain a greater sense of your abilities as new teachers and also help you navigate the challenges specific to your new roles as composition instructors—both in the classroom and within the larger context of the university as a whole.

EXISTING THEORIES OF SELF-EFFICACY

In considering how self-efficacy can benefit new teachers in composition and rhetoric teacher-development programs, we want to first establish how we are defining the terms we are using. Developed by social learning theorist Albert Bandura, the concept of self-efficacy refers to a person's belief in their ability to achieve a specific performance. When Bandura published *Social Learning Theory* in 1977b—introducing the theory of self-efficacy—he was responding to well-established research on operant conditioning, including the work of B. F. Skinner. Theories of operant conditioning presented humans with little agency, constantly reacting and being changed at the whim of their environments; in essence, such understandings of human behavior denied individuals a sense of agency with regard to their decision-making processes. In contrast, Bandura's theory of self-efficacy emphasizes how internal constructs and agency actually play significant roles in influencing personal choices and behavior. In his research, Bandura theorizes and empirically demonstrates that perceptions about one's abilities impact one's performances, explaining,

> There is a difference between possessing skills and being able to use them effectively and consistently under varied circumstances. Development of self-regulatory capabilities requires instilling a resilient sense of efficacy as well as imparting knowledge and skills. If people are not convinced

of their personal efficacy, they rapidly abandon the skills they have been taught when they fail to get quick results or it requires bothersome effort. (1997, 733)

Thus, by reframing how a person's disposition influences their decision-making processes, a theory of self-efficacy fosters a better understanding of a teacher's perceptions of their abilities to achieve specific outcomes, how these perceptions are formed, and what performances are achieved as the result of self-beliefs.

In offering further points for understanding, Bandura also breaks down the larger conceptualization of self-efficacy into two more terms: "efficacy expectation" and "outcome expectancy" (1977a, 193). Efficacy expectation is defined as "the conviction that one can successfully execute the behavior required to produce the outcomes" (Bandura 1977a, 193). For example, a TA may have strong efficacy expectations that they can lead a successful lesson on writing structure. Outcome expectancy is defined as "a person's estimate that a given behavior will lead to certain outcomes" (Bandura 1977a, 193). In this same example, the TA may have the outcome expectation that if they spend adequate time lesson planning and reviewing their plans with a mentor, their first lesson on structure will be successful. In this case, the TA is reflecting a high internal locus of control, or a sense of greater individual agency. They believe their ability to attain certain outcomes, and then their performances, will lead them to success. On the other hand, a TA who believes they have what it takes to teach a good lesson, but that the success of their performance is completely out of their hands (due to scheduled course time, student attitudes, luck or misfortune, etc.), has a different outcome expectancy drawn from a high external locus of control. Given their more specific nature in relation to the larger concept of self-efficacy—and thus their greater ability to be measured quantitatively—these two terms, *efficacy expectation* and *outcome expectancy*, have been used frequently in scholarship on self-efficacy.

Of course, in day-to-day life, people do not usually talk about their self-efficacy toward performance—they talk about their confidence, or feelings that they can or cannot do well or succeed at something (Pajares and Schunk 2001). For example, in considering the experiences of new teachers specifically, estimations of one's abilities come through in a variety of ways, not the least of which is the anxiety that stems from experiencing the fraud complex or imposter syndrome of being a new teacher. While new composition instructors' feelings of doubt or insecurity have been explored in a variety of contexts (Dethier

2005; Pytlik and Liggett 2002; Restaino 2012), within this discussion specifically, we consider *generative teacher self-efficacy* within and in relation to an *affective* framework. In doing so, we want to emphasize how emotions as a TA influence not only your understanding of your teaching experiences but also how you perceive your capacity to enact change within a composition classroom.

It is important to recognize that in discussions on affect, "there is no single generalizable theory of affect: not yet, and (thankfully) there never will be" (Gregg and Seigworth 2010, 3). However, despite (or perhaps because of) this lack of consensus on a precise definition of affect, we find employing such a framework enables us to consider the relationship between instructors' self-efficacy and their emotions in a generative manner. That is, similar to how we want to challenge absolute definitions of self-efficacy that ultimately limit an instructor's understanding of their potential in the composition classroom, we also employ an understanding of affect that yields greater opportunity for understanding—one that recognizes the potential of *all* emotion and feeling in terms of helping instructors develop an awareness of their own abilities to enact change. With this in mind, we embrace affect's fluidity, and throughout the discussion that follows, we actively seek to disrupt any binaries that exist surrounding the notions of emotion or feeling. In other words, we find concepts of positive or negative affect to be problematic and ultimately limiting and instead actively seek to help TAs reframe these notions in ways that will be generative for personal and pedagogical growth.

RESEARCH ON TEACHER SELF-EFFICACY

In this chapter, we discuss teacher self-efficacy, or teachers' beliefs in their abilities to influence student learning toward educational outcomes. There already exists a rich body of scholarship on teacher self-efficacy in primary, middle, and high school. Applying Bandura's (2006) theory of self-efficacy, these studies recognize that teachers' efficacy expectations are informed by mastery experiences, social persuasion, vicarious experiences, and affect. (We discuss these terms and their definitions in greater detail later in this chapter.) When teachers' efficacy beliefs were examined, they revealed relationships to teacher job satisfaction, teaching behaviors, and the success of their students (Gibson and Dembo 1984; Moè, Pazzaglia, and Ronconi 2010; Woolfolk Hoy and Davis 2006). Notably, the self-efficacy of teachers has been repeatedly correlated with teaching strategies; teachers who have high self-efficacy typically teach large groups more effectively, put forth more persistence toward helping struggling students, and design more effective instruction (Ashton and Webb 1986; Gibson and Dembo 1984; Woolfolk Hoy and Davis 2006).

Several researchers have also examined the teaching self-efficacies of college instructors (Burton, Bamberry, and Harris-Boundy 2005; Tschannen-Moran and Hoy 2007). David Morris and Ellen Usher (2011) used a unique qualitative approach to research the complex teaching self-efficacies of twelve award-winning, tenured instructors at research institutions. These professors developed methods of framing negative teaching experiences as part of narratives of development, and after several years as a tenure-track instructor, each "arrived at a more stable perception of their instructional capabilities, at which point their self-beliefs were much less susceptible to fluctuations based on a bad experience or negative comment" (241). In other words, even instructors with PhDs have continually developing perceptions about their worth and abilities. The professors in Morris and Usher's study conveyed that their efficacy expectations were primarily informed by related mastery experiences and social persuasion, and one of their participants noted, "If I hadn't started off so well, I wouldn't have much confidence at all. I mean, I really feel sorry for people who were never TAs for as long a time as I was because it was very helpful. I think the early years are important" (241). We include this perspective not only to help reinforce the value of the TA experience you are currently having but also to help highlight how a generative self-efficacy can affect both immediate and long-term attitudes about teaching.

Given the ways Morris and Usher's (2011) study reflects aims similar to our own (despite their focus being experienced instructors and ours new instructors), throughout our exploration, we will use the concept of "framing" Morris and Usher offer in order to demonstrate how new TAs in composition and rhetoric can come to understand their sense of self-efficacy in generative ways. In other words, we recognize teachers have the power to frame their experiences within narratives. Experiences of failure may be interpreted along a wide spectrum of stories teachers tell themselves about their abilities—one teacher's frame could lead them to believe "this failure is further evidence that I am a horrible teacher," while another teacher's frame could support the idea "this experience with failure is not uncommon, and is part of my continued growth and experiences as an instructor." The experienced, successful teachers from Morris and Usher's study adopted a frame that allowed them to interpret experiences within mindsets of development and consideration for past performances. We encourage TAs to adopt a developmentally oriented frame as well.

In research on self-efficacy, Carol Dweck's (2007) theories of mindsets toward intelligence are also beneficial for interpreting the frames individuals adopt toward skills and tasks. Dweck's theory distinguishes between *growth mindsets* toward intelligence, in which people recognize their potential for learning and development, and *fixed mindsets*, in which people identify with set binary identities—such as good teacher and bad teacher. Dweck found that mindsets impact the choices we make and that social persuasion guides people toward mindsets in different contexts; when others recognize hard work and recognize specific development ("You're really developing as a teacher!"), people are more likely to adopt a growth mindset versus how when social persuasion is framed in terms of set identities ("You're a good teacher!"), decontextualized from work and development, people are more likely to adopt a fixed mindset. With this in mind, we encourage TAs to think about how feedback you are given influences your perceptions of your abilities, how you give feedback to other teachers, and how you can reflect in ways that emphasize your skills rather than labels. In other words, try to promote *growth* mindsets for yourself and others—not *fixed* mindsets that assume you will never grow.

There have also been studies in the fields of psychology, chemistry, and economics to examine the teaching self-efficacy of graduate teaching assistants. This interdisciplinary research demonstrates that TAs typically start with low self-efficacy expectations toward teaching. (So rest assured, if you are feeling anxious about teaching right now, that is completely normal!) However, TAs' beliefs in their abilities increase when they have training, are enrolled in a teaching practicum, and reflect upon their experiences (Dembo and Gibson 1985; Evans and Tribble 1986; Heppner 1994). Regardless of past teaching experience, when TAs across the disciplines gain training and experience related to their new courses before starting, their self-efficacy expectations are significantly higher (Prieto and Altmaier 1994; Prieto and Meyers 1999). For example, as part of TA training, discussions in TA practicums in the field of psychology "helped participants see their fears and anxieties as normal and appropriate" (Heppner 1994, 9). After new TAs start teaching, their self-efficacy expectations begin to rise, but with more experience, their expectations fall again (Dembo and Gibson 1985; Evans and Tribble 1986). So, do not be discouraged if your beliefs in your abilities waver after you get started. This is attributed to "the initial absence of actual teaching experiences, which may temporarily inflate perceived

efficacy until teachers deal with assimilating real performance accomplishments" (Prieto and Altmaier 1994, 486). While TA self-efficacy may
fluctuate, there are things you can do to promote generative dispositions
that instill realistic confidence and encourage your growth as a teacher.

DEVELOPING A GENERATIVE TEACHER SELF-EFFICACY

As this brief review demonstrates, there is a wealth of research on
teacher self-efficacy across various disciplines. However, these studies
typically rely on quantitative measures of teacher self-efficacy, such as
the Self-Efficacy Toward Teaching Inventory (SETI) (Tollerud 1990).
These measures predetermine which beliefs and skills count toward
teacher self-efficacy; for example, teachers rate their ability to "wake
the desire to learn even among the lowest achieving students" (Skaalvik
and Skaalvik 2007, 624). The quantified results of such surveys show
which TA self-efficacy expectations are "low" or "high," or presumably
"good" or "bad" for teachers. Quantitative self-efficacy scales, when used
alone, can fall short in accurately and fully representing self-perceptions
(Schoettler 2017). Our experiences, as well as those of other TAs we
have spoken with, have demonstrated that such binary divisions between
high and low or good and bad or positive and negative effectually over-
simplify the teaching experience. In other words, teaching composition
is a far more complex experience than that which can be determined
by a predetermined set of beliefs or skills or classified as good or bad.
Establishing such labels can actually be detrimental to your perception
and understanding of your teaching abilities. Thus, rather than considering teacher self-efficacy in such absolute terms, we seek to offer
an understanding of teacher self-efficacy that relies on an alternative
method and more nuanced terminology, specifically through reframing
your perceptions of your abilities as generative *and/or* disruptive. We
adopt the terms "generative" and "disruptive" from Bronfenbrenner
and Morris (2006), who recognize that dispositions of learning can
be generative—allowing for productive human development to take
place—and/or disruptive—resulting in an inhibitive impact on the
development of the individual (810). We argue that this framework
of teacher self-efficacy not only enables teachers and teacher mentors
to recognize and assess when experiences are productive for teacher
performance, motivation, and development but also makes room for
more qualitative understandings of teacher self-efficacy—approaches
that can yield such insights and practical suggestions as this chapter
offers. Ultimately, we aim to contribute a framework of generative

teacher self-efficacy situated in the composition and rhetoric TAship specifically; through analyzing the experiences of new TAs, we highlight moments in which these instructors reframe (Morris and Usher 2011) their potentially inhibitive or disruptive pedagogical experiences into generative moments.

In our framework of generative teacher self-efficacy, we draw from Bandura's (1997a) and Frank Pajares's (2003) research on the contributors to self-efficacy expectations to lay the groundwork of our approach. According to Bandura and Pajares, complex self-beliefs come together as a result of several contributors: mastery experiences, social persuasion, vicarious experiences, and affect. Generally, when new teachers have *mastery experiences*—such as leading a lesson in either a pedagogy practicum or the composition classroom itself—experiences interpreted as successful raise self-efficacy expectations. In other words, you will have raised expectations of your abilities to achieve success with similar tasks in the future. In contrast, experiences you interpret harshly as failures can lead to lowered self-efficacy expectations, or a lack of motivation and self-belief. Next, individuals' self-efficacy expectations are influenced by *social persuasion*, and for TAs, this includes feedback from, but not limited to, mentors, peers, and students. Social persuasion has varying impacts on self-efficacy expectations based upon the teacher's value of their performance, the effort they perceived they put forth, and the credibility and value of the persuader in relation to the teacher. *Vicarious experience* occurs when teachers observe others attempting tasks and/or make social comparisons with others. Witnessing successful strategies and achievements of fellow teachers, such as observing a peer delivering a lesson, can raise efficacy expectations; however, normative comparisons with peers can also have a detrimental effect, such as when teachers negatively compare their abilities to other TAs.

The final contributor influencing teacher self-efficacy stems from an instructor's "physiological and affective states, including stress, fatigue, anxiety, and mood," which "can also influence perceived capability" (Morris and Usher 2011, 233). In his original conception of self-efficacy, Bandura (1977b) calls particular attention to the influence of affect on one's perceptions of one's abilities, labeling affective responses as "emotional arousal" and positing these emotions as manipulatable insofar as they can influence one's self-efficacy (82–83). However, scholarship on teacher self-efficacy has since seemed to place this contributor on the periphery of its scope of investigation (DeChenne, Enochs, and Needham 2012; Hoy and Spero 2005). As we seek to demonstrate the complexity of teacher self-efficacy—highlighting the care and nuance with which teachers should approach concepts of their self-confidence, ability, and belief—we place affect at the heart of our discussion. After all, not only do our emotional states heavily influence how we perceive ourselves and our abilities (Ahmed 2004; Damasio 2000; McLeod 1997; Tomkins 1992), but as Bandura points out, one's self-beliefs of efficacy have "effects on cognitive, affective, and motivational intervening processes" (1989, 733). That is to say, affect both influences and is influenced by its relation to teacher self-efficacy and thus should not be considered a peripheral point of inquiry in such discussions. In our analysis of teacher self-efficacy, we bear this in mind, as we seek to understand the experiences of new composition and rhetoric TAs through a lens of self-efficacy *and* affect, recognizing the potential such a juxtaposition offers in terms of your pedagogical development as a TA.

With these four contributors providing the foundation of our conceptualization of generative teacher self-efficacy, we want to offer some practical suggestions such a framework offers for new composition and rhetoric TAs specifically. In the discussion that follows, we share narratives stemming from two sources: our own experiences in the pedagogy course at our shared institution—as both student and mentor—and the results of a year-long case study. In this IRB-approved study with first-year composition instructors at two different universities, qualitative methods were employed, namely conducting classroom observations and a series of open-ended interviews with each of these instructors.[1] The focus of these conversations tended to revolve around how the TAs felt about teaching a composition course for the first time, their level of confidence and ability in the classroom, their feelings of preparation about teaching, and how they might come to better understand the nature of their pedagogical experiences. Throughout these conversations, we strive to represent the complexity of teacher self-efficacy while also demonstrating how such approaches necessarily resist binary labels (such as high and low being equated with good and bad) and thus destabilize such potentially detrimental norms.[2]

REFRAMING SHAME

In our experiences and observations, one of the most important locations to deconstruct and reframe limiting binary labels regarding teacher self-efficacy is in how we talk about shame and failure as composition instructors. Within the field of composition and rhetoric specifically, Kellie Sharp-Hoskins and Amy Robillard claim that "rhetoric and compositionists are ideologically hailed to narrate and interpret pedagogical experiences in binary terms—good teachers and bad, good students and bad—which are secured and enforced through emotion" (2012, 306). Sharp-Hoskins and Robillard suggest that the fear of the shame a composition instructor would experience as a result of not meeting the expectations of what is considered a good teacher then works to limit how they talk about their pedagogical experiences to others. In other words, the good teacher/bad teacher binary can not only influence your teacher self-efficacy but can also restrict how you talk about your teaching. This good/bad binary often serves as a model in an instructor's assessment of their abilities: in their vicarious experiences, they compare themselves to their cohort, whom they may only know as good teachers through the stories they hear; they interpret their mastery experiences as failures because of their inability to meet the standards of the good teacher; and they inevitably experience social persuasion through received feedback they interpret as critical and shaming.

To better understand how the concept of shame can be a significant influence on teacher self-efficacy, especially in light of the good teacher/bad teacher binary, we can look to the experiences of Jessie, a composition and rhetoric international TA teaching her first composition course. During our conversation, Jessie shared that she had low self-confidence as a teacher, and she described how, on her first day as a TA, she had a mastery experience that influenced how she understood her abilities:

> Because I'm so self-aware that I'm teaching in my second language, so I got really nervous and self-conscious and really nervous. Just extremely nervous. And then students also think that I'm so young. Like, all those things, factors, when they come together, my first class did not go well. Especially when I—when I speak. So I asked them, "Does anyone want to write about slang of your hometown?" That is my prompt—asking them to write about discourse community, a huge concept. So, I was asking, "Does anyone want to write about slang from your hometown?" and I think I mispronounced that. I forgot how to pronounce that. And so, the students were like, "Oh! You mean slaaang." And then I smiled, and then other students asked, "What did you say?" And then she pronounced my mispronunciation and then that student laughed. And so I didn't know what to do, so I just laughed it off. . . . And that was my first day.

Clearly, this pedagogical moment stuck with Jessie (as it most likely would with any instructor)—during our conversation, a month after this event, she still remembered every detail of the interaction. She explained she is "so self-aware that [she's] teaching in her second language" that she is constantly self-conscious and nervous about it. She then entered the classroom and had her anxieties confirmed when her students seemed to make fun of her pronunciation. In addition to the social persuasion from her students, Jessie's disruptive teacher self-efficacy was further impacted by social persuasion from another graduate student. After sitting in on her class, the observer told her, "There were students laughing at you again. It was hard to watch." Jessie was "annoyed and hurt" by this feedback, and it made a lasting impact on her teacher self-efficacy.

Jessie also shared that her day-to-day confidence impacts how she teaches—she cannot "pretend or hide" when her self-efficacy is disruptive. However, during our conversation, Jessie arrived at a strategy to respond to her shame. Thinking back to her first class as a TA, she stated,

> I was wondering if I should have a conversation with my students about the benefits of them having an international instructor. I did not do that on the first day because I did not want to make this even more overt. (laughs) So I only told them that I'm from China, English is my second language, I'm getting my PhD, but I did not much emphasize—I kind of only implied that I do have the credentials to teach this course. And also that by having me, you will get so many interesting new insights, like approach things from new perspectives which you might find informing. But I did not say that out loud, so I don't know . . . I think I'm going to do that next time.

Jessie did use this approach to introduce herself to her classes the following semester; she found it both helpful for her students and empowering for her confidence. However, she was not able to arrive at this generative moment until she had thought through it explicitly. That is, at the time of the interview, Jessie's experiences in the classroom had stuck with her in ways that were inhibitive to her development as an instructor. She felt she needed to adapt, as she believed, "After the first class, students are going to think I'm just weak or soft, still wondering if they got a good teacher. I don't know if I'm a good teacher." She needed to understand the nature of the shame she experienced in her first class in order to identify ways of negotiating "the affective cost of not following the scripts of normative existence" (Ahmed 2004, 104). Sara Ahmed (2004) explains that experiencing shame "may be restorative only when the shamed other can 'show' that its failure to measure up to a social ideal is temporary" (107). The inhibitive (often stifling) effects of shame become generative only when either the social ideal one is not living up to or the shame itself are better understood and reframed as part of a narrative.

When Jessie talked candidly about her experiences within the context of the interview, the opportunity served as an experience to reframe her shame. Addressing directly and reframing the social ideal her students may have of teacher helped her deconstruct this notion and reconfigure her own positioning in relation to that ideal. In fact, in the week following our interview, Jessie talked about her experiences with friends, colleagues, and mentors in a similarly candid manner. Seeking feedback from others—including those in her small teaching group in practicum—enabled Jessie to recognize the forces that were constructing her view of the ideal and her capacity to change these influences. In other words, by reframing her experiences of shame through generative social persuasion, Jessie was able to deconstruct the good teacher/bad teacher binary she had previously been using to construct her teacher self-efficacy.

Jessie's experience illustrates the impact of teacher self-efficacy and affect for a new TA in composition and rhetoric. Whereas she had previously doubted her abilities as an instructor, by narrativizing her experiences in a way that situated shame as part of the process (rather than as a result), Jessie was able to develop a generative teacher self-efficacy. In recognizing how such practices can be fostered in teacher-development programs specifically, we can turn to the concept of mindsets toward intelligence (Dweck 2007). In reframing her experiences, Jessie was exhibiting a growth mindset toward intelligence—or a belief that through her efforts she could build upon her performance of teacher rather than be perpetually and disruptively tied to shame as an inhibiting influence. Though Jessie's interaction with a peer, who called her teaching "hard to watch," could have reinforced fixed conceptions of her abilities, other opportunities in her TA training helped Jessie develop a growth mindset and approach.

Within the space of teacher-development programs specifically, there are many ways such generative social persuasion can be fostered. One such possibility is by establishing teaching communities in which TAs meet with one another in a more personalized context—similar to those incorporated into the program at our university. Beginning with Megan's cohort at University A, these teaching groups met once a week with a mentor and worked through a variety of topics, ranging from questions about individual students to assignment development to general feelings about the experience of teaching. Just as Jesse used this space to help her reframe shame in a generative manner for her personal and pedagogical growth, TAs can have the opportunity to talk about and narrativize their pedagogical experiences in a low-risk, more intimate environment that makes space for them to understand the nature of their affective reactions, to negotiate the often complex emotions of anxiety, elation, joy, and shame that frequently can make one feel more vulnerable in a larger-class-sized setting. By creating or joining a teacher community, you can have the opportunity to engage in meaningful conversation that helps you develop as a TA. These conversations can also help deconstruct potentially disruptive binaries while offering vicarious experiences that explore moments of struggle and challenge. It is important that in these teaching communities, TAs try to resist using labels such as *good teacher* and *bad teacher* and that you talk candidly about your successes *and* your failures. While these teaching communities are certainly not the only way to help TAs develop generative teacher self-efficacy as a new composition and rhetoric instructor, they can work especially well to destabilize and reframe the ways you come to understand your capacity in relation to your peers and others in the profession.

REFRAMING COMMUNITY

As is evident throughout our discussion thus far, the tendency for composition and rhetoric TAs to compare their pedagogical experience to others has a direct influence on how these instructors feel about their abilities as a teacher. This makes sense, for within an academic community, you are not only working alongside others going through similar experiences but are also talking about these experiences with these individuals. In other words, your vicarious experiences as a member of this community determine not only how you feel about your experiences but also what you think you should feel about them. Often, when instructors engage in such comparison without recognizing the potentially inhibitive influence of this process, the conclusions at which these teachers arrive are inhibitive and disruptive to their teaching self-efficacy. To elucidate this point, we can call on the notion of the ideal instructor established by the good teacher/bad teacher binary. If new composition and rhetoric TAs are constantly comparing themselves to an ideal they have constructed solely based on narratives motivated by an imperative to be considered a "good teacher," inevitably these new teachers will fall short of that constructed ideal. Such moments of "failure" can then demotivate TAs in their processes of pedagogical development. However, while such methods of comparison are a natural approach to understanding your abilities as a teacher—and are often inescapable—there are ways you can make these experiences more pleasant and generative for your development.

To help demonstrate how these processes of comparison can be made productive for pedagogical growth, as well as the development of generative teacher self-efficacy, we would like to turn to the experiences

of Diego—an instructor in his first semester teaching first-year composition. Through conversations with Diego, it became clear he had
developed a perspective on comparison that helped him negotiate how
he felt about his own abilities as a composition instructor—in other
words, a perspective that fostered generative teacher self-efficacy. Before
exploring this directly, though, we want to take a moment to establish
a difference between Diego and others in his cohort; that is, we want to
explore how he framed his notion of the academic community to which
he belonged. As he explained,

> I think it helped that—unlike some of the other TAs—I had a good rap-
> port with some of the past TAs. . . . Those are the kind of people I share
> approaches with. . . . Yeah, those are the kind of people I am similar
> to—and I talk to them about teaching, and they're like, "Yeah, just don't
> freak out too much." And I'm like okay. That actually really calmed me
> down when I got into the program.

We see here how Diego drew a distinct line between himself and "some
of the other TAs" because of his embeddedness within a different academic community; he related to the "past TAs" more than he did his
own cohort—those are the individuals he shared a pedagogical approach
with and those are the ones he compared himself to. Therefore, in terms
of developing a generative self-efficacy, Diego relied more on the social
persuasion from past, experienced TAs than he did his own cohort, while
also drawing his vicarious experiences primarily from the past TAs' pedagogical narratives. While it is certainly valuable for TAs to confer with
one another and share experiences amongst their cohort, college instructors' teacher self-efficacy tends to become more generative as they gain
more experience (Morris and Usher 2011). New TAs can benefit from
the development-oriented outlooks of experienced TAs, and "verbal persuasion from experienced teachers in the form of encouragement and
advice," which is a potent source for new teachers' self-efficacy (Hoy and
Spero 2005). Given that Diego's pedagogical influences all had more
teaching experience than he did, the advice he received from those instructors seemed to bolster his efficacy expectations in productive ways.
Ultimately, as Diego's reflections on the effect of these influences demonstrate, bridging the gaps between various levels of teaching can help new
composition and rhetoric TAs develop a generative teacher self-efficacy.

When the interview with Diego turned directly to the concept of
comparison, the point came up, "Do you ever question—because you
feel a little bit different coming from a different cohort from every-
body else—do you ever question whether what you're doing is right or
wrong?" To this, he responded,

I think it is what it is. I don't question in respect to some of the other people—the way they do their methodology—because I already have a way I think about writing and a way I think about situating this class, which comes from my influences: the people I've talked to, the friends I was with, the things I've read, and my own things. I don't think I'm ever doing anything right or wrong relative to other people. I think of whether I'm doing the right thing or wrong thing relative to my own. So I think I question sometimes my approach at moments and how complex, how not complex, how I should approach what I'm talking about. That's a thing I think about a lot, but I don't think it's right or wrong—I don't think I'm doing good or bad relative to other people because I had those other people help me figure things out. I think those things really helped a lot.

Diego's ability to recognize that his own pedagogical approach stemmed from unique influences different than those of his cohort ultimately enabled him to develop a generative teacher self-efficacy. Because of the diverse nature of his vicarious experiences, he did not view his teaching as "right or wrong," and he did not consider it as "doing good or bad relative to other people." He viewed his own influences as distinctive from others in his cohort, as he "had those other people help [him] figure things out," and this helped him recognize the multivalent nature of teaching. In other words, Diego did not compare himself to others in his cohort because he recognized it was not an apt comparison, so he instead reframed his sense of community and questioned what he was doing in comparison to his own ideals. His recognition of the difference between his approach and those around him was thus facilitated by the diversity of his vicarious experiences.

As the moments of interaction we include throughout this discussion demonstrate, each new teacher's experience is affected by a variety of influences. As a TA, you should consider ways to recognize these influences and introduce yourself to a wide range of teaching approaches. Reaching out to a multitude of mentors to hear and learn from, for example, can help deconstruct ideal notions of what it means to teach while also allowing you to reframe your perception of the academic community to which you belong. It offers a variety of vicarious experiences through which you can identify the potential of your own pedagogical approaches—as nonnormative as you feel they might be (or perhaps especially in these instances). You can also achieve such vicarious experiences through reading composition-pedagogy articles and narratives that explore a wide variety of pedagogical approaches and the theories that support such methods. Pieces such as those found in this collection can help you recognize not only how you might want to develop your own pedagogy but can also help you understand why these approaches would or would not be successful in various contexts.

As Diego's experience demonstrates, if mentorships are not already implemented in your teacher-development program, you can be active about establishing these relationships—and we strongly encourage you to do so. Such inclusion of a variety of perspectives will not only serve to present you with a multiplicity of narratives to learn from while also helping you reframe your perceptions of their academic community but will also help you develop a growth mindset toward pedagogical development (Dweck 2007). That is, by engaging with more experienced teachers, you will likely be better able to recognize your pedagogical growth as an evolving process rather than a set or stagnant result. Additionally, you can observe these mentors' classes, talk with these veteran instructors, and write reflections about their observations and conversations. Through understanding how you view yourself in relation to instructors outside your cohort, you can come to develop a generative teacher self-efficacy not based on the idea that there is only one right way to teach. Further along these lines, it is important to remember you should not view these experienced instructors as good teachers who represent what is right but rather as models of the wide variety of approaches you can consider as you develop your own pedagogical philosophies and practices. Ultimately, branching out to a diverse, supportive network of experienced educators can be valuable for your pedagogical experience while also creating a greater sense of community within your program as a whole.

REFRAMING FAILURE

As the interactions with both Jessie and Diego demonstrate, talking through your experiences can enable you to recognize your capabilities and influences in relation to your students and larger academic communities. As a TA, you can engage with existing opportunities for such conversations or create your own. Whether it is part of a community or independent practice, one valuable way to foster generative teacher self-efficacy is by engaging in strategic reflection. With this in mind, we want to turn the focus to our own experiences within our pedagogy seminar, specifically in relation to the practice and importance of teaching journals. Teaching journals are designed as an activity in which TAs can slow down to contemplate and grow in the teaching practice, as well as work through challenging affective states associated with being a new teacher. Or, as it was described in our pedagogy seminar syllabus, the TAs were encouraged to view these as "an opportunity to reflect critically on [their] classroom experiences, to learn from [their] own approaches and consider how [they] might implement change in productive ways." It is important to note that these journals should be an extremely low-risk space to reflect and explore vulnerable moments, so if you decide to share your writing, any feedback should be oriented toward your development—not simply critiques of your practice. In other words, it should be made clear and explicit to whomever you share your writing with that these journals are not means of evaluation but are rather a space for you to explore and come to better understand the nature of your teaching experiences. Feeling comfortable about being honest and transparent with this type of reflection results in greater opportunity for learning about and making meaning of particularly complex pedagogical experiences.

As part of her practicum during her first year as a TA, Megan kept such a teaching journal. During her first semester, her reflective entries were shared with the composition director and assistant directors each week and could generate points of conversation for the small-group meetings of TAs. Further, as Sarah Liggett points out in discussing the concept of teaching journals more in depth, "without such records, TAs [are] apt to forget their and their students' specific reactions to particular activities as they [seek] to solve teaching problems" (2002, 304). Indeed, these journals served as a record for our own understanding of the teacher-development seminar, as returning to Megan's teaching journals from the beginning of her master's program was an opportunity for us to see the development of Megan's teaching self-efficacy, the role of reflection and social persuasion in that process, and how Beth specifically informed Megan's perceptions of her abilities as a teacher.

In the process of journaling, Megan realized that writing her TA journal was changing how she was thinking about herself as a teacher. Instructors often use affect to clue them in to how they are performing as a teacher (Morris and Usher 2010), and Megan relied upon this when she first started teaching. Unfortunately, Megan's affective experiences with teaching were often disruptive. Stress and anxiety after teaching a class were often paired with overwhelming thoughts that she had no idea what she was doing as a teacher. Through her teaching journals, she had a chance to think through her role as a teacher, and like Jessie, to begin to narrativize and reframe her development. As a demonstration of this development, we can look to Megan's TA journal from her third week of teaching. She began this entry with a thorough description of a peer-review lesson she gave, including the productive learning of her students. This reflection followed the description of the lesson:

I am very emotionally invested in my teaching. This is good because I think it contributes to the quality of my work, but it can also be dangerously draining. I tend to view my teaching in black and white—I'm "great" or "horrible"—in fact, I've been feeling pretty negative today about my teaching until I started writing about how successful the peer review was. (Their Inquiry 1 drafts were also amazing!)

In Megan's journal, she recognized that reflecting on the meaningful learning moments of her class reframed how she understood her ability as a teacher. The act of reflecting on one successful part of her lesson—the peer review—also prompted her to remember and document that her students had written successful drafts for their first large assignment.

Recognizing her achievements as a teacher was generative for Megan, and exploring her missteps in her TA journal was transformative as well. When Megan wrote about experiences she considered failures, the process of reflective journaling made her examine those experiences with a lens of development. In other words, instead of brooding on mistakes as part of being a "bad teacher" (which she often did), she thought about her teaching experience as part of a normal learning process of a new teacher. A common move Megan made was reframing—or taking a teaching experience she considered a failure (or at best, imperfect) and thinking about it in terms of opportunity for growth, often answering the question "What might I do differently next time?" The following entry from Megan's fourth week of teaching illustrates this reframing:

> The trip to the writing center was ok—I'm glad that I did it—but I will scaffold it more next time. I think I will go into the idea/purpose of the writing center, examples of when I have used it, and a sample of a tutoring session next time. Also, I will have each student write a question down on a notecard for the writing center consultant who speaks to us.

Though Megan's lesson was initially disappointing to her, her TA journal was an opportunity to reflect on the experience and make a concrete plan for the next time she taught a similar lesson. Like Jessie, this reframing allowed Megan to see her failure as temporary—one stepping stone on a long path of her development as a teacher.

What made Megan's journaling particularly powerful for her was the social persuasion she received when mentors responded to her reflections. Every time a TA in Megan's practicum submitted a teaching journal, they received feedback from the composition director and/or assistant composition directors. Consistent with Bandura's (1997) finding that social persuasion is particularly meaningful from sources people consider knowledgeable and genuine, Megan found feedback from her practicum mentors essential to the development of a generative teacher self-efficacy. Megan knew that whenever she was writing a journal entry she had two audiences: first, she was writing for herself to think through her experiences, and second, she was writing for her practicum mentors and instructors. This second audience played an important role—they could show Megan her experiences, including the fears and frustrations, were not unusual and confirm or deny Megan's explorations of her ability as a teacher.

The role of this secondary, persuasive audience is particularly evident in Megan's journal entries from the middle of her first semester. In an entry from her fourth week as a TA, Megan states,

> I really love my profession, but I think a large part of my teaching development will be . . . creating reasonable ways to assess my effectiveness (that don't make me feel horrible). One strategy that I do think works really well is talking with other (especially experienced) teachers. I want to meet with Beth soon to chat. (If you are reading this and have time on Friday, let me know, if not, then maybe Monday?)

In this teaching journal, Megan recognizes the value of social persuasion from mentors in her development as a teacher and explicitly calls for persuasion even beyond what she might typically receive in a typed response to her journal from Beth. Several weeks after this journal entry, Beth was able to observe Megan's class and then have a long debriefing session afterward in which they talked about Megan's lesson and her experiences as a new teacher. Megan documented the results of this meeting in her week-seven TA journal:

> Getting thoughtful feedback and praise from Beth after her observation and receiving feedback from my students in an in-class memo made me feel a lot better about myself as a teacher. I want to hold on to what my students and Beth said to remember—"I am being effective! My class is engaged, learning, and on top of that, students are actually feeling comfortable and having fun!" I'm feeling a bit more confident in myself as a teacher and also getting excited for my next semester (and many years to come . . .) of teaching and adapting lesson plans and assignments to be even more interesting and effective.

In this entry, Megan describes two sources of social persuasion: (1) feedback from a respected mentor who observed her class and (2) anonymous feedback from her students about their learning experiences. Combined, these sources of social persuasion had a powerful influence on Megan's generative teacher self-efficacy. Megan felt not only confident and energized but also recognized her success could be part of a career of growth and successful performances.

Self-efficacy scholars have recognized that "university instructors who experience early failure may be caught in a downward spiral with regard to their self-efficacy beliefs" (Morris and Usher 2011, 241). For Megan, maintaining a reflective teaching journal and staying in conversation with experienced teaching mentors helped her navigate negative experiences and affective states toward a more generative teaching self-efficacy. Specifically, these strategies helped her recognize what she was doing effectively, as well as reframe moments of failure. Like the experienced college professors in Morris and Usher's study of teacher self-efficacy, Megan had moments of failure and then focused "not on what inabilities led to their failure but rather on what skills would ensure future success" (2011, 242). To put it another way, by maintaining a reflective teaching journal during her first semester as a TA, Megan developed a theory of her teaching self. She spent her time throughout the semester not only thinking through her teaching experiences but also recognizing how she felt about those experiences in relation to her own abilities as a teacher. As she was heavily informed by her own research in writerly self-efficacy, by the time she reached her final essay, Megan also wanted to take a moment to articulate where a semester's-worth of self-reflection and teaching experience had led her. In her final entry, she was able to confidently write: "I see myself as a highly approachable, open teacher in my classroom. A lot of students have been visiting my office hours to get extra help, and I get emails from my students frequently, which I think shows that they are invested in the class." Megan's reflection here demonstrates that she was able to recognize her strengths as a teacher, pointing out specific aspects of her pedagogy she found productive for her students and for becoming the type of teacher she envisioned herself to be.

We find it worth noting, however, that while Megan developed a generative teacher self-efficacy toward teaching first-year composition, only some elements of her process would be repurposed to her experiences teaching other courses in other contexts. That is, as the majority of instructors do, she inevitably experienced self-doubt and continued to question her abilities in the classroom. We want to point out that these feelings are simply part of the process of development and that a generative teacher self-efficacy encourages developing a disposition that recognizes this aspect of teaching. (In fact, as Megan is currently preparing to teach a new advanced course, she is already experiencing the self-doubt and uncertainty that comes with this new task. Fortunately, her teacher self-efficacy is such that she still feels motivated to succeed despite the anxiety.) In making this assertion, we also want to call back to the problematic tendency for scholars and researchers to equate having a high teacher self-efficacy with being a good teacher and having a low teacher self-efficacy with being a bad teacher. Megan's teacher self-efficacy will fluctuate, ebb and flow over time; this is part of the process of developing as a teacher, and it is her development and awareness of her generative teacher self-efficacy that has enabled her to become comfortable with this process in productive ways.

We also want to emphasize that, while teaching journals may already be implemented as part of your teacher-development program, in cases where this approach is not included, you can still benefit from such reflection independently and/or amongst your own teaching community. That is, you can take the time on your own to write through your teaching experiences as you seek to understand and learn from your practice. Further, you can exchange these journals with other TAs who might not only be able to offer you generative feedback but might also benefit from reading your reflection. And while it can be extremely useful to get feedback on your writing—whether that is sharing writing directly or using reflections as a conversation starter—even in cases in which you don't feel comfortable sharing your journals with others (for whatever reason), it is also helpful to journal just for yourself. We especially encourage you to adopt this practice given it does not demand many resources but can· have a lasting and significant impact on your development as a teacher.

FINAL THOUGHTS AND IMPLICATIONS

By exploring these TAs' rich moments of development through the framework of generative teacher self-efficacy we have established, our hope is that you will be able to glean insight from this framework and their experiences as you develop your own attitudes and beliefs about teaching composition. Of course, your experiences in the composition classroom will be unique to your personal, social, and institutional contexts, but we know the value of sharing such teacher narratives—not only as a way to acquire vicarious experiences but also as a means of recognizing the potential of that space. With this in mind, we would like to take a moment to emphasize the importance of taking an active role in shaping the nature of your pedagogical trajectories within larger institutional contexts.

As you seek to understand your role as a TA—in your pedagogy seminar and in the composition classroom—we encourage you to remember that both success and failure are generative moments of the teaching experience. Though it is certainly valuable to hear your WPA and mentors share stories from the classroom in which a particular activity or assignment succeeded beyond expectations, these narratives should be balanced with reflections on moments of total and complete failure. Seek out these stories of failure when they are not immediately offered. Try to create an atmosphere in which such deconstruction of Sharp-Hoskins and Robillard's (2012) "good teacher/bad teacher" binary is welcome and valued. And make time to reflect on these narratives and experiences of success and failure. Just as Jessie was able to talk through her experiences in the small teaching groups in a way that was productive and made room for her to share in a low-risk environment, so too was Megan able to explore and develop her own teacher self-efficacy in her teaching journals and in conversations with her mentors. In these instances of reflection, the TAs felt comfortable sharing their doubts and insecurities as they reframed their teaching as a continuing narrative, but they were able to do so because they knew it was the intended purpose of those interactions. In other words, actively seek out and try to create a community in which you and your peers feel comfortable reflecting on *all* aspects of the teaching experience; by having these opportunities for reflection within your process of development as a teacher, you will also be better able to recognize that your perceptions of your abilities and your feelings about your abilities are not peripheral elements of your development as a teacher.

Being a TA can often be a volatile experience—you are entering into a new space and must instantly negotiate a multitude of influences while trying to better understand the liminality of your role, your capacity, and how you feel about all these expectations and responsibilities. In this environment, it is valuable to foster a sense of community and camaraderie with your peers, as well as with your mentors. Such a collaborative and supportive environment ensures TAs (such as Jessie, Diego, and Megan) have people to talk with in order to understand their own feelings about their pedagogical experiences in generative ways. However, it is also important to recognize each teacher-development program will be different; depending on the structure of the program, where it is housed within the department, how the WPA is positioned within this dynamic, the funding and support, and so forth, your teacher-development program will provide its own unique opportunities and limitations.

Inevitably, all these factors influence how a TA feels about teaching; however, we encourage you to draw from the readings throughout this collection to identify ways by which the liminal positionality of a TA in rhetoric and composition can offer you the chance to work within your individual institution to create generative vicarious experiences for yourself and your peers while developing approaches to effectively negotiate the social persuasion inherent to the teaching experience. In other words, while the in-betweenness, the fluidity, the transformations can certainly feel unmooring at times, they can also be generative. Our hope is that TAs in rhetoric and composition are able to recognize the affordances that come along with their liminality, and in the process, come to better understand their capacity to effect change in both their immediate and larger institutional contexts.

NOTES

1. At the time of the observations and interviews, each instructor was in their fourth week of their first semester teaching first-year composition, and though they differ in many ways, both universities have extensive teacher-development programs. At what we'll call University A, when a student is accepted to the graduate school, they are automatically enrolled in a two-week course on pedagogical instruction prior to the beginning of the fall semester for which they have been admitted. Following, there is a semester-long practicum course that meets weekly for an hour and twenty minutes. These courses are cotaught by the director of composition and two assistant directors of composition (experienced doctoral students in the program) and are primarily focused on helping new teachers develop and refine their pedagogical approaches to the composition classroom. At University B, there exists an entirely different structure for the TA program. Here, the graduate students are required to work in the university writing center for a year prior to applying for the TA program (barring a few rare exceptions). Also, as part of their writing center experience, tutors are scheduled to work as an instructional student assistant (ISA) in at least one English course, where they assist the instructor of that class in a variety of ways (as agreed upon by the instructor and the student). Typically, in the second semester of their first year working in the writing center, the graduate students may then apply for the TA program, and once admitted into the TA program, the graduate students are then enrolled in a semester-long pedagogical seminar that begins at the same time as their teaching assignments (Saur 2017).

2. While there were eight TAs involved in this study, for the purposes of our discussion specifically, we highlight and include the experiences of instructors we feel are particularly relevant to the concepts of self-efficacy and affect at the heart of our focus. Such a framework as we develop certainly could apply to any of the teachers interviewed; however, in trying to balance considerations of length and a desire to offer a thorough understanding of the instructors' experiences, we have opted to limit the scope of our inquiry to those most relevant and illuminating. Further, we sought to emphasize reciprocity throughout the data-collection process. We wanted to ensure participants benefited from the experience of being involved in our research—a desire that comes from both our stance as researchers who are concerned about the time and investment of our participants and from our own positionalities as fellow instructors and colleagues. In *Getting Smart: Feminist Research and Pedagogy with/in the Postmodern*, Patricia Lather asserts, "Emancipatory social research practice calls for empowering approaches to research where both the researcher and the researched become, in the words of feminist singer-poet,

Cris Williamson, 'the changer and the changed . . . doing empirical work offers a powerful opportunity for praxis to the extent that it enables people to change by encouraging self-reflection and a deeper understanding of their particular situations" (1991, 56). Such an approach to our own research not only encourages the type of self-reflection that helps participants develop a greater awareness of their situations, but with the emphasis it has on the concept of change and capacity, it also speaks directly to the understandings of affect and self-efficacy we employ throughout this chapter.

REFERENCES

Ahmed, Sara. 2014. *The Cultural Politics of Emotion.* New York: Routledge.

Ashton, Patricia T., and Rodman B. Webb. 1986. *Making a Difference: Teachers' Sense of Efficacy and Student Achievement.* New York: Longman.

Bandura, Albert. 1977a. "Self-efficacy: Toward a Unifying Theory of Behavioral Change." *Psychological Review* 84 (2): 191–215.

Bandura, Albert. 1977b. *Social Learning Theory.* Englewood Cliffs, NJ: Prentice-Hall.

Bandura, A. (1989). "Regulation of cognitive processes through perceived self-efficacy." *Developmental psychology* 25 (5): 729–35.

Bandura, Albert. 1997. *Self-Efficacy: The Exercise of Control.* New York: Worth.

Bandura, Albert. 2006. "Toward a psychology of human agency." *Perspectives on psychological science* 1(2): 164–80.

Bronfenbrenner, Urie, and Pamela A. Morris. 2006. "The Bioecological Model of Human Development." In *Handbook of Child Psychology,* edited by William Damon and Richard M. Lerner, 793–828. New York: Wiley.

Burton, James P., Nola-Jean Bamberry, and Jason Harris-Boundy. 2005. "Developing Personal Teaching Efficacy in New Teachers in University Settings." *Academy of Management Learning & Education* 4 (2): 160–73.

Damasio, Antonio R. 2000. *The Feeling of What Happens: Body and Emotion in the Making of Consciousness.* 1st ed. New York: Harcourt.

DeChenne, Sue Ellen, Larry G. Enochs, and Mark Needham. 2012. "Science, Technology, Engineering, and Mathematics Graduate Teaching Assistants Teaching Self-Efficacy." *Journal of the Scholarship of Teaching and Learning* 12 (4): 102–23.

Dembo, Myron H., and Sherri Gibson. 1985. "Teacher's Sense of Efficacy: An Important Factor in School Improvement." *Elementary School Journal* 86 (2): 173–84.

Dethier, Brock. 2005. *First Time Up: An Insider's Guide For New Composition Teachers.* Logan: Utah State University Press.

Driscoll, Dana, and Jennifer Wells. 2012. "Beyond Knowledge and Skills: Writing Transfer and the Role of Student Dispositions." *Composition Forum* 26 (Fall): 1–12. https://compositionforum.com/issue/26/beyond-knowledge-skills.php

Dweck, Carol S. 2007. "The Perils and Promises of Praise." *Educational Leadership* 65 (2): 34–39.

Evans, Ellis, and Margaret Tribble. 1986. "Perceived Teaching Problems, Self-Efficacy, and Commitment to Teaching among Preservice Teachers." *Journal of Educational Research* 80 (2): 81–85.

Gibson, Sherri, and Myron H. Dembo. 1984. "Teacher Efficacy: A Construct Validation." *Journal of Educational Psychology* 76 (4): 569–82.

Gregg, Melissa, and Gregory J. Seigworth. 2010. *The Affect Theory Reader.* Durham, NC: Duke University Press.

Heppner, Mary J. 1994. "An Empirical Investigation of the Effects of a Teaching Practicum on Prospective Faculty." *Journal of Counseling and Development* 72 (5): 500–507.

Hoy, Anita Woolfolk, and Rhonda Burke Spero. 2005. "Changes in Teacher Efficacy During the Early Years of Teaching: A Comparison of Four Measures." *Teaching and Teacher Education* 21 (4): 343–56.

Lather, Patricia Ann. 1991. *Getting Smart: Feminist Research and Pedagogy with/in the Postmodern.* New York: Routledge.

Liggett, Sarah. 2002. "Evolution of a Teaching Notebook: Contents, Purposes, and Assessment." In *Preparing College Teachers of Writing: Histories, Theories, Programs, Practices,* edited by Betty Parsons Pytlik and Sarah Liggett, 303–14. New York: Oxford University Press.

McLeod, Susan H. 1997. *Notes on the Heart: Affective Issues in the Writing Classroom.* Carbondale: Southern Illinois University Press.

Moè, Angelica, Francesca Pazzaglia, and Lucia Ronconi. 2010. "When Being Able Is Not Enough. The Combined Value of Positive Affect and Self-Efficacy for Job Satisfaction in Teaching." *Teaching and Teacher Education* 26 (5): 1145–53.

Morris, David B., and Ellen L. Usher. 2011. "Developing Teaching Self-Efficacy in Research Institutions: A Study of Award-Winning Professors." *Contemporary Educational Psychology* 36 (3): 232–45.

Pajares, Frank. 2003. "Self-Efficacy Beliefs, Motivation, and Achievement in Writing: A Review of the Literature." *Reading & Writing Quarterly* 19 (2): 139–58.

Pajares, Frank, and Dale Schunk. 2001. "The Development of Academic Self-Efficacy." In *Development of Achievement Motivation,* edited by Allan Wigfield and Jacquelynne Eccles, 16–32. San Diego: Academic.

Prieto, Loreto R., and Elizabeth M. Altmaier. 1994. "The Relationship of Prior Training and Previous Teaching Experience to Self-Efficacy among Graduate Teaching Assistants." *Research in Higher Education* 35 (4): 481–97.

Prieto, Loreto R., and Steven A. Meyers. 1999. "Effects of Training and Supervision on the Self-Efficacy of Psychology Graduate Teaching Assistants." *Teaching of Psychology* 26 (4): 264–66.

Pytlik, Betty P., and Sarah Liggett. 2002. *Preparing college teachers of writing: histories, theories, programs, practices.* New York: Oxford University Press.

Restaino, Jessica. 2012. *First Semester: Graduate Students, Teaching Writing, and the Challenge of Middle Ground.* Carbondale: Southern Illinois University Press.

Saur, Elizabeth. 2017. "Affective Understandings: Emotion and Feeling in Teacher Development and Writing Program Administration." PhD diss., Miami University.

Schoettler, Megan. 2017. "The Development of Writerly Self-Efficacies: Mixed-Method Case Studies of Writers across the Disciplines." Master's thesis, Miami University.

Skaalvik, Einar M., and Sidsel Skaalvik. 2007. "Dimensions of Teacher Self-Efficacy and Relations with Strain Factors, Perceived Collective Teacher Efficacy, and Teacher Burnout." *Journal of Educational Psychology* 99 (3): 611–25.

Sharp-Hoskins, Kellie, and Amy E. Robillard. 2012. "Narrating the 'Good Teacher' in Rhetoric and Composition: Ideology, Affect, Complicity." *JAC* 32 (1/2): 305–36.

Tollerud, T. 1990. *The Perceived Self-Efficacy of Teaching Skills of Advanced Doctoral Students and Graduates from Counselor Education Programs.* PhD diss., University of Iowa.

Tomkins, Silvan S. 1992. *Affect, Imagery, Consciousness.* Rev. ed. New York: Springer.

Tschannen-Moran, Megan, and Anita Woolfolk Hoy. 2007. "The Differential Antecedents of Self-Efficacy Beliefs of Novice and Experienced Teachers." *Teaching and Teacher Education* 23 (6): 944–956.

Woolfolk Hoy, Anita, and Heather A. Davis. 2006. "Teacher Self-Efficacy and Its Influence on the Achievement of Adolescents." In *Self-efficacy Beliefs of Adolescents,* edited by Frank Pajares and Timothy C. Urdan, 117–37. Greenwich, CT: Information Age.

Afterword

STAYING WITH THE MIDDLE

Jessica Restaino

My book, *First Semester: Graduate Students, Teaching Writing, and the Challenge of Middle Ground* (2012) got its start as a dissertation. The manuscript went through a series of revisions, some of them major, before becoming a book. As I now have the honor of closing out a collection of essays written especially *for* graduate student writing teachers, I want to begin with my roots and the drive to do that initial study, one that grew from my own experience of graduate studenthood and that ultimately transported me out of such an identity. Indeed as I think about this idea of movement or transport, I am reminded of the notion of liminality, that in-betweenness unique to being *on the way* and thus neither static nor fully stable. In my case, during my own first semester of graduate school, I was freshly unable to imagine a life's work bound up with, as I had originally intended, the study of postcolonial and feminist literature; at the same time, my attention and my energy were captivated most deeply by the struggle in the first-year writing classroom, especially the frequent disconnect between my students' diverse needs and literacy practices and my underinformed (and perhaps colonizing) efforts to help. In the first writing class I ever taught, my students and I were nearly the same age but for one woman who was decades older and who sometimes brought gifts of home-cooked meals to our one-on-one conferences. We were all vulnerable and, whatever our age, each of us hoped the other would be merciful and generous. Several weeks in I could only imagine one reason to stay in school: my students and the struggle that lived between us. Driven to this edge I discovered the field of rhetoric-composition; I was fascinated and also profoundly grateful for this rich breathing space.

I was also enormously limited, in a sense. My first language for talking and thinking about the composition classroom was mostly just loaded with desire and inadequacy. Of course, over time we develop not just a pedagogical tool kit but also a standpoint, a praxis, a way of thinking

DOI: 10.7330/9781646420896.c008

about what we do and why. But in this moment and at the end of this particular book, I want to argue for the value of that first language and for keeping it close as a kind of thread to carry through our other progressions—those of discipline and perhaps accumulated knowledge, including self-knowledge since our first languages can be loaded with privilege and power we ought to uncover. These become the theoretical frameworks in which we learn to move. As William Macauley writes in his introduction to this collection, the less anticipated themes among these chapters include identity, social condition, homogenization. Negotiation or even critical interrogation of such themes is lifeblood for all kinds of growth, and my sense is that these themes, in and of themselves, tend to root in our first languages. Indeed the more "professionalized" we become, the further we can sometimes float away from wrangling with the very human urgency and inadequacy we experience when the classroom stumps us. The more equipped we are with terminology, with a tested, theorized framework through which to filter our experiences, the more insulated we can be from the raw nerves of our own self-doubt. And I'm not sure that's entirely a good thing. However many years we have been teaching writing, we will always meet, again, that student whose struggle to write perplexes us in a uniquely personal way, undercuts what we thought were our very best practices, and forces us to question the reliability of our allegiances to research, even to language, our own or others'. I want to thus make an argument that recognizes the value of accumulated experience and knowledge while insisting that the presence of self-doubt will always be hopeful news. Self-doubt is where some private sense of ourselves meets with everything else we (think we) are supposed to know or be able to do (and to be fair: labor disparities, and the inadequate preparation or support for teaching common to graduate students and other contingent faculty, can fan unhealthy degrees of self-doubt). The inevitable crash between these (and here I'm thinking about our field's historic embrace of Mary Louise Pratt's "contact zone") can foster productive shifts on either side of the equation. Graduate studenthood—for all its injustices—ought to stay with us.

Over and over the authors in this collection expose these collisions and productive negotiations in ways that make a convincing case for graduate studenthood as a rich site for invention, resistance, and rethinking. In "Multimodal Analysis and the Composition TAship: Exploring Embodied Teaching in the Writing Classroom," Lillian Campbell and Jaclyn Fiscus-Cannaday describe their work with multimodal discourse analysis as "providing an analytical framework for attending to how embodied talk 'index[es] specific discourses about self, writing, [and] academia'" (chapter 2). Campbell and Fiscus-Cannaday study the ways TAs' embodied classroom performances reveal their own ideological positions and pedagogical philosophies, as well as their very wrangling with uncertainties about any of these standpoints. Perhaps most critical is that study of the video footage of teacher performance confirms, for Campbell and Fiscus-Cannaday, "a range of identities." The presence of "range" is of course a kind of liminality and, while we all tend to naturally seek what feels like solid ground, I think there is value in maintaining some fluidity in our ongoing work, even as we move into alternate or more formalized professional identities.

Perhaps in making the case for fluidity and some healthy degree of uncertainty, I ought to also make a companion claim: there is some danger in believing one has ever fully "arrived." For Kylee Thacker Mauer and Faith Matzker (with Ronda Leathers Dively) in their chapter "The Graduate Teaching Assistant WPA: Navigating the Hazards of Liminal Terrain Between the Role of Student and the Role of Authority Figure," efforts to "navigate . . . threshold concepts are necessary experiences that allow grad teaching assistants (TAs) to successfully transition from student to professional, from novice to scholar, and from learner to educator" (chapter 4). The notion of threshold concepts here functions as a progressive pathway towards an advanced professional identity. "Successful transition" is nevertheless a fraught one, or at least I think it ought to be. Exploring earlier discussions of threshold concepts, the authors draw on a notion of thresholds as "between rooms . . . 'neither here nor there,'" and thus thresholds create opportunities to "reconstruct and reimagine our identities." Yet our human tendencies toward fixity often play out and we assign more static power to names and titles, to language, to what we see as "markers" of experience, achievement, or knowledge. Recent critiques around what counts as knowledge in our discipline and, of course, *who gets to say so* continue to push our field towards necessary and fraught conversation.[1] Mauer and Matzker experience similar phenomena around their assigned titles: "We often feel powerless in our position, but TAs view the WSA role as a position of power." What becomes worrisome about all this—beyond the frustrations of graduate students in disempowered administrative roles—is the likelihood that each new identity becomes not so much a new in-between space in which to explore oneself but rather a step in a progression, an assigned expectation of competency and power that can frustrate more than it can enable. It becomes painful to take a step back, to claim uncertain knowledge, to expose the gaps in one's power (after all, TAs look to Mauer and Matzker with hope). Our human impulse, then, can be to accumulate thresholds—like titles—as achievement markers, to walk through doors convinced that going back is a demotion of sorts.

GOING BACK, STAYING PUT: THE VALUE OF IN-BETWEEN

What might graduate studenthood look like if we valued it for its very evolutionary quality rather than its status as a set of markers towards professionalization? And what if—to step further—we carried that very notion of studenthood into our work long after graduate school? How might our scholarship, what we define as research, and our teaching change? My hope here at the close of this important collection on the graduate student experience is that we might consider sustained attention or intellectual commitment to the notion of uncertainty, movement, the sort of hopeful indeterminacy graduate students so often bring to their work. This approach, a praxis to be sure, need not be limited to the study of graduate students alone. In my own recent work, illness and the dying body offer a space for valuing a rhetoric of failure and uncertainty. *Surrender: Feminist Rhetoric and Ethics in Love and Illness* takes as its focus a two-year ethnography I completed with my friend and collaborator Susan Lundy Maute in the last two years of her life with terminal breast cancer. Much of our collaboration is defined by the sort of seeking that—given both the mystery of dying and the boundaries between healthy/ill bodies—ultimately always denies full clarity or certainty. It's here though that I argue for "staying put," for the unique meaning housed in such spaces.

NOTE

1. See Asao Inoue's chair's address ("How Do We Language So People Stop Killing Each Other, Or What Do We Do About White Language Supremacy?") at the 2019 Conference on College Composition and Communication (CCCC) in Pittsburgh.

ABOUT THE AUTHORS

EDITORS

William J. (Bill) Macauley Jr. is a professor of English at the University of Nevada, Reno, and was a TA at Indiana University of Pennsylvania. Bill directed UNR's writing center and writing-in-the-disciplines program and has continued to work in the development and assessment of UNR's innovative Silver Core curriculum. Bill teaches undergraduate and graduate courses, including the TA practicum and an advanced undergraduate writing course on affordable housing/homelessness. Bill has worked directly with TAs from most of the UNR English graduate programs: MA—language and linguistics, literature, public engagement, rhetoric and writing studies; and PhD—literature, rhetoric and composition. English TAs typically teach in the core writing program and have opportunities for hands-on professionalization in composition and communication in the disciplines, core writing, and the University Writing and Speaking Center. Bill has supported TAs in English and other disciplines in the design, development, and assessment of assignments, courses, curricula, and programs; studying writing, the teaching of writing, and research in/teaching of writing in the disciplines; professionalizing in writing center and writing program administration; participating in the development and proctoring of faculty development; and, of course, developing individual teaching, research, scholarship, and service.

Leslie R. Anglesey is an assistant professor at Sam Houston State University in Huntsville, Texas, and earned her PhD in rhetoric and composition from the University of Nevada, Reno, in May 2019. Her research is situated at the intersections of composition theory and pedagogy, feminist rhetorics, and disability rhetorics and focuses on interrogating ableist and gendered assumptions that undergird the teaching of writing. During her TAship, Leslie served as a coordinator for the first-semester first-year writing course in which she organized an ongoing professional-development series for instructors. Later, she served as gWPA, cochairing the assessment committee for the writing program. She also mentored new TAs (formally and informally); participated in TA training and orientation; served on the public-relations committee, working to highlight the work of our first-year students; and collaborated with our writing center to improve our center's accessibility. The work from this collaboration was recently published in *Peer Review*.

Brady Edwards holds master of arts degrees in English and American studies from the University of Nevada, Reno, and Utah State University, respectively. During his time as a teaching assistant at these institutions, he gained valuable experience as an assistant writing program administrator, where he was able to observe and mentor multiple teaching assistants. Additionally, as a veteran TA, he was a regular contributor to the annual teaching-assistant orientation at these universities. Such contributions allowed Brady to share ideas and collaborate with others to improve first-year writing instruction. Besides his teaching assistantships, Brady has interned with the writing center and the Teaching Excellence and Achievement Center at UNR. Working with these centers has broadened his ability to connect with others and to meet the needs of an institution and its constituents. Brady has published essays and reviews in *Peer Review*, *Southern Discourse in the Center*, and *The Journal of Popular Culture*, among others. Brady is a first-time editor for this collection and is thrilled with the prospect of helping to bring so many new (and needed) teaching-assistant voices to the field.

Kathryn M. Lambrecht is an assistant professor of Technical Communication at Arizona State University. She earned her PhD in rhetoric and composition from the University of Nevada, Reno in August 2018. Her research focuses on interdisciplinary writing and the ways disciplinarity informs communication across different types of experts. During her TAship, she worked with faculty from across the disciplines in a WAC/WID program, mentored fellow graduate students as a first-year writing coordinator, and contributed regularly to the TA-training program at UNR, where TAs take a pedagogy graduate course during the first semester they are teaching. In chapter 6 ("From Imposter to 'Double Agent': Leveraging Liminality as Expertise"), she makes the argument that the graduate student identity of expert-in-progress can be an asset, a source of agency, and a foundation for community building within the classroom. Kat's work has been featured in the *Journal of Business and Technical Communication*, the *Journal of Higher Education*, and the *Bulletin of the American Meteorological Society*.

Phillip K. Lovas is a lecturer in the Karen Merritt Writing Program at the University of California, Merced, where he teaches courses in first-year writing and research, professional writing, upper-division academic writing, and interdisciplinary seminars for first-year students. The Karen Merritt Writing Program has an interdisciplinary approach to writing that offers students the opportunity to work with creative writing, professional writing, and writing in the disciplines. His research interests are focused on students' writing in the disciplines, professional and technical communication, genre theories, and how students transfer information beyond the classroom.

CONTRIBUTORS

Lew Caccia earned his PhD in rhetoric and composition at Kent State University. Lew is currently an English professor at Kent State University, Stark Campus, in North Canton, Ohio. Lew received a University Teaching Council Faculty Recognition Award for teaching that made a difference in the life of a Kent State graduate; he has also been thrice nominated for the Distinguished Teacher Award. The values that help guide his pedagogical practice include mentorship, rigor, flexibility, staying current, and technology. For four years, Lew served as visiting assistant professor at Youngstown State University, where he mentored first-year TAs, helped supervise senior projects for professional and technical writing majors, and coordinated the professional and technical writing internship program. In chapter 1 ("Imitation, Innovation, and the Training of TAs"), Lew advocates the use of imitation pedagogy as an explicit component of TA training. Lew's work with TAs suggests they draw as closely from their own experiences as students (and the experiences of peers) as they do from scholarship or direct mentoring. Working with those perspectives by encouraging thoughtful imitation can be a way to help new teachers develop. Lew's current scholarship explores "needfinding" approaches to curricular development in professional and technical writing.

Lillian Campbell earned her PhD in language and rhetoric from the University of Washington (UW) in 2016. She then began her career as an assistant professor of English at Marquette University. Her research focuses on disciplinary writing, with a particular interest in methods for studying multimodality and embodiment. During her time at UW, she taught in the expository writing program, helped train and support about thirty new TAs in that program, and worked as a research assistant for the director of writing across the curriculum. In chapter 2 ("Multimodality and the Composition TAship"), cowritten with her colleague Jaclyn Fiscus-Cannaday, Campbell explores how TAs' disciplinary identities manifest during their classroom teaching through embodied gestures. She argues that the liminal positioning of TAs in both their disciplines and in rhetoric and composition can be explored and unpacked through more attention to these embodied strategies. Campbell's related research can be found in the *Journal of Writing Research*, *Written Communication*, and *Composition Forum*.

Rachel Donegan is an assistant professor of English at Georgia Gwinnett College in Lawrenceville, Georgia. Her research focuses on rhetoric, composition, and writing studies, WPA scholarship, mental disability, and the rhetorical nature of access. During her five years as a TA, she served as a gWPA for two years, working with faculty at all levels to expand and improve accessibility in their writing courses. As a disabled gWPA, she also mentored new TAs and created numerous workshops for faculty on how to support disabled students while adhering to best practices. In her chapter "The Invisible TA: Disclosure, Liminality, and Repositioning Disability within TA Programs," she highlights the precarious balancing act disabled TAs often perform in TA programs and challenges common attitudes towards disabled graduate students in general. Now out of graduate school, Rachel is currently working on an article on being on the job market while invisibly disabled.

Jaclyn Fiscus-Cannaday earned her PhD in language and rhetoric from the University of Washington (UW) in 2017. She then began her career as an assistant professor of English at Florida State University. Her research and teaching are situated at the intersection of composition studies, linguistics, and feminism, broadly exploring how communication works, how people think it should work, and how we might address those ideologies through pedagogy and policy to better work across difference. While at UW, she taught in their expository writing program, and she worked as an assistant director of the expository writing program and as an assistant director the computer-integrated classrooms. Her cowritten chapter, written with her colleague Lillian Campbell, discusses how embodied gestures in the classroom are influenced by TAs' disciplinary identities. Fiscus-Cannaday's related research can be found in *Composition Forum*.

Jennifer K. Johnson is a full-time lecturer in the writing program at the University of California, Santa Barbara, where she prepares new TAs to teach first-year composition. The TA-preparation program she teaches includes a two-week preservice workshop, followed by a practicum course that meets during the TAs' first quarter of teaching. In addition, Jennifer also teaches first-year and developmental composition courses, as well as upper-division writing courses including writing for accounting, writing and rhetoric, and writing for the social sciences. Jennifer was a TA in the English department at California State University Northridge, where she first became interested in studying TA preparation. She earned her PhD from Indiana University of Pennsylvania, and her dissertation focused on TA preparation in the UCSB writing program by examining how TAs' disciplinary backgrounds correlated with their collective responses to the practicum. She regularly presents her work at the Conference on College Composition and Communication and the Council of Writing Program Administrators Conference, as well as at regional and local conferences. Her other research interests include the relationship between composition and literature, independent writing programs, genre theory, and writing about writing.

Professor **Ronda Leathers Dively** received her BA in English (with teacher certification) and her MA in English (literature) from Eastern Illinois University. After gaining a few years of teaching experience in the secondary English classroom, she completed her doctor of arts degree (English—rhetoric and composition) at Illinois State University in 1994 and accepted an assistant professorship in the SIUC English department that same year.

In May of 2019, she retired after thirty-three years as an English teacher. For nine of those years, Dr. Dively served SIUC's English department as the director of writing studies, a role that enabled her to mentor hundreds of first-year writing teachers and numerous aspiring writing program administrators. Her major accomplishments during her tenure in that position included leading the transition of the English 101 curriculum toward standardization and revising the accompanying TA-preparation program to support that new curriculum (a process detailed in a 2010 *Composition Forum* "Program Profile"). Dr. Dively's areas of teaching specialization included composition theory and pedagogy, empirical research methods in composition, and intermediate and advanced composition. She also enjoyed teaching special-topics courses exploring intersections between creativity theory and composition theory—upper-level seminars growing from her primary research interest in the role of invention and incubation in a diversity of writing situations. More specifically, Professor Dively's scholarship investigates how intersections of creativity and composition theory may illuminate how individuals negotiate transitions (i.e., transfer knowledge) between various academic composing contexts—from high school to college classrooms, from general education to discipline-specific writing courses, from status as undergraduate student to graduate student, from status as graduate student to professional. Such interests have generated a book-length empirical study entitled *Preludes to Insight: Creativity, Incubation and Expository Writing* (Hampton Press 2006), a textbook entitled *Invention and Craft: A Guide to College Writing* (McGraw-Hill 2016), as well as various articles and conference presentations. Her latest book project traces the paradigmatic creative process model through a substantial corpus of *Paris Review* interviews, the goal being to identify common composing strategies and shared contextual themes associated with literary production.

Faith Matzker is a PhD candidate in Victorian literature at Southern Illinois University, where she held a position as a writing studies assistant (WSA) for five years. As a WSA, she aided the writing studies director in the development of standardized curricula for composition courses, helped train and mentor her teaching-assistant (TA) peers in best pedagogical practices, and acted as a mediator and liaison in matters concerning faculty, staff, graduate students, and undergraduate students. This position propelled her interests in rhetoric and composition theory, and her research in this field is primarily involved with bridging the divides in diverse discourse communities—particularly in the FYC classroom. In the coauthored chapter offered in this text, "The Graduate Teaching Assistant as Assistant WPA: Navigating the Hazards of Liminal Terrain between the Role of Student and the Role of Authority Figure," she and her coauthors explore the multiple liminal personas inhabited by the WSA and some of the difficulties and complex relationship dynamics this role can produce. She and her coauthors argue that despite the challenges encompassing the WSA position, administrative TA roles provide graduate students with essential and invaluable experience, acumen, and professional-identity development.

Jessica Restaino is professor of writing studies and director of gender, sexuality, and women's studies at Montclair State University. In addition to a number of essays and book chapters, she is the author of two books, *First Semester: Graduate Students, Teaching Writing, and the Challenge of Middle Ground* (2012) and *Surrender: Feminist Rhetoric and Ethics in Love and Illness* (2019); and she is coeditor, with Laurie Cella, of *Unsustainable: Re-imagining Community Literacy, Public Writing, Service-Learning, and the University* (2012).

Tanya K. Rodrigue is an associate professor of English and coordinator of the writing intensive curriculum program at Salem State University in Salem, Massachusetts. She was a TA at Syracuse University during her PhD program. After noticing a dearth of scholarship on TAs in WAC programs, Tanya decided to make TA writing pedagogy and WAC the subject of her dissertation, "Listening Across the Curriculum: TA Preparation in the Teaching of Writing." In addition to exploring existing TA writing-pedagogy models, she conducted qualitative research, interviewing TAs and professors at a large doctoral-granting institution, in efforts to reveal the needs of TAs in the disciplines and propose possible training methods and models for WAC TAs. From this research, she published two articles: "The (In)visible World of Teaching Assistants in the Disciplines: Preparing TAs to Teach Writing" in *Across the Disciplines* and "Listening Across the Curriculum: What Disciplinary TAs Can Teach Us about TA Professional Development in the Teaching of Writing" in *Teaching/Writing: The Journal of Writing Teacher Education.* More recently, Tanya coedited a special journal issue, "Teaching Assistants and Writing Across the Curriculum," in *Across the Disciplines* with Andrea Williams. Although her institution does not grant teaching assistantships, Tanya still works closely with English graduate students, supporting them in studying and practicing writing pedagogy in high school and college.

Elizabeth Saur earned her PhD in composition and rhetoric in 2017 from Miami University in Oxford, Ohio. While pursuing her doctorate, Beth served as the assistant director of composition, where she had the pleasure of teaching and mentoring the incoming TAs in the composition-pedagogy practicum, developing and implementing curriculum changes, and serving as coeditor of *The Teacher's Guide* and *Rhethawks* (programmatic materials distributed to everyone involved in the first-year writing program). Her research interests focus on affect theory, composition pedagogy, and teacher-development practices. In chapter 7 ("Beyond 'Good Teacher' / 'Bad Teacher': Generative Self-Efficacy and the Composition and Rhetoric TAship"), Beth and Megan Schoettler explore how new TAs in composition and rhetoric can develop a framework of self-efficacy that leads to more generative understandings of their own capacity to teach composition. Beth's other publications on affect and teacher development can be found in *WPA: Writing Program Administration* and in a forthcoming collection on the intersection of writing centers and game studies. Beth is currently a lecturer in the writing program at the University of California, Santa Barbara.

Megan Schoettler is a PhD candidate in composition and rhetoric and graduate assistant director of composition at Miami University. Her research focuses on feminist writing pedagogies and rhetorics. Megan started as a teaching assistant in the English department in 2015 while she earned her master's degree, growing from the mentorship of her WPA team, including Beth Saur. Five years later, Megan serves in Beth's past role as a graduate assistant director of composition, which involves mentoring TAs, coteaching a course on composition pedagogy and the TA practicums, and assisting with revisions to the FYC curriculum.

Kylee Thacker Maurer is a PhD candidate in English, with a concentration in rhetoric and composition, at Southern Illinois University Carbondale (SIUC). She is currently writing her dissertation on student engagement in the composition classroom, as well as teaching first-year composition courses. While being at SIUC, Kylee served as a writing studies assistant to the director of writing studies, an instructional mentor, and a teaching assistant for English 502: Teaching College Composition. During her stint as an assistant and mentor, she guided, instructed, and communicated with fellow TAs, providing updates and general information regarding writing studies and answering questions about teaching and policy. She facilitated professional-development and training workshops, preparing TAs to teach new composition courses, as well as observed new TAs, composed observation notes, and conducted follow-up conferences providing valuable feedback. Additionally, she compiled and revised curricular documents for course revisions sanctioned by the Writing Studies Committee. While the assistantships exposed Kylee to complicated liminal terrain, the training also provided excellent administrative experience and strengthened her passion for teacher training and for teaching college writing courses.

Andrea L. Williams directs a writing-in-the-disciplines program, writing-integrated teaching (WIT), at the University of Toronto, where she works with faculty and graduate teaching assistants from over twenty disciplines. Andrea has written about her experience in "Integrating Writing into the Disciplines: Risks and Rewards" in the edited collection *Minefield of Dreams: Triumphs and Travails of Independent Writing Programs*.

INDEX